East Africa and the Indian Ocean

East Africa and the Indian Ocean

EDWARD A. ALPERS

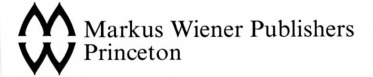
Markus Wiener Publishers
Princeton

For information, write to
Markus Wiener Publishers
231 Nassau Street
Princeton, NJ 08542
www.markuswiener.com

Library of Congress CIP data
Alpers, Edward A.
  East Africa and the Indian Ocean / Edward A. Alpers.
  Includes bibliographical references.
  ISBN 978-1-55876-452-1 (hardcover : alk. paper)
  ISBN 978-1-55876-453-8 (pbk. : alk. paper)
  1. Africa, East—Relations—Indian Ocean Region. 2. Indian Ocean Region—Relations—Africa, East. 3. Africa, East—Relations—Asia. 4. Asia—Relations—Africa, East. 5. Africa, East—History. 6. Islands of the Indian Ocean—History. 7. Islands of the Indian Ocean—Commerce—History. 8. Indian Ocean Region—Commerce—History. 9. Indian Ocean Region—History. I. Title.
  DT432.4.I5A47 2009
  303.48'267601824—-dc22
                                    2008042923

Markus Wiener Publishers books are printed in the United States of America on acid-free paper and meet the guidelines for permanence and durability of the Committee on Production Guidelines for Book Longevity of the Council on Library Resources

TABLE OF CONTENTS

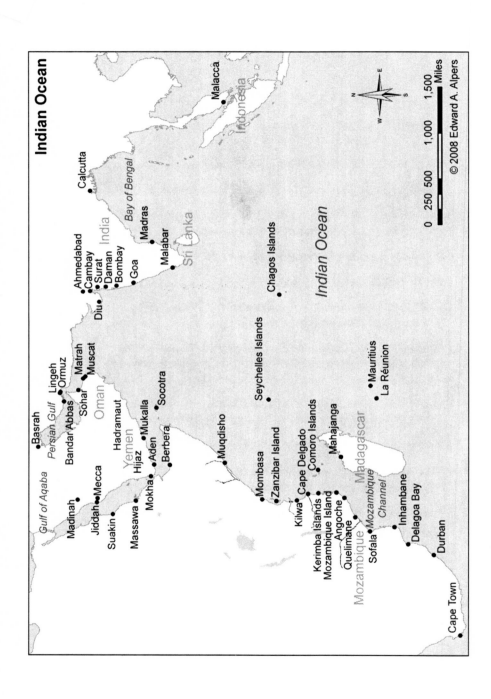

Indian Ocean

Malacca

Indonesia

Calcutta

Bay of Bengal

Madras

Ahmedabad
Cambay
Surat
Daman
Bombay
Diu
Goa

India

Malabar

Sri Lanka

Chagos Islands

Indian Ocean

Seychelles Islands

Basrah
Lingeh
Ormuz
Matrah
Muscat
Bandar Abbas
Sohar
Persian Gulf

Mauritius
La Réunion

Oman

Hadramaut
Mukalla
Socotra

Gulf of Aqaba

Madinah
Jiddah
Mecca
Hijaz
Mokha
Aden
Berbera
Yemen

Muqdisho

Mombasa
Zanzibar Island

Cape Delgado
Comoro Islands

Mahajanga

Kilwa

Massawa
Suakin

Kerimba Islands
Mozambique Island
Angoche
Quelimane
Sofala

Madagascar

Mozambique
Channel

Inhambane

Mozambique

Delagoa Bay

Durban

Cape Town

N E W S

0   250 500   1,000   1,500
Miles

© 2008 Edward A. Alpers

INTRODUCTION

If, as Michael Pearson argues in his major contribution to the historiography of the Indian Ocean, South Asia "was the fulcrum of the ocean around which all other areas swung," then eastern Africa was certainly a periphery of the Indian Ocean World.[1] Or, as Lodewijk Wagenaar suggests in a critical response to Pearson, "in a [sic] M-shaped world (the Indian subcontinent in the centre, East Africa and the Indonesian Archipelago [appear] as 'legs')."[2] Nevertheless, Pearson's recognition that eastern Africa is not without significance in the larger history of the Indian Ocean is itself an important corrective to the too easy dismissal of this vast region of Africa by Kirti Chaudhuri almost two decades before.[3]

In this collection of previously published essays, I consider the significance of the Indian Ocean for eastern Africa, as well as the place of this long littoral, its hinterland, and its numerous islands in the history of the Indian Ocean. Although much of this history focuses on trading networks, those very networks also precipitated broad cultural exchanges and movement of peoples, which in turn created permanent connections between eastern Africa and the wider Indian Ocean world. Following Pearson's adoption of the distinction made by Peregrine Horden and Nicholas Purcell between history *in* and history *of* the Mediterranean Sea, these essays fall under the heading of history *in* the Indian Ocean.[4] Chronologically, although most of the chapters focus on the nineteenth century, several also range considerably backwards in time while others extend into the colonial and post-colonial period. Together, I believe, they reveal important connections and patterns of influence that help to identify the significance of the Indian Ocean for the peoples of eastern Africa.

As is the case for all oceanic studies, historians face various problems of definition. As Kären Wigen notes in her introduction to the recent AHR Forum on "Oceans of History," "*maritime regions every-where are understood to be fractured, fragmented* worlds, unified more by contact among contrasting places than by any purported similarity across their shores."[5] For my part, first, when I speak of eastern Africa I include the entire coastline from the Red Sea shores to the Cape of Good Hope, including the major African islands, a perspective that not only transgresses the territorial boundaries of modern political and internal African studies but also enlarges the concept of Indian Ocean Africa. By adopting such a generous notion of eastern Africa, I also wish to emphasize Wigen's point about differentiated coastal regions *within* eastern Africa and not simply between eastern Africa and the rest of the Indian Ocean region. Second, what exactly do I mean by the Indian Ocean? For eastern Africa, the western Indian Ocean is without question the primary context in which its oceanic history has been played out, but depending on time and place, the eastern Indian Ocean also had relevance for eastern Africa. In addition, for the far northern littoral, the Red Sea and Gulf of Aden were of particular significance, while for the southern reaches of the coast, the Mozambique Channel was of major consequence. Moreover, as we shall see for all regions within eastern Africa, there have been significant elements of what Wigen calls Horden and Purcell's concept of "seaborne connectivity," a broader rubric within which we can situate concepts employed by other Indian Ocean scholars—concepts such as trading diasporas, family networks, and population movements.[6] Accordingly, in what follows I hope to demonstrate that, allowing for shifting boundaries and frontiers over time, eastern Africa has been an integral part of the Indian Ocean world for the better part of the past two millennia.

*   *   *   *   *

Some of the essays in this collection will be familiar to readers; others may not. They span a period of scholarly activity over three decades, from the mid-1970s to 2007. In reproducing them here I have organized them into three parts consisting of three chapters each.

Within each part, I have arranged the chapters by date of publication rather than attempting any chronological progression in their actual content, although to a certain extent there is some convergence.

In the first part, "The Western Indian Ocean," I explore the widest connections of the entire littoral of the region, as well as its many islands, both large and small. Chapter 1 represents an early attempt to understand the role that Indian Hindu merchants from Gujarat played in the ivory trade of East Africa in the three centuries following the sixteenth-century Portuguese assault on Arab trade networks. In the past three decades, several different scholars whose work I cite in my references have similarly addressed this phenomenon. Chapter 2 takes up a still neglected topic—the trade in foodstuffs along the littoral of the western Indian Ocean and across its waters. This essay was previously published only in the conference proceedings of the second of the now defunct quinquennial meetings of the International Congress on Indian Ocean Studies. The last chapter in this part, relating to the Indian Ocean islands of East Africa, adopts a different perspective, suggesting the utility of looking at the African continent from the islands rather than the other way around.

In the second part, "Coastal Eastern Africa," the focus is on various aspects of the modern history of what some might consider to be the Swahili coast, although two of the essays relate, in fact, to the Benaadir coast of southern Somalia. Chapter 4 positions Muqdisho squarely in the orbit of Busaidi Zanzibar, of the urban tradition of the coast, and of the commercial networks of the Indian Ocean and argues for a different sort of Soomaali historical experience than the dominant image of pure camel nomadism. The following chapter, on the indigenous textile industry of Muqdisho, grew out of my fascination with what was in 1980, when I conducted my research in Somalia, still a living, if less than thriving, production center in the heart of the city. In Chapter 6, I try to understand a women's spirit possession cult that was recorded in some detail by an astute Spiritan priest in the 1860s. Piecing together the elements that he describes and making sense of them drove home to me the importance of the extensive cultural networks that wove together different points of the

Indian Ocean littoral, from the African mainland and interior to Zanzibar to northeast Africa to Arabia, as far as Indonesia.

Finally, in the third part of the volume, "The Mozambique Channel," I examine the complex set of connections that link the societies on both sides (and in the middle) of the Mozambique Channel, and that thereby create a subregion of the western Indian Ocean. This zone of activity—involving commercial, political, religious, and familial networks—deserves much more scholarly attention than it has received, but the challenge of mastering a number of different languages, in addition to political unrest at various times in the recent past, has made serious investigation a daunting endeavor. Chapter 7 connects a very specific phenomenon—the Malagasy maritime raids on the coast of eastern Africa—to the wider Indian Ocean slave trade in the early decades of the nineteenth century. Chapter 8 tries to get at the complex set of relationships between the Mozambique coast and the Comoro Islands in the last two centuries. Finally, Chapter 9 tests Michael Pearson's formulation of the significance of littoral society in the Indian Ocean against the specific historical context of the Mozambique Channel.

In preparing these pieces for this volume, I had to make some basic decisions in order to achieve a whole that would be more than a simple reproduction of earlier publications. First, I decided to establish a single format for all the references, despite the differing conventions of the sources in which they originally appeared. Wherever possible I have also added information on publishers. Although I have not replaced any of the original references, in a few cases I have updated them, and in various notes I have added citations of significant scholarly works that have been published or appeared as unpublished dissertations since the original article or book chapter was written. These are usually introduced with a phrase such as "A recent study by . . ." or similar language. Also, to make the present volume more usable, references to my own work that now appear as chapters in this volume are made, in the endnotes, to these chapters, rather than to the journals in which they were originally published.

Second, I decided to try to establish a consistent nomenclature for place names. This was not always easy, and in some cases I might have decided on another form than the one I chose. For example, in this volume I decided to use *Muqdisho* consistently because two of the articles attempt to conform to Soomaali orthography, even though in other essays I had originally used *Mogadishu*. In the same vein, I adopt *Mahajanga* over *Majunga*, the principal trading port of north-western Madagascar in the nineteenth century. Other instances include using the more familiar term *qadi* for the Somali rendering of *kaadi*, *Omani* in preference to *ʿUmani*, *Busaidi* over *Bu Saʿidi*, and *Hadramaut* instead of *Hadramawt*. I also prefer *Ngazija* to *Ngazidja* or *Grande Comore*, the largest of the Comoro Islands. However, in regard to the various names of another of the Comoro Islands, *Nzwani*, I have not resolved this question. It is still officially rendered *Anjouan* and was known to the Anglophones in the nineteenth century as *Johanna*. So while *Johanna* appears only in a few titles in the references, I use both *Nzwani* and *Anjouan* in different chapters, depending on when I originally published them. Such decisions are clearly arbitrary, but once again I think that it makes for a more consistent whole to adopt such nomenclature.

Third, in two instances where I originally concluded a paper with a reference to contemporary politics (see Chapters 3 and 5), I have changed the actual text to reflect the current political situation. Similarly, in a few isolated cases I have changed tenses when referring to some specific example of research assistance or, more frequently, corrected a typographical error in the original text. I hope that these decisions will help to make the collection as a whole more readable.

Although I had been thinking for some time of putting together a collection of my essays on this broad topic, this particular volume would not have come about were it not for the encouragement of and invitation from Markus Wiener, which he proffered during the Cahuita Symposium on Slavery, Culture, and Religion at Cahuita (Limón), Costa Rica, in February 2006. I am most grateful to the various original publishers of my work for granting me permission to reproduce the essays in this slightly different form between these covers. Full references to the original publications can be found in a footnote on the first page of each chapter, respectively. Individual acknowledgments of research support, both personal and pecuniary, appear in individual chapters below. Finally, I am especially grateful to Philip Schlatter for the technical aspects of preparing the maps for this volume. And I am above all indebted to Annie Alpers for helping me to proofread and index this volume, as well as for making invaluable contributions that consistently help me to clarify my writing.

Los Angeles
July 2008

PART I

The Western Indian Ocean

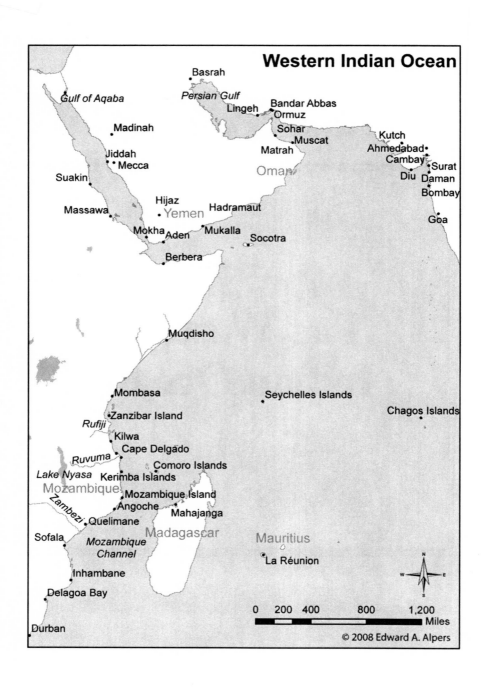

Western Indian Ocean

Basrah

Persian Gulf

Gulf of Aqaba

Bandar Abbas
Lingeh
Ormuz

Madinah
Sohar
Muscat
Matrah

Kutch
Ahmedabad
Cambay

Jiddah
Mecca

Oman

Surat
Diu Daman

Suakin

Bombay

Hijaz
Massawa
Yemen
Hadramaut

Goa

Mokha Aden
Mukalla
Socotra

Berbera

Muqdisho

Mombasa
Seychelles Islands
Chagos Islands

Zanzibar Island

Rufiji

Kilwa
Cape Delgado

Ruvuma

Comoro Islands

Lake Nyasa Kerimba Islands

Mozambique Island

Zambezi
Mozambique
Angoche
Mahajanga

Quelimane

Sofala
Mozambique Channel
Madagascar
Mauritius

La Réunion

Inhambane

Delagoa Bay

Durban

0   200   400   800   1,200
Miles

N
W   E
S

© 2008 Edward A. Alpers

CHAPTER 1

Gujarat and the Trade of East Africa, c. 1500-1800*

One of the more persistent problems confronting historians of East Africa remains the lack of reliable standard histories of the Indian Ocean world. Topics which are especially affected by this lacuna in the historical literature are the problem of Indonesian contacts, the history of Islam on the coast, and the economic history of both the coast and the interior. Only in the case of the Portuguese seaborne empire do we possess a series of studies which places East Africa squarely in the context of the Indian Ocean system.[1] In this respect Indian Ocean studies lag far behind those of the Atlantic Ocean.[2] Although we are aware of close commercial links existing between East Africa and India throughout the better part of the present millennium, we know little about the precise nature of these relations and the organization of trade itself. At the same time, it is quite clear that East Africa never played as important a role in the history of the Indian Ocean world as did West Africa in that of the Atlantic, making the reconstruction of developments in East Africa as they pertain to this larger historical arena doubly difficult. This paper proposes to explore a single topic within this context, the identity and organization of those Indian traders who were most deeply involved in the East African trade from the late fifteenth to the nineteenth century,

* Reprinted from *International Journal of African Historical Studies*, 9, 1 (1976), pp. 22-44.

and to do it in a way which invites the participation of specialists in Asian history in resolving this and similar issues in the history of East Africa.

Before the arrival of the Portuguese in Indian Ocean waters, trade between India and East Africa was based primarily on the exchange of gold from southern Zambesia and ivory from the coastal hinterland of East Africa for cotton cloths from India and glass beads from both India and Venice. The importance of exotic trade goods for East Africa was vividly recounted in an early sixteenth-century Portuguese report, which suggested that "cloth and beads are to the Kaffirs what pepper is to Flanders and corn to us, because they cannot live without this merchandise or lay up their treasures of it."[3] Among the items involved in the trade were rhinoceros horn, tortoise shell, and some slaves from East Africa, grain from India, and Chinese porcelain, which was transshipped in western India. Ibn Battuta says nothing about Indian traders in East Africa, while his description of characteristic landlord-stranger relationships between foreign and local merchants at Muqdisho in 1331 suggests that this method of organizing commerce may have also obtained at Kilwa and Mombasa, the other major commercial centers on the coast in the early fourteenth century.[4] The fifteenth century may have witnessed important changes in both the personnel and organization of trade with the rise to prominence of the Muslim sultanate of Gujarat from 1392 and the domination of Indian Ocean trade by Gujarati merchants, for, as Jean Aubin remarks, Gujarat was the "keystone of the commercial structures of the Indian Ocean."[5]

The heart of the sultanate of Gujarat was Cambay, which was divided into ten territorial administrative units called *sarkars.* Six other *sarkars* lay outside of Cambay but within the Gujarati state in Kathiawar, Kutch, the marches of Malwa and Rajputana, and the country south of the Tapti River. They were economically peripheral and in other respects quite distinct. Cambay produced the cotton cloth, silk, and indigo for which Gujarat gained fame, and there the capital of Ahmedabad was located. Although this state was at the height of its powers at the end of the fifteenth century, and although its rulers had a vested interest in the success of trade, little official control of foreign commerce was held at the center. Gujarat was a land-based state, and its rulers counted their power and influence in their authority over territory and people. So long as maritime trade continued to function smoothly, and those who did their business within the kingdom contributed to the revenue of the state accordingly, the Muslim rulers of Gujarat were content to provide them protection and leave them alone. If it is difficult to determine precisely the extent to which it enriched the state, there can be little doubt that "sea trade was a very important element in the total economy of sultanate Gujarat."[6]

In about 1500 the city of Cambay was the most important international trading port of Gujarat, but as the result of the progressive silting up of the bay on which it is located and the dangerous tides there, it was soon to be surpassed by both Diu (Div), located to the west on an island off the Kathiawar peninsula, and Surat, which lay to the south of Cambay on the north bank of the Tapti River. Indeed, Portuguese relations with Gujarat at the beginning of the sixteenth century were dominated by the rivalry between Diu and Surat, and, in a militaristic solution typical of their creation of an Asian seaborne empire, the Portuguese forcibly seized Diu after many attempts in 1555.[7] By about 1520, in fact, Diu had become the greatest trading port of Gujarat, driving a great traffic with the other Indian ports. "Ships also sail hence to Meca, Adem, Zeila, Barbara, Magadaxo, Melinde, Brava, Mombasa, and Ormuz with the kingdom thereof."[8] In the decade before it fell to the Portuguese its preeminence received official support from the sultan of Gujarat.[9]

The merchants of Gujarat included representatives of all the major trading communities of western Asia. Among the Muslims were Arabs, Turks (especially at Diu), Persians, and Egyptians. Gujarati Muslims also participated in this trade, but to a much less significant extent than their foreign co-religionists resident in the sultanate. The most important Gujarati traders, however, were Hindus and Jains, and among these the predominant group was the *vanias*. Michael N. Pearson carefully points out that the *vanias* were a specific yet diverse group, an important point to remember for students of East Africa, where the term *banian* generally meant any Hindu merchant. Their *varna* was *vaisya,* the third in rank of the four mythical divisions of Hindu society. Of the forty-one strictly endogamous *jati,* or castes, some included both Hindu and Jain sections (called *meshri* among Hindus, *shravak* among Jains), although some were dominated by Jains. Inter-dining was both permissible and common.[10]

What were the factors which made it possible for non-Muslim merchants to achieve and maintain such a commanding position in the maritime and overland trade in a Muslim state? First, they were tolerated by the state despite their religion because of the revenue their business generated. Second, as Pearson also notes, they were a numerically larger group. Third, notwithstanding misconceptions dating back to Weber about the inhibiting effect of Hinduism on Indian economic development, the *vanias* demonstrably constituted a very adaptable class of merchants whose religious beliefs did not prevent them from conducting business profitably.[11] Above all, the high degree of occupational specialization found in the *jati* system is striking.

Characteristically, Tomé Pires provides us with the first detailed impressions of Hindu business practices and training.

> These [people] are [like] Italians in their knowledge of and dealings in merchandise. . . . They are men who understand merchandise; they are so properly steeped in the sound and harmony of it, that the Gujarantees say that any offence connected with merchandise is pardonable. There are Gujarantees settled everywhere. They work some for some and others for others. They are diligent, quick men in trade. They do their accounts with figures like ours and with our very writing.

Of the other merchants of Cambay he notes: "None of these count in comparison with the heathens, especially in knowledge. Those of our people who want to be clerks and factors ought to go there and learn, because the business of trade is a science in itself which does not hinder any other noble exercise, but helps a great deal."[12] Toward the end of the century a rather less flattering but similar description comes from the pen of John Huygen van Linschoten, who declares that the *vanias* of Gujarat "are the subtilest and politiquest Marchauntes of all India." "They are most subtil and expert in casting accounts and writing, so that they do not only surpasse and goe beyond all other Indians and other nations thereabouts, but also the Portingales: and in this respect they have much advantage, for [that] they are very perfect in the trade of merchandise, and very ready to deceive men."[13]

Travelers' accounts of the seventeenth century abound with references to the business acumen of the *vanias*. Jean Baptiste Tavernier, whose six voyages to India spanned the middle decades of the century, was particularly impressed by the training of their children for trade. "They accustom their children at an early age to shun slothfulness, and instead of letting them go into the streets to lose their time at play, as we generally allow ours, teach them arithmetic, which they learn perfectly, using for it neither pen nor counters, but the memory alone, so that in a moment they will do a sum, however difficult it may be. They are always with their fathers, who instruct them in trade, and do nothing without explaining it to them at the same time."[14] John Ovington commented on *jati* exclusiveness and the training which it provided for its children in 1689. "The son is engag'd in the Father's trade, and to maintain the Profession of it in his Posterity, it is transmitted always to the succeeding Generation, which is obliged to preserve it in a lineal Descent, uncommunicated to any Stranger. Upon this account all Marriages are restrain'd to one Sect, and contracted only between Persons of the same Perswasion and Profession."[15]

The application of the *vanias* to business was not only limited to the transmission of individual and family commercial skills; it also included their organization as a community of merchants. Within the main cities of Gujarat the *vanias* were organized collectively in *mahajans,* which in Gujarat "usually meant a body representing a group of people engaged in the same commercial activity, a governing council with an elected or occasionally hereditary headman," the *sheth*. Participation in the *mahajan* usually transcended *jati* membership, as it was concerned exclusively with matters commercial, while religious and social affairs were governed by *jati panchayats*, or governing councils. The *mahajan* dealt only with matters such as prices, internal adjudication, and the representation of all members in their external relations with other *mahajans* and governments. A peculiar feature of commercial organization at Ahmedabad was the existence of a municipal *mahajan* which included representatives of all the occupational *mahajans* in the city and whose head was known as the *nagarsheth*. In Gujarat, then, *jati* specialization was strengthened by wider occupational cooperation in commercial affairs. "This helps to explain," says Pearson, "why such *mahajans* were always stronger in Gujarat than in other parts of India."[16]

When one adds these components together, and reckons in the undoubtedly great commercial wealth which was generated by the Gujarati merchants but for which no figures exist in the early sixteenth century, one has a merchant capitalist system of the first order, particularly by East African standards. Our main sources come from the early sixteenth century and describe a system in full flower. According to Pires, "Cambay chiefly stretches out two arms, with her right arm she reaches out towards Aden and with the other towards Malacca, as the most important places to sail to, and the other places are held to be of less importance.... Malacca cannot live without Cambay, nor Cambay without Malacca, if they are to be very rich and very prosperous. . . . If Cambay were cut off from trading with Malacca, it could not live, for it would have no outlet for its merchandise."[17]Among the "other places" Pires includes none of the towns of the East African coast, which should leave no doubt about the essentially peripheral nature of East Africa in this flourishing maritime commercial system. Only in his description of Aden, the key entrepôt for Mediterranean goods, does he note that its traders and those of Cambay purchased "all kinds of cloth, for trading in Zeila, Berbera, Sokotra, Kilwa, Malindi, Muqdisho, and other places in Arabia." In the same passage he also suggests that there was direct

Cambay trade "with all the other places I have mentioned."[18] Trade
does not, of course, occur between places without the participation of
their people (although historians have a tendency to forget this sometimes), and Pires makes clear the primacy of the Gujarati merchants
in the Indian Ocean of his time. But although he states that they traded everywhere, establishing factories and their own organizations for
trade, he does not mention their presence as a significant body in East
Africa. Their chief concentration outside of Gujarat was Malacca,
where some thousand merchants and four-to-five thousand seamen
lived at the end of the fifteenth century.[19] The Gujarati merchants
were represented by one of their own number, who was appointed as
shahbandar to speak for their community by the ruler of Malacca.
The *shahbandar* of the Gujarati merchants was the most senior
among four such officials, who represented each of the major foreign
trading communities at Malacca. His main task was to look after the
interests of his people, to manage the markets and warehouses, to
insure that standards of measurement were observed, and to adjudi-
cate disputes within his community.[20] Essentially, the Gujarati *shahbandar* of Malacca occupied a position in a foreign port analagous to
the *sheth* of a *vania mahajan,* or perhaps more accurately to the
nagarsheth of Ahmedabad, the Gujarati capital. Pires notes that the
Gujarati traders were followed to Malacca by those of other nations
and that they established companies for trading there. Among these
were "people from Ormuz, Kilwa, Malindi, Muqdisho and Mombasa" and others.[21] Since the three other *shahbandars* represented
merchants from different communities in the rest of the Indian sub-
continent, the Indian archipelago, and East Asia, these East African
merchants in Malacca quite possibly were represented by the Gujarati
shahbandar, as their city-states were intimately tied to Gujarat
through the trade of Aden.[22]

The first unambiguous references to Gujarati traders in East
Africa are provided by the earliest accounts of the Portuguese on that
coast and therefore date to the same period which Tome Pires
describes. In 1500 the Portuguese fleet encountered three two-hun-
dred-ton vessels from Cambay at Malindi. Six years later they

attempted unsuccessfully to burn several unloaded Cambay ships
which were aground in Mombasa harbor, and captured several
Cambay merchants.[23] Duarte Barbosa explicity delineates the commercial links of Cambay to the coastal city-states of East Africa from
Muqdisho to Sofala, and thence to the interior. He also writes that
the busy harbor of Mombasa included ships from "the great kingdom of Cambaya and from Melynde," while the merchants of Malindi itself impressed him even more strongly. "They are great barterers,
and deal in cloth, gold, ivory, and divers others wares with the Moors
and Heathen, of the great kingdom of Cambaya; and to their haven
come every year many ships with cargoes of merchandise, from which
they get great store of gold, ivory, and wax. In this traffic the Cambay
merchants make great profits, and thus, on one side and the other,
they earn much money."[24] How was this trade organized? Did it follow the pattern of landlord and stranger which Ibn Battuta had
observed some two centuries previously, or did it conform on a
reduced scale to that which existed in contemporary Malacca?

Gervase Mathew has suggested that "it might be possible to dis-
cern the office of Shahbandar behind the Portuguese accounts of the
activities of Muhammad 'Ankoni,'" or Rukn-ad-Din al-Dabali. But
his political ambitions do not conform to the characteristic behavior
of Gujarati merchants either at home or abroad, and in any case he
was an Arab, notwithstanding his family origins in western India at
Daybol.[25] In the aftermath of his nomination as sultan of Kilwa by
the Portuguese and his consequent assassination in 1506, however,
Justus Strandes notes that the claim of Rukn-ad-Din's son "was supported by the officials of the Greek trading agency."[26] Strandes's
translator has quite properly noted "Greek?," and as his annotation
was not always rigorous it is difficult to check the sources on which
he based this statement. Armenian would seem much more in keeping with what we know about the trade of the Indian Ocean.[27] Of
greater importance than the nationality of these merchants is the reference to the manner in which they organized their business in East
Africa, which suggests the existence of a factory and a recognized
representative at Kilwa. Here, on however modest a scale, we are

much closer to affairs as they are known at this time from Malacca and other Indian Ocean ports. Considering the relatively large number of Gujarati merchants at Mombasa and Malindi, it seems very likely that they, too, were organized along similar lines, although no evidence is available to determine whether sufficient numbers were resident in either of these city-states to warrant the appointment of *shahbandars* by their rulers.

During the course of the sixteenth century the Portuguese dominated the Indian Ocean and its littoral. Although a great deal of official trade was carried in Portuguese vessels, a *modus vivendi* soon emerged by which the Portuguese granted licenses to Asian merchant vessels plying the high seas. If the Portuguese seaborne empire were to be a paying proposition, it could not rely on the trade of its officials and of private Portuguese merchants alone. Because of its larger struggle with Islam, both religious and economic, however, Portugal was determined to eliminate Muslim merchants, especially Arabs, in the Indian Ocean system. Accordingly, the Hindu and Jain merchants of Gujarat were ideally situated to increase further their domination of the traditional trade of Asia. And as Pearson observes, "perhaps the dominating characteristic, especially as regards Gujarati traders, was flexibility and readiness to adapt."[28] In Gujarat the growing strength of the *vanias* seems to have matured after the middle of the sixteenth century, when the Portuguese were at last secure in their fortress at Diu and were capable of policing the waters of the western Indian Ocean. In the early 1570s the customs revenue of twenty-three Gujarati ports amounted to nearly thrice the total revenue of the entire Portuguese Estado da India a decade later, when it had achieved the very pinnacle of its success.[29] At Diu, which was second only to Goa as a source of revenue for the Portuguese crown, prosperity rose considerably in the second half of the century, customs revenue doubling from 1556 to the 1590s.[30] By the end of the century the Portuguese must have recognized how very dependent on the support of Gujarati merchants they had become, for in 1595 Gujaratis were forbidden to trade beyond the ports of western India, and Hindus were prohibited from acting as agents for Portuguese officials and from holding royal contracts. But like most proclamations of this sort in Portuguese India, which were frequently initiated and typically supported by either the local settlers or ecclesiastics, these were dead letters from the beginning.[31] The Portuguese crown was predictably more concerned with protecting its own revenue and the income of its high-born officials than it was to encourage the emergence of an effective low-born Portuguese merchant class in Asia.[32]

Restrictions against non-Christians would have been effective, however, had not the merchants of Gujarat been successful in voicing their strong objections to such measures. For all of their willingness to accommodate Portuguese imperialism and to endure the insults of the Portuguese in their pursuit of commercial profits, the Gujaratis were neither a submissive nor a defenseless group. This strength they owed largely to their existing commercial organization, particularly the occupational *mahajans*. Pearson cites several sixteenth-century examples of successful action by the Gujarati merchants of Diu as well as the Portuguese recognition of their ultimate dependence on the merchants' presence there. During the seventeenth century the increasing vulnerability of the Portuguese in Asia and the steady attrition of their maritime empire in the face of English, Dutch, and Omani Arab competition made them all the more responsive to protest and pressure from Gujarati merchants upon whose commercial activities they came increasingly to rely.[33]

At the same time as Portugal was consolidating its hold over Diu, the independent sultanate of Gujarat was being incorporated into the Mughal empire as the consequence of Akbar's conquest in 1572. Discussing the independence of Gujarati merchants, Pearson argues that these political innovations in no way changed the nature of their relations with the ruling class, as the Mughals shared the same territorial political values as had their independent Gujarati Muslim predecessors. During the course of the seventeenth century, however, Gujarati merchant capitalists became increasingly involved with the dominant system of agrarian revenue collection which made the Mughal empire uncommonly oppressive for the Indian peasantry. The intermingling of commercial capital derived from foreign trade and that derived from Mughal agricultural exploitation made the fortunes of Gujarati merchants rather more susceptible to changes in the political system of Gujarat than appears to have been the case in the sixteenth century.[34] Yet it also gave these merchants a greater voice in politics than they seem to have enjoyed before the Mughal conquest.[35] Meanwhile, many Gujarati merchants successfully exploited the entrance of both the English and Dutch East Indies Companies into Indian Ocean trade by acting as their brokers and agents.[36] Through all of this they successfully protected their interests through the agency of their *mahajans*.[37]

Determining the impact of these changes on the trade of East Africa is extremely difficult. Tapan Raychaudhuri argues for the whole of India at this time that "there was little or no economic integration as between different parts of the country. . . . Changes in the economic life of one region had very little impact on the economic life of other parts." Yet even he qualifies this sweeping generalization by his statement that "the bulk of the supply [of overseas exports] came from areas around the centres of export," in this case from the cotton textile manufacturing centers of Cambay, Broach, and Ahmedabad. Indeed, B.R. Grover's pioneering and impressively documented study of the contiguous region of North India during the seventeenth and eighteenth centuries suggests very strongly that the commercial life of Gujarat was much more closely integrated than Raychaudhuri's perspective would allow. At the very least, it is impossible to divorce the export trade of Gujarat to East Africa from the economic life of Mughal Gujarat as a whole.[38] What does need emphasizing here, however, is the importance of political factors of empire, both Mughal and Portuguese, in determining the trading connections of Gujarati merchants in East Africa during this period. In this respect both Diu and Surat continued in the historical pattern of Indian Ocean trading emporia.[39]

In East Africa, specific commercial links to Gujarat were equally dependent upon the holders of local political power. Even after the Portuguese took the coast by storm in 1505, they did not achieve effective imperial control of East African trade until the penetration

of Zambesia, which became significant only from the 1570s, the occupation of Mombasa in 1592, and the construction of Fort Jesus in the
following year.[40] Until the end of the sixteenth century they were
unable to direct all the Gujarat trade to their strongholds at Malindi
and Mozambique, which were linked by imperial bonds principally to
Diu. Thus what the Portuguese called "illegal" and "contraband"
commerce between Gujarat and the East African ports which lay outside their control or sphere of influence in the sixteenth century—
Mombasa and Angoche to the south of Mozambique Island, for
example—very likely was in the hands of Gujarati merchants from
Surat.

Throughout the sixteenth century the trade of Portuguese East
Africa was a declared monopoly of the Portuguese captains of the
coast. Despite this, the principal trading goods for the East African
trade continued to be Gujarati cloths. In fact, clear evidence indicates
that the once-thriving cotton textile manufacturing industries of the
East African city-states were before long completely obliterated by
the impact of Portuguese imperialism, with the single exception of
Muqdisho, which lay beyond Portuguese concern and seems to have
had a specialized market in Egypt.[41] Since all authorities agree that
the early sixteenth century witnessed a reduction in the flow of gold
abroad from East Africa, the resulting monopoly which Gujarati
cloths exercised over the East African market does not necessarily
reflect an increase in trade between Gujarat and East Africa. Indeed,
the total export market which Gujarat now controlled may actually
have been smaller than that which it shared with East African textiles
in the fifteenth century.[42] In the later part of the century, only a very
small number of Gujarati merchants seem to have been personally
trading in East Africa, and these few were undoubtedly from Diu. In
1600 there do not appear to have been any Indians resident at
Mozambique, but after the Portuguese secured Mombasa and made
it their capital for the Swahili coast an important small community of
vanias grew up on the narrow Mombasa street which faced the gate
of the fort and is now known as Ndia Kuu. By 1606 Indians from Diu
were also trading at Pate, on the coast north of Mombasa.[43]

This renewed direct participation by Gujarati merchants in the trade of East Africa reflected everyone's disenchantment with its near total monopoly by Portuguese officials in the last decades of the sixteenth century. At Diu, for example, monopolistic practices in the East African ivory trade led to collusion between the Portuguese captain and the head of the *vanias* of that town, who sold ivory to other *vania* merchants on his own terms.[44] Because contemporary Portuguese accounts do not employ the term *sheth* when referring to merchants like this man, usually calling them by the official Portuguese appointive title of captain or simply referring to an individual's prominent position in the community, the presence of occupational *mahajans* has been difficult to ascertain until now. But as Pearson remarks with respect to the lack of direct evidence of *jati panchayats* in Goa at this time, "it would be extraordinary if they did not exist." Captains of the Gujarati *vanias* were at Diu, Ormuz, and Goa in the seventeenth century, and in Goa they lived on their own street. In 1646 the total population of *vanias* resident in Portuguese India was reckoned at about 30,000 individuals, with their headquarters at Diu.[45] In fact, there is evidence beginning in the late seventeenth century and extending to the present to finally enable us to demonstrate the existence of traditional forms of organization among the *vanias* of Diu beneath the umbrella of Portuguese officialdom.

Faced with the declining fortunes of Mozambique, which for most of the seventeenth century had been subjected to a series of futile administrative measures designed to stimulate trade while keeping it in the hands of the Portuguese, and perhaps too in response to the havoc wreaked on Diu by the Omani Arabs in 1669, the viceroy of India in 1686 granted a full monopoly of trade between Diu and Mozambique to a group of merchants at Diu who are described as "the Company of Mazanes."[46] Until recently the identity of this body of traders remained obscure to me, but I am now convinced that they were probably representatives of a city-wide commercial *mahajan* like the one that existed at this time at Ahmedabad. Ahmedabad's unique position as provincial capital and commercial hub of Mughal Gujarat was partially paralleled by Diu's commercial supremacy of the Portuguese Estado da India. And in the middle of the twentieth century, at least, a very much reduced Diu was still dominated by its *vanias,* the richest of whom was Calachand Irachand, "who commanded from Diu a commercial emporium with international relations and credit, and agents in Bombay and Lourenco Marques" and who occupied the office of *nagarsheth.* As Paiva Couceiro, the count of Paraty, correctly indicates, the *nagarsheth* was elected by the commercial communities of Diu as their collective representative to the civil authority.[47] I suggest, then, that the origins of the city-wide commercial *mahajan* at Diu with which Paiva Couceiro was familiar in the middle of the twentieth century may well date to the granting of a monopoly of the Mozambique trade in 1686, or at least to that era.[48]

In contrast to the election of the *nagarsheth* of Diu in modern days, in the late eighteenth century the office of captain of the *banians* (which surely must correspond to the *sheth* of the *mahajan* in Gujarat, outside Portuguese control) was hereditary within a single family, although the *vania* notables seem to have had a voice in determining who among the legitimate heirs should hold office.[49] And like the other towns of Portuguese India, the *vanias* apparently resided in a specifically designated neighborhood, so that their strong sense of community expressed itself in spatial as well as structural terms.[50] Clearly none of these interpretations of the economic, social, and political organization of the Indian trading communities of Diu can be regarded as proven. The evidence is far too fragile to be other than suggestive. But there exists now a basis for further research in the archives of Goa and among the people of Diu which has previously been lacking.

To assume, however, that there was no direct Gujarati participation in the trade of Mozambique before the organization of the Company of Mazanes in 1686 would be incorrect. In 1653 Nicholas Buckeridge noted the arrival of "seaven vessells hither this yeare 6 from Goa: vizt 3 for the Governors owne Accountt, 2 for other marchants & one for Accountt of Bannians & one from Dew." Moreover, if the examples of both official and private Portuguese trade at Diu and Cambay apply here, it is likely that Gujarati capital was behind the trading accounts of all or some of the Portuguese vessels Buckeridge encountered.[51] The commercial prosperity of the Swahili coast during the seventeenth century was apparently no less due to the activities of the *vania* merchants of Diu.[52] But the trade of that coast, which was centered around Mombasa, probably began to slip after mid-century, when the Omani Arabs began raiding into East African waters. In 1660 and 1661 they raided Mombasa itself, sacking Ndia Kuu, where the *vania* merchants resided. Six years later a British visitor to Mombasa wrote that "It is a place of no great traffic, the evidence of which I imagine is the poverty of the inhabitants who (although as well Portuguese as Banyans) are so squeezed perpetually by the Governor that they seldom or never come to be worth anything of an estate. Nor are they suffered to trade for twenty pieces-of-eight without the Governors license, which to be sure is never when he can get anything by it himself."[53] This sort of competition for control of trade in the Estado da India remained an endemic problem until the modern period, and may have been another contributing factor to the granting of a monopoly to the Company of Mazanes in 1686.

No matter who was doing the actual trading, the products of Gujarat clearly continued to dominate the trade of East Africa during the seventeenth century, and most of the products of East Africa were consumed by Gujarat. In 1630 Jean Mocquet noted that *bertangil*, a cotton cloth dyed blue or dark purple, was the proper trading cloth for the East African market. This seems to have been a specific kind of plain white calico, or *bafta*, which was taken, bleached, to Agra and Ahmedabad, near the source of indigo, to be dyed blue, black, or red. For the decades after 1630 Tavernier notes that "these kinds of cotton cloth, which cost from 2 to 12 rupees the piece, are exported to the coast of MELINDE, and they constitute the principal trade done by the Governor of MOZAMBIQUE," about which he was unusually well informed.[54] Most of these cloths were probably obtained by the correspondents of *vania* merchants in Diu and Goa who operated in the main towns of Mughal Gujarat. But there also was a certain amount of direct trade in Portuguese vessels with Cambay, and perhaps other Mughal ports, for the

Mozambique market.[55] Yet exaggerating the volume of this trade would be a mistake; in 1600 it was probably no more than about four percent of the total export trade of western India.[56] East Africa's share of this trade was probably not much different at the end of the seventeenth century. But if the trade of East Africa was peripheral to that of Gujarat as a whole, it was absolutely central to that of Diu. Raychaudhuri argues that an "increase in export almost certainly meant an increase in production," particularly "a concentrated increase in comparatively small areas for which the quantitative changes involved might have proved to be significant." The proliferation of local industries at Diu in textile production, ivory and tortoise shell carving, and goldsmithing appears to bear out his general statement and to testify to the importance of East African products in the total economy of Diu.[57]

Very little is known about the organization of the Company of Mazanes at Mozambique in the first years of its operation after 1686. In 1752 it was represented there by Deuchande Seuchande, who was assisted by the curate judge of the company, by law the rector of the College of St. Francis Xavier in Mozambique. Thus, as a consequence of the active mercantile policy of the Society of Jesus, the Company of Mazanes enjoyed the protection of the Jesuits, with whom the *vanias* of Diu had long-standing amicable relations, although any advantages this union brought were completely nullified by Pombal's ruthless suppression of the order by 1760.[58] At mid-century, however, the colonial economy of Mozambique was completely dominated by the ivory trade to Gujarat, and this was exclusively in the hands of the Company of Mazanes and a handful of *vanias* and Muslims from the much less important Portuguese port of Daman in Gujarat, as well as Goa.[59]

In the late 1750s the Indian community of Mozambique, most of whom were Gujarati *vanias,* numbered more than two hundred individuals and was apparently larger than that of the Portuguese settlers. Although we do not know the composition of the community, the Portuguese governor general was petitioned in 1758 by forty gentiles, undoubtedly all *vanias,* and fourteen Muslim Indians, and this mix very likely represents the relative numerical strength of each community. The ownership of shops by merchants and goldsmiths in 1764 and 1765 reflects about the same proportions.[60] Two decades later the Indian population had increased by half, and there were extensive *vania* holdings on the mainland opposite the island capital, but it was now slightly smaller than the total Portuguese population on both the island and mainland.[61] This was probably the maximum size attained by the Indian community of Mozambique, most of whom were men without their families. By 1830, when Gujarati control of the colonial economy of Mozambique was being altered by the domination which European capital exercised over the booming slave trade, an official census counted a total of two hundred Indians on the island, all of whom gave Diu as their homeland. Ten were Parsees, five Muslims, the rest *vanias,* so there had been a marked decline in the Muslim Indian population of Mozambique since the 1760s. Seventy-seven were traders, twenty cashiers, and the rest artisans. Most were reported to work alone, while others had as many as six assistants. "Related individuals are grouped by houses, that is, the name of a merchant is indicated together with his associates, cashiers, cooks, etc." There were ninety such houses at Mozambique. Finally, all except two of the Gujaratis were slave owners, with one Fattechande Getta holding the largest number, seventy-six.[62] Presumably they resided in a specific neighborhood on the island, but none of the maps which I have seen includes this sort of detail. Finally, a detailed census of the Indian population of Diu in 1794 reveals that a total population of 6522 included 1645 *vanias,* more than twice the number of any other *jati* or non-Hindu group. Of the total *vania* community, 577 were men over the age of fourteen. By comparison, the *vania* population of Mozambique during this period was certainly a tenth as large and, given its predominately adult male composition, probably about a third the size of the adult male *vania* population of Diu itself.[63]

In addition to the representatives of the Company of Mazanes at Mozambique, the *vanias* of Diu also had their own captain and leading merchants there. In the 1760s the most prominent of these was Ponja Velgi, who as "the principal trader of that Market" and the "principal head of the traders of that Market" sought permission in 1762 to appear in public wearing a hat and being carried in a palanquin. A more precise indication of how important Ponja Velgi was in the commercial life of Mozambique comes from this same petition. In it he computed the customs duties paid from March 1760 to December 1762 on his imports and exports there as 134,114 *cruzados* and 095 *reis,* a striking figure when compared to the total income of the royal treasury of the island capital in the fiscal year 1760-1761, which amounted to 124,015 *cruzados* and 128 *reis.*[64] Although the documentation is silent on this point, he was almost certainly the captain of the *banians* of Mozambique. Whether or not he was also representative of the Company of Mazanes is not known, but the multiethnic character of the company (which I have argued above) may well have meant that this office was quite separate from individual community leadership at Mozambique. During the eighteenth century the Muslims of Gujarat also had community leaders at Mozambique. In 1723 the paymaster for the government was a Muslim Indian named Bashira Mucali. In 1759 one Abdul Razaca was named "Lieutenant of the Asian Muslims," a title which probably reflects the fact that their community was less important in the life of Mozambique than was that of the *vanias.* A few years later another wealthy Muslim Indian, Anangi Monagi, bid successfully for the leasing of the customs house and was also named inspector of ivory (*tareiro*) at Mozambique.[65] As the number of Muslims dwindled, however, positions such as these must have fallen increasingly into the hands of the *vanias.*

We have no direct evidence to indicate how the *vanias* came to drive their Muslim counterparts out of the Mozambique market, where they clearly were an important commercial force at least as late as the 1760s, but the circumstances are probably to be found in the 1777 dissolution of the Company of the Mazanes monopoly of the Mozambique trade from Diu. Within a few years the number of *vania* merchant vessels annually plying this route rose from one or two to as many as five.[66] The trade of Portuguese Daman probably also became even less important to Mozambique after the declaration of free trade at Diu. What emerges clearly through all of this, however, is that during the seventeenth and eighteenth centuries the trade of Gujarat with Portuguese East Africa, including both Mozambique and the Swahili coast, was almost entirely mediated through the agency of the Indian merchants of Diu, especially the *vanias*.

After the expulsion of the Portuguese from Fort Jesus, Mombasa, in 1698, the Swahili coast trade suffered a severe depression as the result of very unstable conditions during the first half century of haphazard Omani Arab hegemony there.[67] But during these years a different body of Gujarati merchants began to make their mark along the Swahili coast. In the late 1720s, for example, three of the vessels used to transport Omani troops to East Africa were borrowed from *vanias*. These were most likely provided by the *vania* community at Muscat, who, like so many others in the ports of the Red Sea and South Arabia, were part of a general expansion of *vanias,* Jains, and other Hindu merchants in this region during the seventeenth century.[68] Indeed, as early as 1653 Buckeridge remarked that the towns of Muqdisho, Marka, and Baraawe on the southern Somali coast, which "have been long free from any Tribute to ye Portugalls... are yearly traded to with 4 or 5 Tourins, or smale vesails from Suratt, which bring thence A good quantitie of such goods as are usualie brought from Mombasse & Pate." Seventy-five years later the same pattern of avoiding imperial domination along the Swahili coast was reported from Pate in the annual trade of three ships from Surat to Barawa, where they could carry on their business without fear of Omani interference.[69] With the coming to power of the Busaidi dynasty in Oman after 1744 and the development of the East African empire based on Zanzibar after 1750, these Gujarati merchants were at last able to extend their operations to this market. Most of them undoubtedly had strong connections with Surat at this time, where the dominant group were the Muslim Bohras, for despite its impending collapse after the merchants' revolt between 1730 and 1732 Surat remained in the 1740s "one of the best, the finest, and richest and greatest marts, not only of the Mogul's country, but of all the Indies. . . . It is here that the Indians constantly embark to go and trade on the coasts of

Persia, Arabia, Egypt, and Africa, even to the Cape of Good Hope, and in the Island of Madagascar."[70]

The collapse of the Mughal empire in the 1750s, the emergence of British Bombay over Mughal Surat, and the rivalry for political and economic command of the Swahili coast between Mazrui Mombasa and Busaidi Zanzibar, unresolved until the fourth decade of the nineteenth century, must have discouraged the domination of any single Gujarati trading group there. Indeed, recent studies of Indian merchant capitalists in East Africa during the nineteenth century demonstrate that while most of them were Gujarati, among Hindus the predominant group were *bhattias* rather than *vanias,* and that Shia Muslims, mainly Khojas and Bohras, were more numerous, though less significant economically. For most of them, however, their origins in East Africa generally do not antecede the final Omani Busaidi victory over Mombasa in 1837 and the movement of Seyyid Said ibn Sultan's capital from Muscat to Zanzibar in 1840. With the exception of Catholic Goans, most of these Gujarati merchants had their closest ties with Bombay and Kutch and were British subjects.[71]

During the second half of the eighteenth century, then, commercial organization and the personnel of trade between Gujarat and East Africa underwent important changes; patterns established in the early sixteenth century by the intervention of the Portuguese in the Asian trade gave way to new ones which emerged after the collapse of the Mughal empire and the rise of the British in India and the Omani Arabs on the Swahili coast. But despite these changes Gujarati textiles continued to dominate the East African trade into the early decades of the nineteenth century, when first American and then British cottons seized the market, decimating the Indian cotton textile manufacturing industry. Although Gujarati merchants continued to play a vital role in East Africa after this time, they no longer operated as independent merchant capitalists, but as compradors for Western industrial capitalism.

CHAPTER 2

The Western Indian Ocean as a Regional Food Network in the Nineteenth Century*

Introduction

The focus of most economic historians of non-Western societies is the expanding world market and the trade carried on between their particular study area and the capitalist economies of Western Europe and North America. At the level of world market analysis there is therefore very little room left for the kind of trade which I discuss in this paper.[1] Even in relevant area studies the dominant concern among economic historians is with the impact of the West.[2] Without minimizing that impact, I think it is possible to penetrate this larger topic in order to reveal not only the existence of a vigorous regional food network, but also its relationship to capitalist penetration in the nineteenth century. Once we get beyond questions about the destruction of indigenous manufactures and the increasing exports of colonial agricultural crops that dominate the literature, we can see that there was a great deal of commercial activity that was carried on throughout the century in indigenous foodstuffs.[3]

* Reprinted from I.C.I.O.S. II: International Congress on Indian Ocean Studies, Perth, Western Australia, 5-12 December 1984, *Proceedings Section A: Resources, Environment and Economic Development*, 20pp.

23

Questions, Sources, and Definitions

As a starting point, we need to ask about the identity and provenance of these items of trade; about the organization of production; about the direction in which these items were traded, as well as the means by which they were transported; about the composition and dimensions of this trade, not to mention its capitalization; about the development of markets for foodstuffs that stimulated this traffic; and, finally, about the implications of this phenomenon for regional economic history. I cannot hope to answer all of these questions satisfactorily in this initial, tentative essay, but I can at least seek to tackle the problem in a manner that emphasizes the internal, regional vitality of the Western Indian Ocean without ignoring the impact of the expanding capitalist world market.

James de Vere Allen has remarked that "the historian turning to the Indian Ocean area is faced with a far larger amount of documentary evidence than is often realized."[4] Indeed, no one is more aware than I of the fact that I have barely scratched the surface. As an historian of eastern Africa my sources are naturally richer, though by no means exhaustive, for the African side of things. Nevertheless, they point towards the kinds of rewards that remain to be ferreted out from a similar combing of the larger corpus of printed and archival primary sources that bear upon the other principal areas that I discuss below.[5]

Before proceeding to the body of my text, I think it useful to clarify certain basic definitions. First, having decided to examine the regional food network of the Western Indian Ocean, I had to determine more precisely what items to include under the heading of foodstuffs. About foodgrains and fruits there are no problems, but with oilseeds and oils, sugar, coffee, and tea, for example, I found it necessary to distinguish between those intended for the world market and those destined for the regional market. Indeed, this same division reflects the fact that foodgrains became an important item of export outside the region later in the century, and also helps to factor out all provisions that entered the regional network from Western Europe and North America. In these terms, then, I make no distinction between what might be called subsistence and cash crops, because once provisions entered the regional market they were, by definition, commodities. Similarly, for the sake of this paper, at least, so long as the foodstuffs were produced and consumed within the region I have not distinguished between them on the basis of the organization of their production. Thus, peasant and plantation crops in both the indigenous and European spheres are included in my survey so long as they conform to this fundamental definition. For the present I have also decided not to include spices in my analysis, though I may want to do so at a later date.

Finally, there remains the problem of defining the region. By the Western Indian Ocean I mean to include the coast of eastern Africa as far south as Delagoa Bay, the Red Sea, southern Arabia, the Persian Gulf, and the western coast of the Indian sub-continent. With respect to the entire littoral, I naturally include their hinterlands as far as these were directly connected to the prevailing system of production and exchange. I also include all of the islands of the Western Indian Ocean, but exclude Sri Lanka, which strikes me as being much less a part of this regional system. That said, the fact remains that this cannot pretend to be an exclusive definition and there are interesting linkages within the wider oceanic basin that make their presence felt even in this preliminary paper.

The Emergence of a Regional Food Market

There were five basic categories of demand for foodstuffs at work in the nineteenth century. Some were already in existence and some were entirely new; some could be supplied effectively by their own area hinterlands, while others had always depended at least partly on regional maritime supplies; but taken together they stimulated an unprecedented regional provisioning network in the nineteenth century.

First, the nineteenth century witnessed the growth of a new series of urban concentrations which required provisioning. Aden, Muscat, and Zanzibar Town are perhaps the most notable of these, but there were several other commercial entrepôts that arose during this period along the African coast which contributed to this demand. Similarly, the continued food dependence and growth of urban areas such as Port Louis, Mozambique Island, Jiddah, Mecca, and Madinah must also be added to this development. So, too, must the many coastal villages and small towns that dotted the shores of the Western Indian Ocean. The reasons for the growth of these urban concentrations vary, but most reflect a combination of commercial and political stimuli that derive from the general growth of world trade in this era.

Second, the expansion of the plantation sector in non-subsistence crops at Zanzibar and Mauritius was a contributing factor that both supported the urban growth of Zanzibar Town and Port Louis and made it impossible for the islands themselves to provide the provisions necessary for the urban population of those places.

Third, the provisioning trade for every sort of shipping increased throughout the nineteenth century. It can be argued that not all of these provisions were consumed within the context of the regional economy, but certainly many of them were. The rule of thumb that I have applied in this instance takes into account both the provenance of such supplies and their consumers. If they were produced in one place and exported to where they were required, then I include them. By this standard, for example, the role played by the Comoro Islands in provisioning mainly British vessels taking the inner passage to India is excluded. But the coastal provisioning of regional shipping is included because its consumers were inhabitants of the region.

Fourth, the steady demand of Muslim pilgrims making the *hajj* during the nineteenth century was another critical factor.[6] In the case of the major towns of the Hijaz, this was probably also a stimulus to their own urban growth during the century.

Fifth, and finally, cultural food preferences had a role to play in creating a regional food network.[7] The extensive population movement that attended these interrelated processes, but especially the dominant one of urbanization, created a regional dispersal of people who required foodstuffs that could not be satisfactorily supplied locally. African slaves throughout the region and Indian merchants dominating virtually all of the regional trade and concentrated in all of its towns were the principal actors in this aspect of demand. But the demand by indigenous populations for specific foods that could not be adequately supplied locally must also be taken into account.

How these preferences developed historically is not at issue here, though this certainly reflects an aspect of deeper cultural exchanges within the Indian Ocean region as a whole. But it is appropriate at this point to emphasize the importance of the ocean itself as a highway of communication and transportation, for without the maritime technology of the region's peoples this food network could not have come into existence or been sustained.

The Regional Food Network

Let me now turn to the evidence for the regional provisioning of several of the most important centers of demand for foodstuffs in the nineteenth century. By taking these in turn clockwise from south to north, I hope to reveal the complexity and sophistication of the supply network as it actually functioned.

Following the British conquest of Mauritius it was no longer possible for that colony to be provisioned from Réunion. The increase in population that attended the importation of indentured Indian labor to work on the island's sugar plantations aggravated what was already a serious problem. As Auguste Toussaint has noted, "From the outset, the question of provisions loomed large." While Africans produced their own manioc locally, "the Indians ate rice, ghee, dholl and flour. . . . all articles that had to be imported." By 1870, Muslim merchants dominated the provision trade and were deeply involved in "the exportation of sugar to India and the importation of beef from Madagascar, a trade that developed in importance as the population increased, locally raised livestock being insufficient to meet requirements."[8]

This latter aspect of provisioning Mauritius was not a new development. A French traveler in 1801 observed that the island took "the greatest part of its beef from Madagascar."[9] Indeed, Madagascar was initially also the principal source of its rice supplies. Similarly, although Réunion continued to supply much of its own provisions, earlier in the century Madagascar was a significant source of supplementary supplies.[10] Hurricane damage was also a persistent problem which frequently necessitated purchasing "rice from India or from Madagascar at a very elevated price." According to one French traveler, "It is from Madagascar that our colony takes a great part of the provisions of which it has need," notwithstanding that "the cattle are exhausted by a journey that is sometimes long and fatiguing; the poultry is not worth more and are very costly; finally the rice is of an inferior quality."[11] That said, it would be interesting to know how the local population reacted to the suspension from 1815 to 1853 by Queen Ranavalona of the Madagascar coastal trade to both French and British shipping, "including the almost indispensable bullock traffic on which Mauritius and Bourbon depended."[12]

In the early 1850s, Osgood implied that some of the needs of Mauritius that were once supplied by Madagascar were "now procured from the more distant African coast," while fifteen years later another traveler mentions that a flourishing salted beef trade had opened up at St. Augustin's Bay to supply these markets.[13] In any event, from the perspective of Imerina, the dependency of the French on Madagascar's supplies was not in doubt, for during the Franco-Malagasy war of 1883-1885 the Malagasy government shut off the rice and cattle trade to outsiders, an action which devastated French traders at both Mahajanga and Tamatave, and was resumed thereafter.[14]

If Madagascar was a critical source of provisions for the Mascarenes, it was no less an integral part of the supply network for Mozambique Island. In particular, the trading center at Bombetoka Bay figures prominently. According to a British naval officer who visited there in 1802, it was "supplied with as fine beef as any in the world, at the moderate price of from one to two dollars each bullock." Salted beef and rice were also plentiful, and the port was frequented by Arabs from Muscat.[15] Two years later, a Frenchman at Mozambique noted that Arab traders sometimes carried slaves from Mozambique to Bombetoka and returned with cargoes of rice.[16]

Virtually all visitors to this port commented on one aspect or another of this trade in provisions, although they did not always specify the direction of such trade.[17] In fact, the trade of Bombetoka Bay extended to direct traffic with European vessels. but primarily with those coming from Surat, Muscat, Zanzibar, and Mozambique.[18] According to the Bishop of Mozambique in 1822, although the Malagasy sometimes traded directly to Mozambique, the overwhelming bulk of this trade was in the hands of Arabs.[19]

This particular branch of the provisioning trade to Mozambique Island is especially well documented for the period after 1829, when we possess some official licenses to trade and cargo manifests from the Portuguese customs house. These reveal that the typical cargo consisted of some combination of cattle and rice, either in the husk or cleaned, although in one instance poultry were also declared.[20] Commenting a decade later on the export trade in beef and rice from western Madagascar, Guillain specified that while fresh beef was shipped to Mozambique, only salted beef was sent elsewhere.[21] By the early 1850s, one observer believed that "About eighty or ninety tons of rice are exported annually, which is generally bought up by a Portuguese trader for the Mozambique market, who supplies it to the Government of that place at one dollar for one hundred pounds weight."[22]

We must careful, however, to set this traffic in its proper regional context. Muslim traders from north of Cape Delgado carried a "prodigious quantity" of provisions to Mozambique without which its population could not survive. Coastal shipping from Arabia, Mombasa, Malindi, Kilwa, Mafia Island, the Comoros, and Madagascar traded sorghum, rice, coconut oil, some cattle, and salted meats all along the coast.[23] An 1830 cargo manifest for a *pangaio* from Madagascar vividly reflects this wider network in microcosm, for it carried not only thirty-six head of cattle, but also ghee, salted fish and beef, almonds and other nuts, as well as tallow and nails.[24] Indeed, the typical coasting pattern of these vessels was to ply their trade between a number of different ports within the region, carrying some goods from their point of origin to their farthest destination and exchanging others more locally along the way.

Also significant was the role played by the Comoro Islands, which supplied Mozambique with rice, sorghum, finger millet, an unspecified food called *sambo*, which was consumed by slaves, some oats, beans, mung or green gram, coconuts, coconut oil, ghee, honey, goats, and cattle.[25] The same great variety of provisions was furnished by the Muslim coasting trade from the nominally Portuguese-controlled Kerimba Islands and the Swahili coast beyond them to the north, although millets clearly predominated and wheat and sugar were also noted.[26] Direct shipments of provisions to Mozambique were also recorded during the 1830s from Diu and Daman, in Gujarat, and there was some additional help to be found from trade in Muslim and Portuguese shipping that linked the Portuguese East African capital to its outlying posts at Quelimane, Inhambane, and Delagoa Bay.[27] That the very existence of Mozambique depended upon the provisioning trade of the Muslim dominated region is vividly attested to by the letters written by the Governor-General of Mozambique to the rulers of Madagascar, Bombetoka, Nzwani, and Ngazija, asking them "to send their *pangaios* with provisions and cattle to Mozambique" during the famine of 1831.[28]

A careful survey of the agricultural production and commercial movement undertaken in 1858 by the Portuguese Governor of the Cape Delgado district makes possible an even keener appreciation of the kind of interchange that typically took place in an area which was both an importer and exporter of foodstuffs. Imports from India included sugar, tea, ghee, and wheat, while flour came from Mozambique and fresh peppers were taken from Zanzibar. Exports included cattle to Mozambique; both raw and clean rice, sorghum and finger millet, and tobacco to Mozambique and Zanzibar; and sesame to both of these places and Bombay. The difference between the total agricultural production (78,377 *panjas* equivalent to about 1,295,101 kg) of the district and its local consumption (66,870 *panjas* or about 1,104,960 kg), that is, 11,507 *panjas* or approximately 190,142 kg of various grains, pulses, and vegetables, "was regularly exported for Mozambique, Zanzibar, and other points." This did not include 3,000 *panjas* (some 49,572 kg) of sesame exports.[29]

At Zanzibar the linkages between East Africa and the northern reaches of the Western Indian Ocean emerge more distinctly. In 1819 exports of finger millet from the island in vessels from Muscat, Surat, and Bombay which had come down from the north carrying sugar, coffee, and dates, among other items, were noted.[30] In the early 1830s this inventory of foodstuffs was expanded to include coconut oil, rice, millet, and ghee from eastern Africa and wheat, dates, raisins, salt, and dried fish from Muscat.[31] It is the evidence from the middle decades of the century, however, that really brings into sharp focus the complexity of the food exchanges that centered on Zanzibar.

The rise of a plantation system dedicated to clove production on Zanzibar and the associated urban development of Zanzibar Town combined to transform that agriculturally rich island into a net importer of food. Rice, in particular, the provision of which was demanded by the new urban elite, was cited by both Osgood and Rigby as an example of a former export which by the 1850s had become the principal imported grain of that port.[32] Vast quantities of rice, totaling some 18,640,000 lbs. in 1859, were imported primarily from India and western Madagascar, but also from the Comoros, Pemba and some of the coastal ports. By the end of the century sup- plies from the Rufiji River flood plains had emerged as a sufficiently important source for that area to acquire the nickname of "Little Calcutta." Sorghum and finger millet were imported for local mass consumption from the entire length of the African continent, as well as a little *bajri* from India. Maize also came from the African ports, and small amounts of wheat came in from Muscat in 1859; these other grain imports amounted to 3,831,000 lbs. In the same year 175,000 lbs. of ghee was supplied from India, Mafia, Mombasa, and Pemba, as well as the Benaadir coast. Goats and sheep came mainly from this last place and from Berbera, and occasionally from the Mrima coast opposite Zanzibar. Honey was funneled in from the en- tire coast, and some even came from Arabia. Dates, raisins, almonds, coffee, salt, and salt-fish continued to be shipped to Zanzibar from Arabia and the Persian Gulf, while some salt-fish was also imported from the Benaadir. Sugar and molasses also were supplied from

India; some vegetables were brought over from Pemba, but onions had to be shipped in from southern Arabia.[33]

The generally accelerated level of regional trade in all commodities prompted the intensification of grain production in the coastal hinterlands of eastern Africa by both independent agriculturalists and slave labor on small and large plantations to such an extent that there emerged an important direct export trade in grains to southern Arabia and Oman. Cooper has reconstructed both the dimensions and social organization of this process for Malindi and Mombasa, the former of which was referred to by one commentator in the 1870s as "the granary of Eastern Africa" and which became known locally as *Mtama*, "Millet." Ylvisaker has documented this development for the Lamu Archipelago, while I have done the same for the Benaadir ports, which a visitor in the 1840s described as "the grain coast for the supply of Southern Arabia."[34] Tanga is also known to have exported millet directly to Arabia.[35] Millet was nevertheless still being exported from Zanzibar throughout the nineteenth century. French sources suggest that the traffic probably declined from the 1840s to the 1860s, but in the latter decade cereals were still going off to Arabia and even in some years to Kutch and British India.[36]

Sesame was also an important regional export from eastern Africa. The best supplies to Zanzibar were from the Kilwa coast in the south, and Guillain estimated in the 1840s that about 2,000 tons were annually sold on the Zanzibar market and re-exported to Mokha, Mukalla, Muscat, and India. By the 1860s, however, most of the sesame was being exported to Europe, although a small amount was still being taken by Arabia.[37]

Perhaps the most intriguing evidence for the food interdependency of this part of the Western Indian Ocean, like its counterpart from Mozambique, dates to a period of crisis. An Alsatian missionary at Zanzibar in the late 1870s attributed the shortage and consequent high cost of provisions there to the great famine that devastated India during this period. The mission, he lamented, was experiencing unprecedented financial difficulties as a result of the "ruinous prices" of provisions. "Last year foodstuffs were exported to India. This year they are again being exported to southern Africa, which has suffered a terrible drought for the past eighteen months."[38] Two years later the situation was complicated by drought in continental eastern Africa and the lingering impact of famine in India and China.[39] Fragmentary as this evidence may be, it suggests the emergence of a much wider regional market for grains than had previously existed before the integration of the Indian Ocean into the world economy.

Although the Red Sea comprised a more enclosed sub-region within the Western Indian Ocean before the opening of the Suez Canal in 1869, it was not entirely distinct. Milburn indicates at the beginning of the century that Jiddah, Quseir, and Massawa were the limits of Indian vessels coming from the south and that those departing from Suez stopped at Jiddah, which he calls "only a mart between Egypt and India," an observation echoed a few years later by Burckhardt. Milburn estimated that not less than 20,000 tons of grain were sent annually from Suez and Quseir to Arabia, but also noted that grain was imported in 1805 from Madras and Bombay. Under the rubric of grain, Burckhardt includes wheat, barley, beans, lentils, durrah (sorghum), and rice from Egypt, although he adds that

> Most of the rice used at Djidda is brought as ballast by the ships from India. The best source comes from Guzerat and Cutch: it forms the chief article of food among the people of the HedJaz, who prefer it to the rice from Egypt . . . The India rice is rather cheaper, and is transported from Djidda to Mekka, Tayf, Medina, and thence as far as Nedjed.[40]

In the late 1840s, cereals were also considered to be "a lucrative trade in which nearly 300 vessels of from 80 to 100 tons were engaged" from Massawa, although by the last decades of the century it was more notably an importer of rice.[41]

The Hijaz imported coconuts from India and the Somali and Swahili coasts. By the same token, almonds, coffee, even a little grain, raisins, and shark fins were sent to India. Large baskets of date paste were exported to India, as well as consumed locally, although smaller baskets of pressed dates were also imported from Basrah because "this kind is preferred to every other."[42]

A major trade in ghee was also carried on between the Red Sea ports. That from sheeps' milk was exported from Suakin, but the best and most came to Jiddah from Massawa and was called "Dahlak butter." According to Burckhardt, "whole ships' cargoes arrive from thence, the greater part of which is again carried to Mekka." Ghee from buffalo's milk was also imported at Jiddah from Quseir. But throughout the century Massawa retained its primacy as the chief supplier of ghee to Jiddah, exports rising to more than 500,000 kg per year in the middle of the century and continuing to dominate the trade of that place right into the Italian period.[43]

In the early decades of the century a similarly complex system of food exchanges fed Muslim pilgrims who approached Madinah by way of Yanbu. Coasting vessels between there and the Gulf of Aqaba traded Egyptian provisions at Bedouin camps for cattle, butter, and honey which they then carried to Yanbu or Jiddah.[44]

The Gulf of Aden is an area which experienced perhaps the most intense development of the provisions trade in the nineteenth century as a consequence of the British occupation of Aden in 1839. At the beginning of the century, although it was the chief seasonal port for the collection of gums from the Soomaali coast, Aden existed in the shadow of Mokha, which was the center of both the world and regional market trade in coffee. In addition to supplying coffee from the Ethiopian highlands, the principal Soomaali entrepôts of Zeila and Berbera also dealt in livestock, ghee, sorghum, and some wheat.[45] Even before the British seized Aden, however, the annual fair at Berbera attracted up to one hundred vessels from India to trade for goats, ghee, coffee, and gums.[46] Traders who touched along the Hadramaut coast mainly exchanged rice and sugar for salt fish and shark fins. At the principal port of Mukalla food imports included rice from Bombay, dates and dried fruits from Muscat, millets from Aden, coffee from Mokha, sheep and honey from Berbera, Quseir and other African ports.[47]

The absolute dependency of British Aden for its food supplies on overseas sources caused it to look to the Soomaali coast for livestock products, to India for grains, and to the Persian Gulf for dates. There is a great deal of evidence for these trades, as well as for the role that Aden played in the re-export of food supplies, both overseas and inland, especially during regional periods of famine, which plagued the Hadramaut, eastern Africa, and western India in the 1860s.[48] Aden's development as a steamer port from this decade further stimulated its food requirements and re-exports. Indeed. F.M. Hunter's meticulous inventory of Aden's supplies in 1875-1876, which is too extensive to be cited in detail here, makes plain that the volume and diversity of the provisions trade was quite remarkable.

Virtually the entire region had some share in supplying Aden. Most rice came from Calcutta, but some also arrived from Madras and Bombay; sorghum mainly from Persia, but also from Zanzibar, the ports of the Yemen, Kutch and Bombay; wheat was supplied from Bombay, but also from Kutch and Persia; pulses came from a variety of ports in the Red Sea, Persian Gulf, and Arabian Sea; potatoes and onions were shipped in from Bombay and Egypt. Most supplies of fruit were local, but "from Zanzibar large quantities of oranges and pine-apples are received; and from Bombay, mangoes. pumaloes, and oranges." Finally, so great was the increased demand for sheep and cattle that in 1875-1876 some 63,262 sheep and goats, and 1,104 cattle were imported from Africa.[49] This pattern remained unchanged in subsequent years, with large imports of grain, dates, and sugar from India and the Persian Gulf continuing, on the one hand, and livestock products from the Soomaali ports holding their own, on the other hand. In 1883, for example, Berbera yielded 15,605 sheep and goats, 1,239 cattle, and 12,090 kg of ghee, and a decade later one visitor to Aden remarked that "sheep and goats are weekly shipped in large quantities from Berbera, Bulhar, and Zeilah . . . ."[50]

On the Soomaali coast the exchange of provisions was clearly complementary, as exports of livestock and ghee were weighed against imports of grain and dates from India.[51] Those smaller ports that were farther east along the Gulf of Aden drew upon direct exchanges with their counterparts in the Hadramaut. In the early 1870s exports of livestock and ghee had been interrupted by the effects of the 1868 famine, but by the 1880s they had reached levels of perhaps 5,000 to 6,000 sheep and cattle, plus 13-15,000 kg of ghee. *Mulji*, the fruit of the Doum palm, was carried over to southern Arabia, while sorghum and dates were imported from there, as was maize from the Swahili coast. Shark fins were another item of export along this coast.[52] By the 1880s the volume of food imports at Berbera and Zeila had apparently increased considerably, with grain. dates, and sugar leading the way.[53]

Although I have no data on the trade of the eastern Hadramaut ports after mid-century, in the 1840s they drove a lucrative trade in grain all along the coast at places like Sayhut and other towns controlled by the Mahra. The region imported an immense quantity of dates from the Persian Gulf, as well as rice from the Malabar coast and sorghum from Zanzibar. Exports included salt and salt-fish to the latter and shark fins to the east.[54] Finally, standing within this orbit but apparently somewhat outside its trading network because of its close political links to Muscat was the island of Socotra, which in the 1830s is said to have carried on an important business in dates from Muscat for local ghee, which was then carried on to Zanzibar, where it was exchanged for grain and slaves.[55]

The centrality of Muscat to the luxury trade of the Persian Gulf in the nineteenth century is well known. Not surprisingly, provisions were also an important category of commodities, particularly exports of dates and salt fish, as well as almonds, raisins, honey, sheep, and cattle. Some of these came from the interior of Oman or from the immediate coastal waters, but some reached Muscat through the maritime trade of the Persian Gulf. Omani ports such as Matrah and Barka, as well as Omani-controlled Persian ports such as Bandar Abbas and Lingeh directed provisions to Muscat either for internal consumption or for re-export.[56] In the 1840s halwa manufactured in the interior at Nazwa and at Muscat was exported to both India and Persia.[57] In the later decades of the century, although the luxury trade of Muscat declined, that in basic necessities, including foodstuffs, persisted. Dates, in particular, dominated exports, typically earning more than Maria Theresa $750,000 annually.[58]

If I am able to say less about other parts of the Persian Gulf, there is scattered evidence from Basrah and al-Hasa. both of which were noted for the exceptional quality of their dates, for continued direct exports in the nineteenth century. Indeed. Lorimer's accounting of the Persian Gulf date trade at the end of the century leaves no doubt about its continued vitality.[59] Together with the Red Sea and the Hadramaut coast, the Persian Gulf also remained a center of the trade in sharks' fins, tails, and maws, which when dried in the sun were shipped to Bombay for eventual export to China.[60]

Finally, I do not propose to say much at all about the trade of the Indian sub-continent during the nineteenth century because its regional dominance in all aspects of commercial organization is so well attested. Even a survey of the available printed official sources of its trade is certain to yield a mass of data reflecting this fact and detailing the particular significance of its regional export trade in rice. But as a careful scrutiny of Milburn's commercial handbook indicates for the very beginning of the century, we must remember not to overlook the labyrinthine maritime exchanges of provisions that occurred within this region from Sind and Gujarat right down to Cape Comorin and, to be sure, beyond.[61]

Conclusions

However tentative and imbalanced this survey might appear, I feel confident that at the very least it has demonstrated the existence of a flourishing regional food network in the nineteenth century. To fully comprehend its operation will require a much more exhaustive examination of the entire corpus of available sources, so that quantitative measurement, changes in composition and direction, fluctuations in prices, and problems of capitalization and production, among other questions, can be properly addressed and answered.

One answer that can provisionally be put forward concerns the apparent collapse of this system during the early 1900s. For although there is evidence that this regional maritime trade in provisions lingered far longer than most realize, it was clearly overwhelmed during the course of the present century.[62] Here we must look to eastern Africa and Madagascar, I think, for our principal explanation. A decade of natural and imperial violence beginning in the 1890s thoroughly disrupted indigenous systems of production, whether free or slave, which were then replaced systematically by colonial economic systems that reassigned labor in a multitude of ways that undermined the structure of indigenous subsistence production. While our measures are extremely crude, eastern Africa, including Madagascar, seems to have moved during this period from being a net exporter of provisions within the region to a net importer within the world economy. The implications of this hypothesis are important not only for historians, but also for those who must plan the future development of the region's peoples.

CHAPTER 3

Indian Ocean Africa: The Island Factor*

"Zanzibar is a large and splendid island some 2,000 miles in circumference."[1]
                                        —*Marco Polo, late 13th century*

"We came to the island of Mambasa, a large island two days' journey by sea from the Sawahil country."[2]
                                        —*Ibn Battuta, 1331*

"The island of Kilwa . . . lies half a league from the mainland, opposite to a peninsula formed by the confluence of two large rivers. It has three safe ports, which are very vast and in which the anchorage is good."[3]
                                        —*Jean-Vincent Morice, 1776*

"Yesterday morning, shortly after day-break, we descried this interesting island [Nzwani]. . . . We coasted for some time along a bold shore, defined by an even line, like a wall, and in many places appearing inaccessible . . . [until] Before us was an extensive bay, scarcely ruffled by the breeze."[4]
                                        —*James Prior, 1812*

"Mauritius is a small island, and it is also one vast sugar factory."[5]
                                        —*Captain Colomb, R.N., 1873*

*Reprinted from *Emergences: Journal for the Study of Media and Composite Cultures*, 10, 2 (2000), pp. 373-386.

"I had not known we were to visit Kwale Island. I had never, indeed, heard of the place until that moment. No one had mentioned it, and it was too small to be on our small-scale chart. Kwale is a low island lying close to the Tanganyika coast, by the northern end of the Rufiji delta. Though I had never heard of it, it is a place much frequented by Arabs bound to the south."[6]   —*Alan Villiers, 1940*

Most scholars would today agree that we can no longer continue to restrict our understanding of African History to the continental land mass known as Africa. Renewed attention to Africa's role in world history and, particularly, its relationship to the African diaspora have led historians to identify three major world historical contexts in which to situate Africa: Atlantic Africa, Mediterranean Africa, and Indian Ocean Africa. Of these three differently defined Africas, only Mediterranean Africa does not include a significant island factor insofar as the peoples of Africa are concerned. No serious scholar would attempt to understand Atlantic Africa or the Black Atlantic, however, without making reference to the role that islands have played in that history. From Cape Verde to São Tomé to the Caribbean, islands are widely understood to have played a major role in defining Africa's place in the Atlantic world. Although islands have certainly been recognized as an important factor in the Indian Ocean world by any number of scholars, no one has previously attempted to locate all the islands of the Indian Ocean in their relationship to the history of eastern Africa. At first glance, this might seem an obvious task. After all, historians of Africa include Madagascar, the great African island, within their purview; Swahili historiography is to a very considerable extent focused on island societies such as the Lamu Archipelago, Zanzibar, Kilwa, and the Comoros; and students of the slave trade in the southwest Indian Ocean have focused on the Mascarene Islands. Nevertheless, while individual scholars have discussed specific island settings in the context of their work on Indian Ocean Africa, the kind of overview and synthesis that I have in mind has not been attempted. This is the objective I have set for myself in this essay.

Because the islands I am discussing are situated in the Indian Ocean, the obvious place to begin is with studies of the vast region as a whole to see if there is any help on that horizon. All who write on oceans must acknowledge the influence of Fernand Braudel, who attributes great importance to the islands of the Mediterranean, noting that "The Mediterranean islands are more numerous and above all more important than is generally supposed." Braudel also expands the definition of island to include peninsulas, or "Islands that the sea does not surround."[7] To take an influential example from Atlantic Africa, John Thornton's major contribution on Africa's role in the making of the early modern Atlantic world specifically cites Braudel as his starting point. Thornton also accords central importance to the Atlantic islands in the creation of an Atlantic system and in that ocean's plantation economy.[8] But while Africa lies at the center of Thornton's Atlantic world, it is to varying degrees marginal in the major available histories of the Indian Ocean world. The first general modern history of the Indian Ocean, for example, by the late distinguished archivist of Mauritius, Auguste Toussaint, both pays homage to Braudel and centrally locates islands in his interpretation of the region. In particular, Toussaint regards the widely separated island groups of the central Indian Ocean - the Chagos, Seychelles, and the Mascarenes - as the ideal place "to be initiated into the life of the Indian Ocean."[9] But Toussaint's patriotic conceptual scheme places far too much interpretive weight on these small island societies for them to bear, especially when one considers that they were only populated from the seventeenth century onwards. K.N. Chaudhuri's impressive study of the pre-modern economic history of the Indian Ocean adopts a continental perspective and only discusses islands in passing.[10] For him, Africa lies at the extreme margins of this universe. Kenneth McPherson's more recent history of the Indian Ocean seeks to go beyond these two works by establishing "the relationship between maritime trade and processes of cultural diffusion and interaction" and focusing on littoral societies as the thread that bound together the region's history. McPherson accords East Africa a reasonable amount of space in his interpretation of this world region and acknowledges the islands of the Indian Ocean, but he grants them no special place in his frame of reference.[11] Several collections of historical essays on the Indian Ocean fare no better with respect to the recognition they accord to islands.[12] Finally, there are a few geographical and scientific studies of the Indian Ocean islands, even in association with the African continent, but their disciplinary focus renders these less useful than one might hope.[13] There is one important exception, however, in the comprehensive new analysis by Jean-Louis Guébourg, who recognizes the historical significance of cumulative cultural mixing in his conclusion that "Dans ces îles de l'océan Indien, les hommes ont transposé des <parcelles de civilisation> sur un espace limité."[14]

The negative stereotype of Africa as "the dark continent" incorrectly construed the continent as insular and isolated. In thinking about the concept of Indian Ocean Africa, Braudel and Thornton's approaches bear more promise than any of the earlier histories of the Indian Ocean because they both subvert and expand the prevailing notion of Africa from one that is continent-bound to another that emphasizes quite different historical and cultural connections. Similarly, Guébourg's synthesis also points in a useful direction by underscoring the extraordinary cross-fertilization of cultures, traditions, and languages that characterizes the islands of the Indian Ocean. My purpose here is to integrate what are often referred to as the African islands of the Indian Ocean into a broader interpretation of East African history that explores the ways in which the history of cultural exchange throughout the region I have defined as Indian Ocean Africa might significantly alter the conventional understanding of Africa. To accomplish this I will discuss five aspects of island history as it relates to Indian Ocean Africa:
  • the commercial integration of East Africa into the
    Indian Ocean world;
  • the islamization of coastal East Africa;
  • the peopling of Madagascar;
  • the slave trade of the southwest Indian Ocean; and
  • the economics and politics of colonial and independent
    East Africa.

The Commercial Integration of East Africa
into the Indian Ocean World

Coastal Eastern Africa is marked by a number of offshore islands that range in size from the minuscule to the semi-continental. These islands also vary in distance from the shore to those that can be reached by swimming to those that lie well beyond immediate sight. The coast was well known to the merchants of the ancient Indian Ocean world from no later than the writing of the 1st century C.E. Alexandrian commercial guide, the *Periplus of the Erythraen Sea*, which described these links as "ancient."[15] Discovery of the workings of the monsoon winds made it possible for merchants to sail along the coast on a seasonal basis that integrated the entire littoral of the Western Indian Ocean. Non-African traders needed to move cautiously along these foreign shores, so they naturally looked for islands as stepping stones. The major coastal emporia noted in the *Periplus* have eluded positive identification, but we do know that the island of Socotra, off the Horn of Africa, was an important transit point and the Pyralean Islands (possibly the Lamu Archipelago, in northern Kenya) are also mentioned. Farther south lay the commercially insignificant island of Menouthias, probably Pemba.[16]

The full integration of this part of the African littoral was not accomplished, however, until the rise of Islam, the starting point for Chaudhuri's history. Combining literary and archaeological evidence we can readily see the significance of islands in the commercial integration of the coast into the Western Indian Ocean. To be sure, not all significant settlements were on islands. Mogadishu, at the northern edge of the Benaadir coast of southern Somalia, is situated on the coast at an open roadstead, yet had emerged as one of the two most important city-states by the time of Ibn Battuta's visit in 1331. But many were. Manda, Shanga, and later Lamu (all in the Lamu Archipelago); Mombasa (although before the modern bridge was built that links it to the mainland it was possible to ford it from the northwest), Mtambwe Mkuu (off Pemba Island), Unguja Ukuu and Kizimkazi on Zanzibar, Kisimani Mafia, Kilwa, Mozambique

Island, and Angoche (to the north of the Zambezi River delta) are all located on islands, although certainly not all flourished at the same time. And while not all of these were major entrepôts, most were. As Mark Horton has observed,

> A particular feature of the early sites is their strongly maritime character. Often located adjacent to shallow but hard beaches and set close to sand-dunes, it is clear that their economic base derived from the sea. Indeed, many are located on islands or at the ends of narrow peninsulas.[17]

To return to Ibn Battuta, after he left Mogadishu, he spent a night at Mombasa before continuing on his way south to the dominant economic and political power on the coast at that time: Kilwa. The Kilwa that Ibn Battuta visited is today known as Kilwa Kisiwani, Kilwa on the island, to distinguish it from its nineteenth-century successor town of Kivinje, just north on the southern Tanzanian coast, which is today called Kilwa Kivinje. Beyond Kilwa, trade links extended past Cape Delgado to the coast of modern Mozambique as far south as Sofala, the coastal outlet for the gold-bearing regions of the Zimbabwean plateau. Mozambique Island and Angoche Island were critical way stations for this commercial expansion and both owed something to the commercial and political hegemony of Kilwa in the 14th and 15th centuries. To the southeast of Kilwa, seaborne traders had extended their reach to northwest Madagascar utilizing the Comoro Islands as stepping stones across the northern end of the Mozambique Channel.[18] Clearly, merchants needed partners with whom to exchange goods, as they could not permanently expect to do sustained business without regular contact. But as they were operating in foreign lands beset with many hazards, it is little wonder that the relative security of islands particularly appealed to these commercial adventurers.

When the Portuguese intervened in this Islamic commercial system at the end of the 15th century, the East African world they encountered coming from the sea was thoroughly dominated by island polities. Not surprisingly, after destroying Kilwa and taking over Sofala, they established their center of operations at Mozambique Island, which remained the capital of their East African holdings until the end of the 19th century, when it was removed to Maputo (then Lourenço Marques) and re-oriented towards the mineral wealth of South Africa. In the later 16th century, they similarly established a northern base at Mombasa Island. At both Mozambique Island and Mombasa the Portuguese built massive fortifications, like a pair of goal posts marking their maritime empire in East Africa.[19] The political entanglements that witnessed the last century of Portuguese hegemony north of Cape Delgado involved intrigues and alliances based largely on the various city-states of the Lamu Archipelago and Zanzibar. To the south of that promontory, the Kerimba Islands, which are strung out along the coast down to the mouth of the Lurio River, became an intermediary area of Portuguese presence.

Both the Portuguese and the Dutch at the Cape sought to exploit Madagascar commercially, although neither succeeded in establishing a significant foothold on the great island. During this period, however, the British, in particular, utilized the Comoro Islands, especially Nzwani (Anjouan) as a way station on the voyage out to India. The long history linking these islands to the African continent thereby rendered them yet another example in the tangled web of island connections that integrated East Africa into the commercial affairs of the Indian Ocean. When the French occupied La Réunion (initially named Bourbon) in the 17th century, then Mauritius (initially Île de France) in the second decade of the 18th century, and finally the Seychelles in the later 18th century, the stage was set for the complete integration of these African islands into the commercial life of East Africa and the Indian Ocean.

It took a Swahili-Omani Arab alliance finally to drive the Portuguese permanently south of Cape Delgado in 1728-1729. Thereafter, rivalry for coastal hegemony focused on the Omani-derived Mazrui of Mombasa and the upstart Busaidi dynasty at Muscat in Oman. In the end, the Busaidi overwhelmed their Mazrui rivals in 1828 and with them all Swahili opposition to their claims to dominate the coast. Intimately connected to the rising British power at Bombay and especially indebted to the Gujarati merchant community that linked that port-city to Muscat, Busaidi Zanzibar and Zanzibar Town became the pivotal place for incorporating East Africa into the expanding capitalist world economy. Omani ruler Sayyid Said ibn Sultan's permanent relocation of his court from Muscat to Zanzibar Town in 1840 sealed this transition and made it the center of international trade in this part of the continent until European invasion at the end of the century redrew the map of the continent and with it the commercial significance of its Indian Ocean islands.[20]

The Islamization of Coastal East Africa

As we have seen, although the commercial integration of East Africa into the Indian Ocean antedated the rise of Islam, it was greatly energized and expanded after that momentous change in world history. It is, accordingly, difficult to separate one from the other. But the expansion of Islam beyond the itinerant collection of Muslim traders who ventured to coastal East Africa was a slow process, tracing its roots to the late 8th century, when the first simple mosque was built at Shanga.[21] Over the next centuries, as witnessed by the increasing number of mosques that have been excavated elsewhere along the coast and on the Comoros Islands and northwest Madagascar, as well as by the increasing size of those mosques, we can begin to see the slow growth of an African Islamic community.[22] The second oldest dated *qibla* (A.H. 500/C.E. 1107) in East Africa is in a mosque that is still in use at Kizimkazi, at the south end of Zanzibar Island. (The earliest, dated to A.H. 498/C.E. 1105, is at Baraawe on the Benaadir coast of southern Somalia.)[23] Many other Muslim communities were also located on offshore islands. When Ibn Battuta visited Kilwa, there was no doubt in his mind that he was in Dar al-Islam, although the mainland of Kilwa was inhabited by non-believers against whom the pious ruler of Kilwa waged *jihad*.[24] The Comoro Islands emerged as a particularly important center for Islam, most of the Arab families and many of the petty sultanates that dominated the islands tracing their roots to the Hadramaut in South Arabia.[25] Although Islam, like the trading entrepôts with which they were initially associated, also took root on the mainland, perhaps islands were regarded as particularly nurturing environments for the development of the *'umma* or community that lies at the center of Islamic practice.

With the exception of some very limited activity up the Zambezi and into the Zimbabwean plateau in the 15th and 16th centuries, in East Africa Islam was for many centuries restricted to the coast and offshore islands, where it became an integral component of defining Swahili and Comorian culture. During the 19th century, however, Islam traveled into the interior with Arab and Swahili caravans, becoming a preamble to the rapid expansion of Islam that marked the very end of the century and the period of colonial rule that followed. The principal vehicles for this expansion of the faith were the Qadiriyya and Shadhiliyya *turuq* (sufi ways) and its two principal bases were initially Zanzibar Town and Moroni, the largest town on Ngazija (Grande Comore). Although the main secondary centers for *tariqa* growth into the interior of Tanzania and Malawi were coastal towns like Bagamoyo and Kilwa Kivinje, in Mozambique both the Qadiriyya and Shadhiliyya established their initial centers at Mozambique Island and expanded inland from there. Even today the various branches (there are now eight in all) of these two *turuq* have their main houses on the island, while the principal branch of the Shadhiliyya maintains very close connections to their founder's *zawiya* at Moroni.[26] Thus, islands were central to the development and expansion of Islam in East Africa and remain important regional centers for connecting East African Muslims to the wider world of Islam.

The Peopling of Madagascar

The peopling of the largest African island, which probably dates to the second half of the first millennium C.E., remains a subject of great scholarly controversy.[27] No one questions that its modern population is made up of both African and Indonesian peoples. Rather, it is the composition of these different populations and how exactly they interacted historically to produce Malagasy society and culture that defy consensus.[28] One aspect of this controversy concerns the route or routes by which Indonesian immigrants reached Madagascar. Some scholars embrace a Kon-Tiki interpretation, looking to Austronesian expansion in the South Pacific and the open sea route across the Indian Ocean as the shortest itinerary between their place of origin and their final destiny. Others consider that the Indonesians more probably followed the same coasting route that marked maritime voyages in the Indian Ocean more generally, sticking relatively close to the shore, taking advantage of the monsoon winds, and island hopping. A local tradition recounted in the late 19th century by a man of the Antalatotse, a Muslim coastal trading people sometimes compared to the Swahili, around Boeny Bay in northwest Madagascar suggests, for example, that their ancestors were "'Arabs who had come from an island near the Comoros. This island sank in a hurricane of wind and rain. The inhabitants sought refuge in their boats, and set sail for Madagascar.'"[29] Proponents of this thesis point to the early dissemination of Southeast Asian food crops such as banana, coconut and sugar cane to eastern Africa and later of outrigger canoes (and, more controversially, the xylophone) as evidence of Indonesian presence along the African littoral. Although there is no archaeological evidence to sustain either of these interpretations, the latter has always seemed more probable in the wider context of maritime navigation around the Indian Ocean. Assuming this to be the case, then, it is highly likely that in coming from an island environment, the Indonesian immigrants who brought their language and culture to eastern Africa utilized the islands that dot the African coast and the Comoro islands in finding their way to the island of Madagascar upon which they settled.

The Slave Trade of the Southwest Indian Ocean

Islands were absolutely central to the rise of the export slave trade in the Southwest Indian Ocean. The earliest example focuses on Madagscar as a source of bonded labor for the Dutch colony at the Cape and even on occasion for the Americas in the 17th and early decades of the 18th centuries.[30] But the real beginnings of sustained slave trading in this part of the world date to the occupation of the Mascarenes by the French and the development of plantation agriculture on those islands. French planters looked first to Madagascar as the nearest source of servile labor and then to Mozambique Island, Zanzibar and Kilwa Kisiwani. As sugar became the crop of choice at Mauritius, the demand grew accordingly and the French expanded their activities to include the Kerimba Islands and Zanzibar.[31] Eventually, the Seychelles also became a part of this system. The laborers themselves overwhelmingly came from the interior of the African continent or the island of Madagascar, but the export system as a whole operated almost entirely as an insular network. The British seizure of the Mascarenes during the Napoleonic Wars did not put an end to this traffic. Although Mauritius and the Seychelles became British colonies in 1814, abolition did not occur until 1834; meanwhile Bourbon reverted to French authority as part of the peace and did not abolish slavery until 1848. As a consequence the Mascarenes continued to sustain a vigorous illegal slave trade that rivaled the annual rate of imports during the previous decades.[32] During these early decades of the 19th century the proportion of slaves coming from Madagascar and East Africa (who were known as "Mozambiques") shifted dramatically from the former to the latter. To avoid official measures against the slave trade, French slave traders invented a system that took slaves who were purchased on the Mozambique coast and shipped them either to the Comoros or the Seychelles for a short period of "seasoning" during which they were taught a few words of French and became "*francisés.*" Thus prepared, newly bonded Africans were introduced illegally to Bourbon and Mauritius as the domestic slaves of French planters. Others were carried to the northwest coast of Madagascar and marched across the northern plains of the great island to ports on the East coast where they were re-embarked to the Mascarenes. Later in the 19th century, this system of disguised slave trade persisted under the guise of a "free labor emigration" or "*libre engagé*" system.[33]

Madagascar itself occupies an important place in this system as both an exporter and importer of slave labor, not unlike Zanzibar (for the northern Swahili coast and Arabia) and the Caribbean islands (for North America). From being a source of labor in the 18th century, the expansion of the Imerina empire transformed Madagascar into a net importer of labor during the 19th century.[34] The export trade was largely carried out by French and Portuguese merchants, while the import trade persisted late into the 19th century aboard Arab, Swahili, and some Indian vessels. Bridging this significant shift was a short period beginning at the very end of the 18th century and continuing into the first two decades of the 19th century during which Malagasy maritime raiders in outrigger canoes conducted a series of slave raids onto the Comoro Islands and coastal East Africa, where they focused their activities on the Kerimba Islands and the Mafia Islands, which lie between Kilwa and Zanzibar.[35] In this context, too, we should note that, following his defeat in 1824 by Radama I, king of Imerina, the Sakalava monarch Andriantsoli of Boina in northwest Madagascar withdrew to Mayotte, the nearest of the Comoro Islands, where he established himself as its overlord. Today Malagasy is still spoken on Mayotte.[36]

The final link in this complex network are the Comoros, which not only served as transit points for slaves from the African continent to the Mascarenes, but also absorbed some of these peoples into their own populations. Although many of the descendants of these 19th-century forced immigrants remain outside the mainstream of coastal town society in the Comoros, they stand as a reminder of the African roots of the original Comorian populations, who probably originated among the matrilineal peoples who migrated centuries before from the same opposing shores.

The Economics and Politics of Colonial
and Independent East Africa

In some respects, this is the most novel category to include in this overview of the island factor in Indian Ocean Africa. There is a general tendency to regard the colonial era almost as a complete break in the historic patterns of Indian Ocean communication, even though scholars certainly recognize the continued significance of East African linkages to South Asia, Oman, and the Hadramaut. Despite the absence of almost any reference in the historical literature to the role of the islands during this century, however, they continued to occupy an interesting place in this African region.

Perhaps the most obvious aspect here is the presence of and connections between different communities of South Asian origin in Indian Ocean Africa. South Asians had long been present in East Africa as merchants and some had eventually settled at places like Mozambique Island before the 19th century. The rise of Busaidi Zanzibar attracted many more to that thriving commercial center, while still others settled in former British East Africa as laborers and small shopkeepers. A parallel community developed further in colonial Mozambique.[37] A similar cluster of merchants settled at the northwest coastal entrepôt of Mahajanga and eventually as traders throughout the towns of colonial Madagascar.[38] In the aftermath of emancipation and the increased demand for labor by the expanding sugar economy at Mauritius, in particular, many more came to the Mascarenes as indentured laborers.[39] At the same time, many others were indentured to Natal, South Africa, and its booming sugar plantations, while a better-educated group of so-called "passenger Indians" voluntarily emigrated to Durban to seek their fortunes.[40] Today, these far flung Indian diaspora communities maintain links both with South Asia and among each other, bound primarily by commercial and financial bonds, but also by those of ethnicity and religion, whether Hindu or Muslim. The island communities have always been a vital part of this diaspora, but with the secondary diaspora of so many South Asians from East Africa in the 1970s, the central place of Mauritius, especially for Hindus, who comprise some 52% of the island's total population and control its politics, stands unchallenged.

The Mascarenes play a rather different role in relation to the African continent today than they did during the era of the slave trade, when their populations were overwhelmingly derived from mainland populations. Mauritius and the Seychelles have highly developed tourist industries that cater to visitors from South Africa and Kenya (both Kenyan citizens and Euro-Americans tourists to East Africa), as well as from Europe. Madagascar seems less a part of this circuit, although it attracts eco-tourists from far afield; even Ngazija, despite its great political instability, has been an outpost of lower end South African tourism. Here, too, it is worth mentioning the importance of Lamu, known internationally as a "living museum" of Swahili culture, and Mombasa to Kenya's tourist industry, while Zanzibar is working hard to develop its own standing as a site for international tourism. Taken together, as a consequence of their very difference from continental Africa as exotic tropical islands, they continue to play an integral part in the commercial economy of the region as a whole. The traffic is not, however, only one way. In common with so many island societies, Mauritians tend to be very mobile and many have lived and worked overseas, including in Africa. Similarly, a number of middle class Indo-Mauritians have begun to send their children to university in South Africa, particularly to the University of Cape Town.

A somewhat different economic role being played by Mauritius arises from the relative strength of its economy and its desire to become the Singapore of the mid-Indian Ocean. Mauritian capital has become the driving force behind the resuscitation of Mozambique's shattered sugar industry and, if the World Bank can restrain itself from crushing the necessary protectionist measures designed by Mozambique to ensure its survival, this capital investment is sure to strengthen the historic bonds between these two countries. Also arising from recognition of the historical connections linking the peoples of Mozambique to Mauritius through the slave trade is the cultural agreement that exists between the two governments.[41]

On the political front, islands were not of any real significance to Indian Ocean Africa until World War II, when the British used Sri Lanka (then Ceylon) to station and train regiments of the King's African Rifles (which recruited troops from its Eastern African colonial empire) who served in the Burma campaign. After the war, a regiment of the KAR was posted at Mauritius from 1943 to 1956. The barracks where they were stationed now houses the Mauritian Special Forces, but it is still known (although erroneously) as the "Camp des Zoulous." African troops from Mozambique were also posted to Madagascar during the same war, where there is evidence of connections with the descendants of enslaved Mozambicans on record.[42] More recently, the Comoros have sometimes played a perverse political role as a consequence of their Islamic character. During the war against the Mozambique liberation forces led by Frelimo, the Portuguese sought to enlist the *mufti* of the Comoros in support of their campaign to rally the leaders of the sufi *turuq* against the specter of what they perceived as godless communist nationalism.[43] Similarly, when Renamo had become a client of apartheid South Africa and was fighting against Frelimo in the 1980s, the Comoros were occasionally used as a conduit for introducing arms to their guerilla units in northern Mozambique.[44] More positively, the African island nations of the Indian Ocean all belong to the African Union, although the AU has had limited success in trying to resolve the latest political crisis in the Comoros.[45] Much more hopefully, the Indian Ocean Rim Association for Regional Cooperation seeks to build an effective regional economic and strategic organization along the lines of other regional organizations on the African continent and elsewhere. Because of their status as French Overseas Departments, however, both Mayotte and Réunion maintain closer formal economic and political ties to France than to their neighbors, although there is continual movement between Réunion and Mauritius and the Seychelles on business, personal, and family affairs.

*   *   *   *   *

In this short paper I have not sought to address the so-called African islands of the Indian Ocean either on their own terms or as exotic tropical paradises. Breaking with both these more familiar genres, I have instead attempted to establish the integral role that these islands have played and continue to play over several millennia in the history of Indian Ocean Africa. As islands, they stand apart from each other and from the continent, but as human societies they owe much of their unique character to Africa. By the same token, as a continent, Africa has its own internal dynamics, but its history is impossible to separate from the Indian Ocean world of which its eastern marches are surely an indispensable part, as are its islands.

PART II

Coastal
East Africa

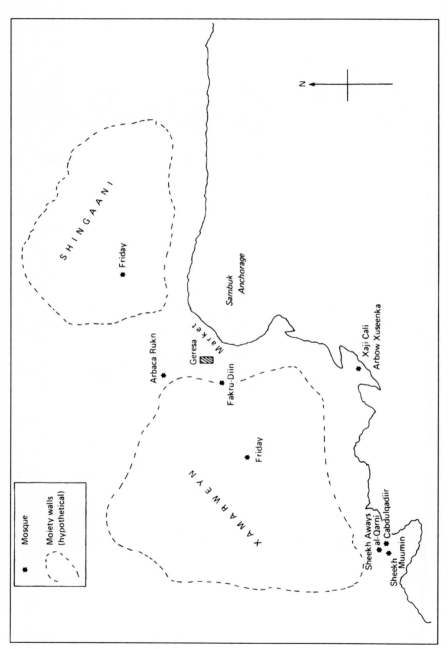

Nineteenth-century Muqdisho

CHAPTER 4

Muqdisho in the
Nineteenth Century:
A Regional Perspective*

Recent contributions by James de Vere Allen have introduced an
entirely new perspective into the long-standing debate about East
African coastal towns.[1] Reacting to earlier assumptions that their cultural characteristics were primarily Asiatic, Allen has built a commanding case in a series of original and important essays for the
specifically African character of these communities, which he depicts
as being thoroughly integrated into the East African hinterland.[2]
Without minimizing the great significance of his pioneering scholar-
ship, I would argue that Allen pays less attention to the critical leav-
ening of Islam in the shaping of coastal civilization than is warrant-
ed, as the more integrated approach taken by Randall Pouwels suggests.[3] Whatever one's position on this important debate, however, it
seems clear now that historical analysis of the coastal towns must
seek to extend itself beyond these confines. Specifically, we need to
come to grips with the class structure of the towns if we are ever to
understand their internal dynamics and the nature of the relationship
between town and country on the coast.

Important empirical beginnings in this direction have been made
by Frederick Cooper and Marguerite Ylvisaker, but my own thinking

* Reprinted from *Journal of African History*, 24, 4 (1983), pp. 441-459.

has been most significantly influenced by the theoretical insights of Ramachandran Menon, who argues that Zanzibar Town depended for its very existence on the exploitation of the town's countryside by means of a dominant slave mode of production.[4] However one might criticize this problematic,[5] it allows one initially to situate nineteenth-century Muqdisho in a much wider context of comparative analysis, both regionally and continentally (as well as theoretically), and at the very least enables one to avoid the kind of parochialism that has isolated Muqdisho and the other towns of the Benaadir coast from most wider considerations of coastal history.

That Muqdisho in the nineteenth century was a shadow of its former splendid self is a generally accepted fact. One has only to compare the famous description of Ibn Battuta of the town in 1331 to those of its visitors five centuries later to realize that its heyday was long since past.[6] When the Portuguese entered the Indian Ocean, Muqdisho was apparently still a wealthy community which drove an important overseas trade based on its complementary relationship with the Ajuraan imamate of the interior.[7] How its prosperity might have been affected by the Portuguese intrusion simply is not known, as the entire Benaadir coast lay outside Portuguese influence.[8] Certainly, there was no commercial collapse, for in the middle of the seventeenth century its principal towns—Muqdisho, Marka, and Baraawe—traded independently with small vessels from Surat.[9] During this period, however, the gradual infiltration of Muqdisho by Hawiyya Soomaali groups of the hinterland brought about a major transformation of the town, including the abandonment of certain quarters which had existed in medieval times and an apparent reduction in its total population. By about 1700 the entire political structure of the town was altered with the ascendancy of a new line of Abgaal Yaaquub imams who resided in Shingaani (the northern moiety of the town), but whose power base remained among the people of the interior.[10]

The Abgaal domination of Shingaani left the older elite of Xamarweyn (the other town moiety) without significant allies in the interior. One important consequence of this predicament, as well as an important indication of the internal dynamics of town history, was that direct commercial contact between the coast and Luuq, the most important trading emporium for southern Ethiopia, was established in the late eighteenth century by a man of the *reer* Faaqi, one of the principal family groups of Xamarweyn.[11] This initiative may also reflect the general growth of trade at Zanzibar, which dates to the domination of the Busaidi dynasty of Oman from 1785.

By the early years of the nineteenth century Muqdisho and the two other principal towns of the Benaadir coast, Marka and Baraawe, seem to have settled into a pattern of regular if modest trade with boats plying the maritime routes between India, Arabia, Lamu and Zanzibar. Exports included cattle, slaves, ivory, and ambergris.[12] From two Soomaali traders from Baraawe whom he encountered at Zanzibar, Commander Thomas Smee learned in 1811 that Muqdisho "is not very considerable, may contain 150 to 200 houses [by this he presumably means stone houses], it has not any river near it, and has but little trade." He was also informed that it was governed by "a Soomaulee Chief named Mahomed Bacahmeen," probably the reigning Abgaal imam.[13] Despite its modest circumstances, Muqdisho was clearly larger than either Marka or Baraawe, the latter consisting of only about 100 huts (as opposed to houses). By comparison, it is also worth noting that Smee's informants could tell him that Luuq had some 300 huts.[14]

This situation probably remained little changed until the following decade, when the fortunes of the Benaadir towns began to intertwine with the ambitious plans of Seyyid Said ibn Sultan for his East African legacy. Muqdisho, in particular, figured in two incidents which clearly established an atmosphere of mutual suspicion with the Omani rulers of Zanzibar. First, it seems, an Omani vessel ran aground north of Muqdisho and its entire crew was sent to that town for sale as slaves, only to be ransomed after a year in captivity by friends in Zanzibar, "who sent some stout negroes to replace them." Then, in 1823, the Omani fleet that was sent to subdue Mombasa dropped anchor at Muqdisho and its commander, Abdullah ibn Sulaiyim, kidnapped two community leaders who came on board his ship and imprisoned them at Zanzibar. A ransom of 2,000 Maria Theresa dollars was fixed for their release, though they were eventually freed by the Governor of Zanzibar at the request of the headstrong British naval captain W. F. W. Owen.[15] Owen hoped to raise the entire Benaadir on behalf of the British cause in East Africa, as he saw it, and while he appears to have had some success at Baraawe, none was forthcoming from Muqdisho.[16]

Owen provides the first detailed eyewitness account of Muqdisho since Ibn Battuta, Smee having only viewed it from the sea, and is worth quoting at length:

> Mukdeesha, the only town of any importance upon the coast is the mistress of a considerable territory.... At a distance the town has rather an imposing appearance, the buildings being of some magnitude and composed of stone. The eye is at first attracted by four minarets of considerable height, towering above the town, and giving it an air of stilly grandeur, but a nearer approach soon convinces the spectator that these massive buildings are principally the residences of the dead, while the living inhabit the low thatched huts by which these costly sepulchres are surrounded. It is divided into two distinct towns, one called Umarween, and the other Chamgany, the latter of which may with justice be called "the city of the dead," being entirely composed of tombs. Umarween has nearly one hundred and fifty stone houses, built in the Spanish style, so as to enclose a large area. Most of the Arab dows visit this place in their coast navigation, to exchange sugar, molasses, dates, salt fish, arms, and slaves, for ivory, gums, and a particular cloth of their own manufacture, which is much valued by the people of the interior.[17]

Despite his tendency to overstatement, Owen's testimony includes the first documented reference to the town moieties by name and is accurate in so far as Shingaani does contain a larger number of monumental tombs than does Xamarweyn. It is also noteworthy for its reference to the importation rather than the exportation of slaves at Muqdisho and the particular importance of *futa Benaadir,* the locally woven cloth, for the interior trade.[18] His description of the respectful, yet firm, manner in which his ship's officers "were subjected to a manner of imprisonment, being immediately shut up in a house, but with liberty to ramble about according to their inclinations within it," also bears witness to the enduring coastal custom of managing the visits of strangers through local mediators (variously called "landlords" or "brokers" in the West African literature), who were drawn from the ranks of the community notables and were known in Somalia as *abban.*[19]

The combination of insulting incidents, which disrupted the smooth transaction of business between Muqdisho and Zanzibar, and foreign interest in the Benaadir coast, is what probably gave rise to the naval bombardment and sacking of Muqdisho by an Omani fleet under Hamed bin Ahmed in 1828.[20] This initial display of Omani sea power and the decision by the leaders of Muqdisho to sue for peace and to offer the town's submission to Seyyid Said did not, however, immediately affect its future to any appreciable degree. A much more serious challenge to its equilibrium occurred about seven years later, when an epidemic of plague which was introduced from Sohar apparently coincided with a long period of drought and consequent famine, thus ravaging the weakened population.[21] Natural calamity was soon followed by disruption of the interior trade routes that fed Muqdisho's export ivory trade as a consequence of the militant phase of the Baardheere *jamaaca,* which lasted from 1836 until its defeat by the combined forces of the Geledi sultanate and its allies in mid-1843.[22] Thus, the period from about 1835 or 1836 until the early 1840s must have been one of considerable trauma for the community as a whole, but especially for its dominant class.

This hypothesis would seem to be borne out by the succession struggle which followed the death of Imam Maxamed (Cusman?) late in 1842.[23] Ideally, succession was determined by primogeniture, but as an early Italian governor of Somalia explained in 1907, "Resulting from numerous marriages contracted among blood relatives by them, by brothers, by sons and by nephews, their bonds of kinship with the more important Yaaquub of the interior are always more intimate, so that now there are many claimants."[24] Thus, whenever there was no direct heir who was also a man who commanded wide communal respect, there was plenty of opportunity for factional struggle. According to Guillain, the conflict in 1842-3 involved the son of the deceased imam, one Axmed Maxamed, and the latter's nephew, one Axmed Maxmuud. The details of the relationship between these rival claimants, which conflict with the genealogies reproduced by Robecchi-Brichetti and Caniglia, require further clarification, but the basic facts are that the nephew, Axmed Maxmuud, sought recognition of his authority in Xamarweyn, where he apparently had relatives among the important *reer* Sheekh Muumin, while Axmed Maxamed secured the support of the imam's traditional base in Shingaani.[25]

While there is no clear record of armed struggle between the forces of the two Axmeds, their prolonged duel was apparently sufficiently disruptive to cause the intervention of the powerful sultan of Geledi, Yuusuf Maxamed, who early in 1843 appeared with an army of some 8,000 warriors at the gates of Xamarweyn to act as mediator between the two parties. Christopher reports that although Sultan Yuusuf regarded the chief and people of Xamarweyn as his enemies and completely dominated the Shingaani imam, he decided not to enforce his will militarily for fear of a division within his own army, members of which had family ties with the people of Xamarweyn.[26] Finally, later in that year, Axmed Maxmuud seems to have succumbed to pressure from all parties, most likely led by Sultan Yuusuf, who was also his uncle, and agreed to withdraw to the interior. Guillain claims that Axmed entrusted the leadership of Xamarweyn to his relative, Sheekh Muumin Xasan Cumar, head of the *reer* Sheekh Muumin, which had especially influential religious and commercial connections inland with Luuq through the settlement of Buur Hakaba, where the tomb of its namesake was an important regional centre of veneration.[27]

Indeed, Guillain's letter of introduction from Seyyid Said of Zanzibar to "Cheikh Moumen-ben-Hhacen, Cheikh A'ounem-ben-Din-Nous, Cheikh Nous-ben-Din and all the elders of Hhameurouine" would seem to indicate his status as *primus inter pares.*[28]

In any case, the conflict between the two rivals to the title of imam had now expanded to become an intense rivalry between the two quarters of the city. Both Christopher and Guillain note the hostility between the two moieties and were careful to make their initial entries into Xamarweyn well armed. Christopher makes no mention of any physical partitioning of the town, either internally or externally, but by Guillain's time, only a few years later, entry from Shingaani into Xamarweyn was controlled by a gate, which implies that the latter was now protected by an intervening wall of some sort.[29] Once again, it is Guillain who provides the critical testimony. Tracing the decline of the town as a whole back to the seventeenth century, he concludes:

> Its division into two quarters was produced by the abandonment, then the collapse of the intermediary buildings, and the disunion between the inhabitants of both became easier when the existing government was no longer sufficiently equitable or respected to maintain them in harmony of views and interests. Nevertheless, it is only in the last years that the inhabitants of Shingaani have ceased attending the mosque of Xamarweyn.[30]

On the basis of the literary evidence, then, it would appear that the long process of differentiation into two spatially separated moities, so that from the sea they appeared as two distinct villages, was brought to a rapid climax during these troubled years.[31] With the establishment of a second Friday mosque, Muqdisho had joined the ranks of other important coastal towns, notably Lamu and Mombasa, where moiety competition yielded similar results.

The final act in this mid-century struggle for supremacy between the various factions of the ruling class of Muqdisho witnessed the

elders of Xamarweyn petitioning Seyyid Said to send a governor to
their town, presumably to counterbalance the influence and hostility
of Sultan Yuusuf of Geledi in town affairs. The sultan of Zanzibar
had, in fact, sent an emissary to the Benaadir coast in 1842 to gather
intelligence about trade and to establish tariffs, the first exercise of
authority that he had attempted there since the bombardment of
1828. Always ready to establish a toehold on the Benaadir coast,
which remained throughout the century a politically weak link in the
Zanzibar empire, Seyyid Said appointed a Soomaali named Cali
Maxamed as governor and customs officer on 5 April 1843. He arrived from Zanzibar with only two soldiers sometime after Christopher's departure at the end of that month, but claiming an insufficient salary he soon abandoned his duties and left for the interior, perhaps sensing the precariousness of his situation in the midst of the
still intense conflict between Xamarweyn and Shingaani.[32] Nevertheless, the stage was set for the continued insinuation of the sultan of
Zanzibar into the affairs of the town, as we shall see presently.

It can be argued that the succession crisis in the imamate, whatever the inherently limited political and economic role that the imam
exercised outside his own family group, provided a crucible in which
many of the major elements in the town's history during the remainder of the century were forged. Through it we can see the significance
of intertwining links of blood (and implicitly of marriage) among the
ruling class of the community which not only operated within each
quarter of the town, but also cut across residential boundaries and
extended into the interior. We can also observe the way in which different factions of the ruling class sought to ally themselves with powerful external partners both in the interior and from overseas. In this
last respect, surely, Muqdisho was absolutely typical of virtually every
coastal town from Lamu right down to the Comoro Islands.

Given the various disruptions of this fluid decade, it is not surprising that when Christopher visited the town in April 1843 he described
most of its inhabitants, whom he guessed numbered some 3,000-
4,000, as living in "filth and poverty" and commented that its buildings were "half in ruins." Yet for all that Christopher also remarks

that there were still some "substantial stone houses," including that belonging to his *abbaan,* who was an Arab merchant of the Ashraaf families living in Shingaani.[33] Guillain's impressions of Muqdisho four years later differ little from those of his British predecessor. Notwithstanding a few new or restored buildings, most of the old stone houses were in a state of disrepair, while the beehive stick and mud huts of the Soomaali, with their straw roofs, were scattered among them "like the nests of sparrows crouched among the ruins." The total population, including slaves, he estimated to be about 5,000, a vague enough figure that we should not surmise a dramatic increase since Christopher's visit. Of these, Guillain reckoned, three-quarters resided in Xamarweyn, which he lauded for its tranquility under the firm rule of Sheekh Muumin Xasaan, in contrast to the unsettled state of Shingaani, where he was quartered in a house belonging to his *abbaan,* Shariif Siid Xadaad (Sid-Hhadad), who was probably also Christopher's *abbaan.* Guillain's conclusion, which must be respected in consideration of his exceptional knowledge of the entire coast and Madagascar, was that "the state of misery and depopulation where it is found today," would lead in fifty years to the total collapse of Muqdisho if the process of decay were not halted.[34]

Manifestly, Muqdisho did not collapse. In fact, it experienced a significant revival in the second half of the nineteenth century which was based on the steady integration of Muqdisho and its hinterland into the economic orbit of Omani Zanzibar through the medium of Indian merchant capital. More specifically, there is a strong case to be made for the proposition that this upswing in the fortunes of the entire Benaadir region was based upon the rapid development of commodity production based on slave labor.

While we lack reliable statistics both for the commerce of the Benaadir and for the growth of slavery there, such a hypothesis is reflected in the available evidence from the 1840s into the early twentieth century and also accords well with what we know was happening elsewhere in coastal East Africa during this critical era.[35] Part of the commercial growth was derived from the expanded market at Zanzibar for the traditional pastoral products of the Soomaali economy, especially hides and ghee.[36] It would also appear that the ivory trade with southern Ethiopia through Luuq was an important element in this process. Indeed, one of the key factors in the struggle between Geledi and Baardheere in the late 1830s was the prohibition by the jihadists against the ivory trade.[37] For his part, Guillain noted in the late 1840s that "all the inhabitants of the Benaadir who have some means, principally those of Baraawe, Marka, and Muqdisho, send their slaves in caravan to Ganane [Luuq] to trade for ivory."[38] But the most critical aspect of economic activity in the Benaadir was the remarkable growth of agricultural exports produced by a system of plantation slavery.

Christopher commented in 1843 that grain (primarily millet) "supplies the whole coast of Hadramaut and Oman" and that the Benaadir "may be styled the grain coast for the supply of Southern Arabia."[39] Four years later Guillain reckoned that nearly 20,000 *jizla* (an Arab measure of capacity equal in grain weight to about 159 kg 12), that is, perhaps some 3,182,400 kg of millet were exported from Muqdisho to Zanzibar and southern Arabia. He also records that between 150 and 250 *jizla* (23,868-39,780 kg) of sesame seed, which could be harvested twice annually in the Benaadir, was sold overseas.[40] Twenty years later there were no recorded imports of cereals from the Benaadir at Zanzibar, but those of sesame seed were valued at M.T. $30,000 and constituted 30 per cent of all such imports that year.[41] By the time of Kirk's visit to the Benaadir ports in May 1873 there can be no doubt that a roaring business was being done in agricultural products, mainly through Muqdisho and Marka.

At Muqdisho, Kirk "was much struck with the number of large dhows at anchor . . . We found twenty vessels from 50 to 200 tons, all filled with or taking in native grain, which I learnt is largely grown on the river behind, near Geledi."[42] He also found a similar number of vessels engaged in the grain trade at Marka. Finally, Kirk continues, "To this must be added . . . crops of the best kind of sesame oilseed, that forms a very important item in the Zanzibar trade."[43] It is difficult to resolve Kirk's impressions with the available statistics for imports at Zanzibar in 1873 and 1874, which are given only in value and not in volume. In both years grain imports were valued at M.T. $1,000, while sesame seed imports shot up from M.T. $2,000 in 1873 to M.T. $45,000 in 1874.[44] Presumably, most of the grain exports from the Benaadir continued to go directly to the Arabian peninsula, as was apparently the case in the 1840s. Whatever the pattern of exports, agricultural produce continued to play a dominant role in the export trade of the entire region right into the early colonial period. In 1896-7 millet was overwhelmingly the dominant cash crop, yielding exports of 5,729.3 tons worth M.T. $ 125, 512.25, with sesame seed occupying a distant second with exports of 3,684 quintals (of 100 kg each) worth M.T. $22,576.75.[45]

This remarkable development of grain and oil-seed production for export in the Benaadir parallels exactly what Cooper has meticulously analyzed for Malindi and Mombasa during the same half-century,[46] as does the progressive reliance of the Benaadir export economy on slave labor. Christopher's description of the labor regime in the Benaadir coastal hinterland makes clear the fact that slavery was both extensive and intensive. In the coastal plain behind Marka he observed "many thousands of men employed in cultivation," while in the neighborhood of Baraawe, which was marked by a system of artificial irrigation, "the slaves and their wives [were] the laborers."[47] Although the general impression of the slave trade of the Benaadir coast which was formed by the British during the following quarter-century reflected the abolitionist preoccupation with the trans-shipment of cargoes north to Oman and tended to ignore the importation of labor to southern Somalia itself,[48] this was certainly mistaken. When British intelligence was increased in connection with the anti-slave-trade treaty that was imposed upon the sultan of Zanzibar in 1873, however, this notion was immediately corrected. Kirk's visit to the Benaadir convinced him that it was the labor requirements of the local plantation economy which "explains why Somali-land takes so many slaves, that are not exported to Arabia as is popularly imagined, but retained for work in the land itself,"[49] an opinion which was subsequently repeated in testimony before Parliament.[50]

The dimensions of this trade remain difficult to quantify, as

Martin and Ryan are careful to emphasize,[51] but Kirk repeated a figure of some 4,000 annually in 1873 and apparently believed that this
was a minimal estimate. More impressionistically, he asserted that
"the demand for slaves in that country itself has been one of the chief
supports of the Quiloa Slave Trade," and Bartle Frere reported in the
same year that "the demand for southern negro slaves is increasing,
and their price this year has been higher on the Somali Coast than at
Muscat."[52] As Cassanelli points out, this influx of slave labor helped
to restore a population which had been seriously decimated by warfare during the Baardheere *jihad* and by the terrible cholera epidemic
of 1858.[53] But it did more than that, replacing an integrated and cul-
turally homogeneous population of Soomaali and non-Soomaali
clients with a substantial slave population of non-Muslim non-
Soomaali Bantu-speaking peoples whose very size facilitated a transformation of the existing social relations of production.

Unfortunately, little is known about the slave population of
Muqdisho until the end of the century. Georges Revoil, who spent
several months there in 1882, notes only that two-thirds of the town's
population was either slave or *habashi,* which he defines as the liberated great-grandchildren of slaves.[54] He also comments that due to the
high price of camels at Muqdisho, the numerous sesame-seed oil mills
in the city were powered by slave labor.[55] But it is not until 1897, when
the Italian administration was directly confronted with the problem
of slavery throughout its new colony, that we get any sort of detailed
picture of what had become a developed slave-labor economy.
According to the Royal Commissioner, Giorgio Sorrentino, "The
fields are cultivated by slaves, who also take care of all domestic
duties; the arts and crafts are the work of the same slaves, of Arabs,
of *vanias,* and Indians." He specifically notes the continued use of
slaves in the production of sesame oil, where some 160 were
employed, and in the textile industry, where some 300 worked under
Soomaali artisans, a claim which finds support in local tradition
today.[56] If the use of slave labor among the artisans of Muqdisho was
more pronounced at the end of the nineteenth century than previously, however, this did not represent a major disruption of the social

division of labor, as all artisans – ironsmiths, carpenters, masons, weavers, etc. – did work which was regarded as being "undignified" and "shameful" for a free man to do.[57] In this respect Muqdisho was typically Soomaali and quite distinct from the situation that Allen depicts for the Swahili towns of the East African coast.[58] Sorrentino also provides an important additional clue to the relationship of the town to the interior in his recording of the case of an inhabitant of Xamarweyn who employed slaves at Jesiira, just south along the coast, "to cultivate the land around the wells." Finally, he suggests that despite the paternalistic nature of slavery in Muqdisho, slaves were often mistreated under the regime of the sultan of Zanzibar, whose governor there was little inclined to support the claims of slaves against their masters.[59]

Writing in 1903 on the eve of abolition in Somalia, the Italian anti-slavery campaigner, Luigi Robecchi-Bricchetti, confirms the fairly common practice of town dwellers employing slaves in the country-side by his casual comment that of five prominent *sambuk* owners in Muqdisho, "all these possess diverse slaves in the city and in the inte-rior in the environs of Geledi."[60] Robecchi-Bricchetti actually made a careful census of the entire slave and liberated population of Muqdisho in order to illuminate the problem for the Italian public and claims that the results give "an approximate and realistic figure of the true free and slave population of the country." The results of this remarkable document, which he also duplicated for Marka and Baraawe, reveal that out of a permanent population of nearly 6,700 more than 31 per cent were still slaves, while another 4 per cent included in the free population had been liberated since 1894.[61] Summing up his research, Robecchi-Bricchetti concluded that the entire wealth of the Shabeelle valley was due to slave labor and that slavery was accordingly regarded as "natural and indispensable" throughout the Benaadir. However one chose to mince words by call-ing this "domestic slavery," he adds, slaves were hereditary property, the real source of private wealth which in the hands of their owners became "an easy monetary unit" when put into circulation.[62] Indeed, this sentiment is echoed by an elderly Soomaali leader from the

Marka hinterland in 1903, who pleaded to the Italian governor that "We can do nothing without our slaves."[63] In the light of this evidence it can be argued, I think, that the development of agricultural slavery in southern Somalia enriched the dominant economic class throughout the region and that there existed a class alliance between its various factions in the towns of both the coast and the interior that worked to the mutual benefit of each.

Table I. Population of Muqdisho, 1903

	Free	Slave	Total
Shingaani	1,750	835	2,585 (38.61%)
Xamarweyn	2,850	1,260	4,110 (61.39%)
Total	4,600	2,095	6,695 (100%)

By itself, however, this hypothesis does not explain the driving force behind the transformation of Muqdisho and its hinterland in the second half of the nineteenth century. For a complete appreciation of this process we must return to the role of the Indian merchant capitalists. Here, too, the evidence is incomplete, but it generally points to the increasing domination by their trading houses of the commerce of the entire Benaadir. The groundwork for this domination was laid in the mid-1840s when Seyyid Said replaced his first, ineffectual governor at Muqdisho with an old Arab who also served as customs officer for Jairam Sewji, the leading merchant capitalist at Zanzibar who rented the customs farm from the sultan from 1834 to 1853.[64] As Cooper points out, "The customs master was not only able to collect vastly more duties than he paid for the privilege, but he was able to use his position to establish close contacts with merchants for his personal business."[65] Jairam Sewji commanded a vast personal fortune and many merchants up and down the coast were deeply in his debt. It would have been remarkable had he not also extended his commercial and financial operations to Muqdisho.

One of the immediate effects of the imposition of the collection of customs duties by the representative of the sultan of Zanzibar was to cut into the revenue of the Yaquub imam. Guillain reports that previously the imam collected tariffs of M.T. $25 on each ship that came to trade at Muqdisho, sometimes increasing to M.T. $35 if the merchants were known to be wealthy. Even boats forced to take port by the weather paid a nominal fee of M.T. $2. At the time of Guillain's visit the cabotage fee was still reserved for the Imam Axmed, but Seyyid Said's more detailed and profitable tariff schedule upset him by removing half of his former revenue from the taxation of the export trade.[66] Guillain and all subsequent visitors to Muqdisho emphasized the very limited political influence exercised there by the sultan of Zanzibar. Indeed, twenty years later it was reported from Zanzibar that responsibility for order along the entire Benaadir coast was effectively in the hands of the governor of Lamu, and there was certainly no official Zanzibar political presence at Muqdisho when Rigby visited the town in 1861.[67] But the fact that the sultan maintained official control of the city's export trade and was recognized by both moieties as nominal overlord, despite the dissatisfaction of the leading authority of Shingaani, indicates the great significance of Zanzibar's economic influence.[68] It also suggests that the balance of power within Muqdisho had now tipped towards Xamarweyn, which it will be recalled had initially petitioned the sultan to send a governor, and that despite the support of the sultan of Geledi for the imam and Shingaani in matters political, it did not affect the economic policy of Sultan Yuusuf Maxamed and his successors, who clearly realized that the commercial authority of Zanzibar promised greater rewards for all of them. Final proof of this state of affairs came in the early 1870s when Imam Maxamed Benyamiin refused to let Seyyid Barghash bin Said build a garrison at Muqdisho. His intransigence was overcome by Sultan Axmed Yuusuf's threat to impose a boycott on Shingaani market by Geledi and its allies and by the agreement of the sultan of Zanzibar not to send his officials inland as a price for the sultan of Geledi's support.[69] Given the circumstances, it is perhaps not coincidental that the Zanzibar *garesa* was built closer to Xamarweyn than to Shingaani.

I have not yet discovered any evidence of Indian merchant activity at Muqdisho for the decades following Guillain's brief notice, but

Frere commented on a clutch of Bohras at Marka, where the sultan of Zanzibar also had "a governor in the fort with a small Arab garrison, and a customs house managed as usual by a 'Banian'," who would have been an agent of Jairam Sewji's associate and successor as customs master of Zanzibar, Ladha Damji.[70] The situation is unlikely to have been much different at Muqdisho. Certainly, by 1882 the Zanzibar garrison was strong enough to keep peace at the central market in front of the *garesa* and to police daily friction between the two moieties, although Revoil reveals little about the actual operation of either this market or the two separate markets of Shingaani and Xamarweyn, each of which had its own specific interior trading partners.[71] By the beginning of the last decade of the century, however, a much clearer picture of Indian merchant capitalist domination of Muqdisho's commerce emerges.

According to Robecchi-Bricchetti, in 1891 the ivory trade of the entire Benaadir was almost completely in the hands of Indians and *vanias* (i.e. of Muslim and Hindu Asians). There were few Soomaali and Arabs, he reports,

> who possess sufficient money to acquire an appropriate piece of cotton stuff to serve as medium of exchange. The Soomaali accordingly take themselves to the Indians to have a certain quantity of cotton goods on credit; and as the ivory trade is rather risky . . . thus the Indians, who know how to manage their affairs very cleverly, begin by assigning to the cotton goods a value superior to their real value, and then, on the arrival of the ivory from the interior, they regain their credit with the exchange of the merchandise, which comes estimated at a value inferior to that obtaining just then on the market. With this system their profit is doubled.[72]

European criticism of Indian traders in East Africa for the manipulation of exchange values in the circulation of commodities dates back to the sixteenth century, but it reveals the pivotal importance of having large credit reserves available for the successful pursuit of international trade, and this only the Indians possessed at this time in Eastern Africa.

In fact, when Robecchi-Bricchetti made his observations of the operation of local Indian merchant capitalists on the Benaadir coast, the entire financial structure of its trade was dominated by Tharia Topan, the millionaire who had succeeded Ladha Damji as customs master of Zanzibar in 1876 and who was "probably the wealthiest man in all of East Africa when he died in 1891."[73] Referring specifically to Marka, Sorrentino records that its trade was monopolized by Tharia Topan, "who had invested immense capital on the Benaadir and was himself the great patron of the market, thus preventing the establishment of minor houses. When Tharia Topan died his heirs ended the trade and Marka remained almost entirely without money," although it gradually recovered with the arrival of new Indian trading houses from Zanzibar.[74]

Unfortunately, nothing yet is known about Tharia Topan's involvement in the trade of Muqdisho, but as customs master he undoubtedly had important dealings there. By 1897, however, there appear to have been four principal Indian firms based in Zanzibar and one Arab firm based in Aden which dominated the Muqdisho trade. One of these may have been the house of Kanji Chianji, whose representative at Muqdisho was one Fadi Lashi. A major debtor of this house from Muqdisho named Abubakr-bin-Aood, who had been drawing hundreds of dollars of credit from them for three years and was involved with the liquidation of the Filionardi concession there, was arrested with all his goods and letters of credit while on business in Zanzibar. Sorrentino also records the fate awaiting a much smaller Soomaali trader, one Cabdaala Nasiir, who had owed M.T. $70 for trade goods received on credit nearly two years previously from a *vania* named Fadi Berdan. Trade could not function if people did not pay their debts, Sorrentino was told by the Chief *Qadi*, who represented the final court of appeal for all commercial disputes in the city, which were normally dealt with in *baraza* and were presided over by the Zanzibar Governor and the Italian Resident in the presence of all the town notables. In the case of Cabdaala Nasiir, it was determined that if he did not settle his debt by the end of Ramadhan, which was less than two weeks away, his goods and his slaves would be auctioned off and receipts put at the disposition of his creditors.[75] In a word, there was no doubting the commercial dependence of the entire Benaadir on Zanzibar, and Sorrentino states simply "that it is, as is well known, the important place where the export goods from the Benaadir are exchanged for import goods." Finally, Sorrentino also mentions that the fluctuating value of the Maria Theresa dollar, which was accepted specie on the Benaadir coast, with respect to the rupee of Zanzibar, where it was not, created difficulties for local merchants, although these informed him that "the trade of that place and the Benaadir is almost entirely conducted through the exchange of merchandise."[76] In view of Robecchi-Bricchetti's description of Asian credit mechanisms at Muqdisho and the presence there of a significant number of Muslim Indian and *vania* merchants, it seems unlikely that the city's commerce was any less dominated by Zanzibar's merchant capitalists than it had been in previous years.[77]

It remains to say something about the persistent problem of moiety competition in Muqdisho. Revoil provides plenty of evidence for the sharpness of the rivalry between Xamarweyn and Shingaani in 1882, and took care "to preserve an absolute neutrality in order not to offend the sensibilities of the hostile parties of Muqdisho." He was impressed by "the wall erected to protect Xamarweyn against the hostile incursions of the inhabitants of Shingaani" and by the fact that the doors of the ancient Fakru Diin mosque, which faced the *garesa* and bordered the central market area, had been walled up so that "the mosque was absolutely reserved to the inhabitants of Xamarweyn."[78] A decade later Robecchi-Bricchetti similarly was struck by "the rivalry between the two villages . . . [which] often leads to quarrels and wars, which disturb the momentary and precarious calm of the country."[79] The intensity of this rivalry, which may possibly reflect the steady integration of the town into the evolving world economy, was as complementary as it was divisive, although Allen takes issue with me here.[80] One can argue that it was indicative of the general vitality of the community as a whole during a period of renewed commercial prosperity, as Pouwels has argued for Lamu and Mombasa in the previous century. Competition, he suggests, "was the hallmark of town civilization" and "the prime mover of coastal history" and expressed itself at all levels of community life.[81]

One element in this pattern of competition may prove to be the willingness of each moiety to conclude external alliances in order to overcome the dominant position of its rival. For example, in the 1840s Shingaani seems to have been still considered the more established, if perhaps not dominant half of the town, and there was apparently no obvious challenge from Xamarweyn to the imam's appointment of an *abbaan* for both Christopher and Guillain from the Ashraaf of Shingaani. But Guillain was much more favorably impressed by the reception he received from Sheekh Muumin Xasaan than he was by Siid Xadaad, whom he describes as "the principal trader of the town" and whom he complains was always after the French for something. Moreover, when he left Muqdisho Guillain carried with him a letter from Sheekh Muumin offering his services to the French as *abbaan*.[82] By contrast, Revoil's *abbaan* resided in Xamarweyn and the Frenchman was able to excuse himself from being placed under the protection of the imam, who recalled for him his predecessor's hospitality to Guillain, by claiming "the proximity of the house of Salem as indispensable to the organization of my expedition." In the end, however, Revoil was obliged to admit that the imam and his family

> would have certainly better aided me and would have shown themselves, without great effort, more courteous than the chiefs of Xamarweyn, who had, shortly before, received me at Zanzibar with the warmest welcome. They disdained to give me the least little attention, even on the day when I took up residence. Imam Maxmuud, to the contrary, presented me with a superb bull for having taken care of one of his sick children.[83]

Xamarweyn's indifference to Europeans, which was based on its combined domination of the trade of the interior and the official Zanzibar connection, ultimately turned into outright hostility as the nineteenth-century political economy of the town was increasingly threatened by European colonialism. In 1891 Robecchi-Bricchetti was menaced at the gate of Xamarweyn and called that quarter "anti-European," while six years later the Italian Governor's residence had been built in Shingaani, where all the European inhabitants of Muqdisho resided, because it was believed that Shingaani had always been less hostile to whites than its rival. In the critical year following the disastrous Italian expedition to Lafoole, Imam Benyamiin pressed this advantage by offering to intervene with the sultan of Geledi on behalf of the Italians, although he may have had opposition from other interests within Shingaani. A decade later Cerrina-Ferroni reiterated the opposition of the leading families of Xamarweyn, which he correctly attributed to the near monopoly they had of the caravan trade.[84] The larger history of resistance and realignment in the hinterland of Muqdisho, including its bearing upon coastal town politics, has been carefully reconstructed by Cassanelli.[85] The point to be made in the context of this discussion is that quite apart from any other considerations, familiar interpretive questions of resistance and accommodation or collaboration must also be understood in light of the nineteenth-century tradition of intense moiety competition between Xamarweyn and Shingaani.

One critical element of town competitiveness that has tended to be overlooked in the literature concerns the social institutions "peculiar to it which cut across the divisions between houses [and moieties] and which unified the town in relation to other comparable communities along the coast."[86] We know almost nothing about these and any unambiguous picture can only emerge after extensive collection of oral data, but both Revoil and Sorrentino provide us with descriptions of communal festivals which emphasize town unity while incorporating elements of ritual battle. Revoil witnessed a festival which he called *Lab* involving the dry-docking of local ships during the height of the monsoon winds. In the morning the ship-owners recruited hands to help with the work, while the actual hauling was done in concert to the accompaniment of dancing and singing by _habashi_ women. When the task was completed, the men—now armed— aligned themselves on the beach according to their family groups. "In peacetime," Revoil continues, "the two quarters of Shingaani and Xamarweyn accept a mutual support to execute the _lab_ together." The two ranks now formed a single regiment and after moving as one along the beach "separated themselves into two battalions to return to their respective quarters" in a rhythmic step and singing a common war song. Each quarter's rank was headed by its elders and followed by the dancers, "who simulated a duel with spears or knives, or even contented themselves with holding in their hands some green branch- es which they balance gracefully."[87] This occasion was probably a Muqdisho variant of the Persian solar New Year celebrations of _Neyruus,_ which was known locally also as both _Istaaqfurow_ and _Ciid fircoon_ ("Pharoah's festival") and more widely among the Soomaali as _dabshiid._ It was also celebrated as a major event at Marka and at various other East African coastal towns.[88]

Sorrentino's description of the "great native festival" that he wit- nessed on 20 November 1897 is much less complete than that of Revoil, but it clearly incorporates many similar elements. He notes that this was the first time that it was allowed to be held since 1894, when the mock battle got out of hand and some 150 Soomaali men were imprisoned by the colonial authorities. This time, however, there were no such problems as the men of each _reer_ paraded past the Royal Commissioner without incident, chanting and displaying their spears and shields over their heads in the characteristic Soomaali fashion. Finally, after a simulated battle between the men of Xamarweyn and Shingaani, general festivity continued into the night. Sorrentino also describes in some detail the slave dances, in particu- larly, of a second festival which took place in Muqdisho some three months later on 7 March 1898 (2 Shawal) and which he compares to Carnival.[89] This was the end of Ramadhan and is similarly marked by general rejoicing all along the coast.[90] Indeed, the whole problem of an emerging slave subculture remains to be addressed for Muqdisho, where slave dances apparently predominated over all others in the later nineteenth century.[91]

Finally, we need to learn much more about the operation of the town *baraza* in this context of unifying institutions, just as we must try to understand those life-crisis ritual occasions, such as funerals, that apparently served to emphasize moiety over family solidarity.[92] Nor can we ignore the other communal celebrations of Islamic holy days, such as *Mowliid* or *Ciid* (the Prophet's birthday) and *Arafo* (the 9th of Alhaji, when pilgrims ascend Mt. Arafa near Mecca), and which also link Muqdisho once again to the other towns of the East African coast.[93] It is hoped that oral testimony will continue to enhance our imperfect understanding of these communal festivals, but the integrative significance of them—cutting across class, family, and quarter—cannot be doubted, though even here competition sometimes manifested itself elsewhere on the coast.[94] Future research must also attempt to elucidate the more mundane, yet critical, question of how Muqdisho was actually run. To sum up, whatever the patterns of urban development in Muqdisho in earlier times may have been, it clearly conformed to wider coastal East African dynamics during the nineteenth century, when the intensified penetration of Indian merchant capital under the overlapping umbrellas of British India and Omani Zanzibar began the process of transformation that would lead ultimately to Italian colonial rule. And while it is also evident that the process of Hawiyya penetration that dates back to the seventeenth century gave Muqdisho a resolutely Soomaali cultural tradition that marks it off from the major towns of the Swahili coast, it is equally certain that the urban characteristics of Muqdisho place it firmly in the regional context of the coast of East Africa.

CHAPTER 5

Futa Benaadir:
Continuity and Change in the
Traditional Cotton Textile
Industry of Southern Somalia,
c. 1840-1980*

Despite the recent appearance of several major studies on African textiles, we still do not know much at all about traditional textile production outside of West Africa.[1] This is much to be regretted, particularly in the case of southern Somalia, which has a history of cotton textile manufacture dating back hundreds of years. According to Muqdisho oral tradition, "The establishment of the industry is associated with the construction of the *jamac* [Friday] mosque in Xamarweyn," which is dated by an inscription above the door by which one enters the minaret to 1 Muharram 636/14 August 1238.[2] This assertion is by no means a far-fetched claim, for when Ibn Battuta visited Muqdisho in 1331, he observed, "In this place are manufactured the woven fabrics called after it, which are unequalled and exported from it to Egypt and elsewhere."[3] For more than five centuries after Ibn Battuta's visit, however, we have not a single notice of the cotton textile industry of the Benaadir coast. According to

* Reprinted from Laboratoire <Connaissance du Tiers-Monde>, *Entreprises et Entrepreneurs en Afrique, XIXe et XXe siecles* (Paris: L'Harmattan, 1983), I, pp. 77-98.

Guillain, who visited Muqdisho in 1847 and 1848, the manufacture of
toob or *futa Benaadir,* as the cloth was known locally, was the only
industry practiced by its people and the only item which the city itself
exported, as opposed to those goods which came to it for export from
the interior. Beginning with the Portuguese intrusion, which cut its
markets to the south, and especially with the invasion of the Abgal
Soomaali from the interior in the 17th century, which disrupted the
entire socio-economic base of the medieval city and led to a precipi-
tous decline in its fortunes, the manufacture of this cloth suffered
accordingly.[4] Nevertheless, this handicraft industry did survive, as it
does to the present [1980]. In this paper I shall present a preliminary
reconstruction of its history over the past century and a half in the
context of the penetration of the world capitalist system in this cor-
ner of Africa.

Guillain attributed the survival of the textile industry in Muqdisho
during the centuries following its apparent medieval apogee to the
fact that since production was in the hands of the lower class and
slaves, an observation which was echoed by Revoil in 1882, it could
survive in very restricted circumstances.[5] But the fact that he reckoned
there to be nearly a thousand weavers in the two moities of the city,
Xamarweyn and Shingaani, out of a total population of about five
thousand, was a direct consequence of the general expansion of the
Indian Ocean market during the early 19th century as it became pro-
gressively incorporated into the world capitalist system of production
and exchange. In particular, it was the growing economic domination
of Zanzibar and its Indian merchant capitalists from the early 1840s
which fueled the commercial revival of the entire Benaadir region.[6]
For although the product of their labor was worn in Muqdisho,
Guillain remarked that most of the annual production of this cloth
was either exported overseas to the Swahili or northern Soomaali
coasts or, especially, sent by caravan to the inland markets as far as
Luuq, on the upper Juuba River at the edge of Oromo country. At the
same time, Guillain was also the first in a long line of doomsayers
who predicted the total decline of this locally produced cloth following the penetration of its markets by modern industrially manufactured textiles.[7]

To understand exactly why his prediction and that of virtually everyone after him was incorrect, we must now look more closely at the organization of production from the 1840s to the beginning of the colonial era in the 1890s. Christopher provides an important note of the sexual division of labor among the Soomaali of the Benaadir which illuminates the social relations of production of cotton textiles. "The occupation of the inhabitants may be shortly enumerated; the women are the spinners of cotton, wood and water fetchers, and cooks; the men weave, go on journeys, and cultivate the ground, although female slaves assist in cultivating if also not taught to spin."[8] Guillain confirms this description and adds some important details to it. The spinning, he tells us, was done "by means of a very simple spinning wheel" with which the women produced "four different threads." These were woven by the men into "six qualities of white fabric, all of nearly equal dimensions, about three meters by 0,65 meter."[9] The same involvement of the entire household of men, women, and slaves was noted fifteen years later by the French commercial agent at Zanzibar.[10] Additional details are provided by Revoil, who spent several months at Muqdisho in 1882. Revoil notes that the ginning of the raw cotton was accomplished by rolling the bolls between two wooden cylinders, after which it was carded by beating so that it resembled cotton packing, and then worked into twists before being spun into thread by the women. Once the raw cotton had been processed into thread, it became the province of men and boys. The boys were responsible for winding the thread into skeins, which they did by taking the bobbin in one hand and making a figure eight with the thread around a small wooden fork. Next the skeins of thread were tied to the loom heddles as warp threads and sized with a paste of maize flour which was applied with a brush made of couch-grass. Finally, the heddles were attached to the loom, "which is almost touching the ground, while the operator is seated in a hole."[11] This cumulative description is completed by Robecchi-Bricchetti, who in 1891 observed that "the worker is seated in a pit dug in the ground underneath the loom and moves the treadles, which serve to raise the threads of the warp, with his feet."[12]

At the technical level, this evidence confirms for the nineteenth century the employment of the double-heddle or "pit treadle" loom by Benaadir weavers, which is still used today. The origin of this loom, which is widespread throughout Africa, where it is always used only by men, may be obscure for West Africa, but in Muqdisho it is remembered as being introduced by traders who went to India and learned the skills there.[13] Certainly, the modern technology of weaving in Muqdisho today varies little from that described recently for a community in Gujarat, the principal region of western India with which the Benaadir coast maintained commercial links throughout the pre-colonial era, and practiced elsewhere around the northwestern rim of the Indian Ocean.[14]

At the socio-economic level, what we have here is a typical example of expanded household production involving everyone except, it seems, female children. Production within each household was organized independently under the direction of its male head. It some cases, the unit of production may have numbered only a man, his wife, and their male children, but in others it was increased by a man's ability to support multiple wives and their male offspring, both male and female slaves, and freely attached apprentices. Certainly, there was no uniformity in the size of household production units and again we must assume that individual skills in all aspects of production, but especially in the weaving of the cloth, were an important variable, as well as the capital resources which any family head could invest in increasing his labor pool. What is even less clear is the relationship that these master weavers had with the merchants who marketed their product. Here, too, we must accept the probable reality of a variety of situations, ranging from the notion of a successful weaver whose household production was relatively large and who enjoyed strong kinship or marital links with one of the major Soomaali trading families of the town to that of small producer who was barely able to eke out a living and who was consequently in debt bondage to some Indian representative of a powerful Zanzibar trading house. Indeed, the greater success of some weaving families and the relative impoverishment or even failure of others seems axiomatic in a petty capitalist enterprise such as this one, particularly in an urban context such as Muqdisho, where weavers lived entirely by their craft and did not produce their own foodstuffs.[15]

Although no figures exist, I believe that we can safely assume that labor costs were minimal in the Benaadir textile industry. No wages were paid to household workers, so that the only expenses involved were the provision of food and shelter, as clothing was presumably supplied by the domestic production unit. It seems reasonable to assume, then, that the major cost of labor was the daily reproduction of its labor power by feeding everyone in the household. Similarly, the simple technology of spinning and weaving meant that there was no great expense involved in the material factors of production and their upkeep, though it is not yet known if weavers in the 19th century made their own looms and spinning wheels or purchased them from local carpenters, or did both, depending on circumstances.

If the social organization and technology of production were clearly factors in minimizing costs and enabling the Benaadir textile industry to survive the competition of increased foreign imports, they were not the only ones. For the 19th century, at least, the key variable appears to have been the raw material. According to Guillain, raw cotton was imported from Kutch, which would have necessitated the intervention of a series of merchant capitalists taking their profits between the weaver and the producer of his raw material. This cotton was sold on the coast at a price of Maria Theresa thalers (hereafter M.T.$) 2-2.25 per *frasila* (16 kg 20 g). Christopher similarly noted that at Geledi, some thirty kilometers inland from Muqdisho on the Webi Shabeele, "they depend on India for cotton in its raw state." Elsewhere, however, Christopher comments that the Sultan of Geledi was attired in "his dress of cotton, the growth and manufacture of the country," and he earlier describes the inhabitants of Torre, a small coastal community just north of and under the influence of Baraawe, as being "herdsmen and growers of cotton," an observation which is independently confirmed by another European traveler in 1843.[16] Four decades later, Revoil makes no mention of imported raw cotton from India, noting only that it was brought to Muqdisho by nomadic

Soomaalis from the interior.[17] By the next decade, southern Somalia was actually exporting raw cotton to India, and in 1891 Robecchi-Bricchetti specifically attributed the ability of *futa Benaadir* to compete successfully with American cottons to the "extremely low price of the cotton which is cultivated in the neighboring regions and by the limited cost of labor."[18] In fact, the tremendous expansion of cotton cultivation in the inter-riveraine area of the Benaadir during the second half of the 19th century has completely eradicated all local memory of there ever having been a need to import raw cotton from India for the indigenous textile industry.[19]

According to Robecchi-Bricchetti, two kinds of cotton grew naturally in the Benaadir, *Gossypium arboreum*, a tree which attains a height of between five and seven meters, and *Gossypium herbaceum*, which grows as a low shrub. He calculated the annual production in the fertile valleys of the Juuba and Shabeele Rivers at about 1,000 tons, which was worth about M.T. $20,000 on the local market. The most extensive areas of cotton cultivation were in the territory of the Abgal, around Baraawe; of the Bimal, around Marka; and of the Wadan, behind Muqdisho. A certain amount was carried in its raw state to the major interior emporium at Luuq, some was consumed locally by weavers in the areas of production and at Baraawe and Marka, with the remainder going to Muqdisho, where it was marketed under rather different conditions in Xamarweyn and Shingaani. "The Indian merchants buy this product as the Somalis carry it to the coast, and when they are thus successful in collecting a certain quantity, they hire a small vessel at Zanzibar, which comes with the monsoon, to load these goods and carry them to Bombay." A small amount was also exported to Zanzibar and all exports of raw cotton were taxed by the Sultan of Zanzibar's customs master at Muqdisho at a 5% *ad valorem* rate. In 1895 Soomaali exports of raw and semi-cleaned cotton, the latter representing no more than a tenth or twentieth of the total, came to 139,986 kg worth M.T. $10,678.[20]

Without pretending to understand the intricacies of the Indian cotton and cotton textile markets, it seems likely that the demand for Soomaali cotton in western India was generated by the handloom industry there, which experienced rising raw cotton costs after 1885 as a result of the expansion of domestic exports and the rise of domestic industrial mills from the time of the cotton famine which was caused by the American Civil War.[21] At the very least, we can rest assured that the cost of cotton production in southern Somalia was sufficiently low to make exportation of raw cotton profitable to the merchants involved.

The key to the low cost of production in the Benaadir region and to its general boom in agricultural commodity production, including millet and sesame, as well as cotton, was slave labor. The available evidence points to the emergence of a dominant slave mode of production in precisely those parts of the Benaadir which were the centers of cotton production in the second half of the century.[22] Large numbers of slaves were settled in the fertile lands of the inter-riveraine region and basically left to fend for themselves and to produce specific commodities for market. One would like to know more about the economics of the slave trade, the nature of organization for production and the maintenance of discipline, and the composition of the class of slave owners, who so far as we know were wealthy Soomaalis of both the coastal and interior towns – the kind of knowledge which we currently possess only for plantation slavery in Zanzibar and on the Kenya coast.[23] Above all, one would like to know in this case how the entire system of plantation slavery emerged in the Benaadir. It is my hypothesis that the stimulus and capitalization came from agents of the great Indian commercial houses at Zanzibar who totally dominated all the export trade of the Benaadir by the 1890s, but this remains to be demonstrated empirically.

The combination of slave production of the raw material and household or expanded household production of the finished product served to assure the Benaadir textile industry a more or less steady level of output during the second half of the 19th century. There are no statistics to sustain this assertion, but the number of weavers and looms in operation in Muqdisho remained stable during this period at about 1,000, a figure which accords well with current oral sources.[24] Guillain reported that annual production of *futa Benaadir* amounted to some 360,000 to 380,000 pieces, while observers in the 1890s noted that production levels were about 50,000 pieces per year. There is no basis for verifying either of these figures, but a decrease of that dimension during an era of expanded trade with a relatively steady production force suggests that either the former figure is too high or the latter too low. Moreover, at least one source indicates that weaving may have been a seasonal activity in Muqdisho, which further complicates any attempt to resolve such discrepancies.[25]

During the 19th century, if not before, the main market for *futa Benaadir* was among the peoples of the interior, both Soomaali and Oromo, with whom it was exchanged for ivory, skins, and other items.[26] By the last decade of the century, however, plain white *futa Benaadir* had been completely replaced by *merikan*, as the grey sheeting manufactured in the United States was known, done up in the standard dimensions of its indigenous predecessor so that it could be worn as the traditional wrapped garment, which was variously known in Soomaali as a *toob, maro, tomonyo,* or *futa.* According to Bòttego, in 1893 a *toob* of *merikan sold* for M.T. $1 in the interior and was accepted as a cloth currency equal to that coin, while a complex system of fractions and multiples reflected the sophistication of the Luuq market, as is confirmed a few years later by Ferrandi and a decade later by Chiesi for the interior, in general.[27] The acceptance of the *toob merikan* as a standard monetary equivalent by the early 1890s suggests strongly that this system of cloth currency had emerged sometime earlier in the century with the expansion of the export trade of the Benaadir hinterland (as is implied by Jablonski in 1862) and that, therefore, it was probably based on the traditional hand woven *toob* of *futa Benaadir.* In this context it is significant that Ferrandi records a tradition among the town elders of Luuq that trade with the coast for *futa Benaadir* was inaugurated in the late 18th century by a man of the *reer* Faaqi, one of the principal family groups of Xamarweyn. In 1896, however, fewer than 600 pieces of *futa Benaadir* were imported at Luuq.[28]

The timing of this new development is important to emphasize, for it provides an essential clue to the Benaadir weavers' ready willingness to convert production from exclusively white to primarily colored cloths, as one finds them today. When Revoil travelled from Muqdisho to Geledi in 1882, the only two kinds of cloth that his caravan carried for gifts and exchange in the interior were *merikan* and *kaniki,* a solid blue cloth which was imported from India.[29] Robecchi-Bricchetti's comment in 1891 about the competitiveness of *futa Benaadir* against *merikan* (see above) suggests that he was witnessing the very end of an era when the economies of production which had protected the former during the previous half century were still effective. As the evidence from Luuq indicates, however, these were very rapidly undermined and the Benaadir was soon inundated with imports of *merikan.* In 1895, for example, imports of *merikan* totaled 2,096 bales worth M.T. $147,496, while other imported cloths were worth only M.T. $24,278. Figures for 1896-1897 indicate that the floodgates were only beginning to open, as imports of *merikan* jumped to 3,245.50 bales worth M.T.$224,892.50 (Muqdisho alone accounting for just over 45% of the total), while other cloths accounted for an additional M.T. $74,643.30.[30] A decade later *merikan* imports were up to 6,079 bales worth M.T. $613,086.22 and the value of other imported cloths was M.T. $142,355.91, the value of *merikan* alone accounting for over 51% of the total imports for the entire colony.[31]

How had all this come about? There seems not to have been any conscious attempt to drive out *futa Benaadir* by either the Indian merchant class or the Italian colonial officials after 1895, so one must look to market forces for an explanation. Since my research on this topic is still preliminary, I can only surmise that a combination of lower costs in overseas production and transportation plus higher costs in the Benaadir, however marginal these may have been, spelled disaster for the future of the traditional plain white weave. On the basis of present evidence about all I can say is that the cost of *toob merikan* in the early 20th century was probably about as inexpensive as the less desirable qualities of *futa Benaadir* had been a half century before.[32]

Coterminous with the sudden domination of *merikan* and the

impending destruction of the Benaadir weaving industry was the strategic carving out of a new market both locally and especially among the interior peoples for a new style of *futa Benaadir* which ensured its survival to the present. Traditionally, as already noted, *futa Benaadir* had been exclusively plain white. But a century ago some colored cloths were being produced by dyeing finished white *futa Benaadir* after it had been purchased for export by local merchants. Revoil noted that "as for the colored cloths, they receive their final preparation in the houses of the traders from the markets of Zanzibar or of Bombay." One of the most popular colors was yellow, which was extracted from Bastard Saffron (*Carthamus tinetorius*), which grew wild as an annual along the banks of the Webi Shabeele.[33] The implication here is that the stimulus for Soomaali craftsmen to begin to think about manufacturing colored *futa Benaadir* may have come from seeing their finished product transformed specifically for overseas export, while they continued to produce plain white stuff for the home markets that they were soon to lose to *merikan*. At about the same time, however, Soomaali weavers also began to incorporate colored threads from India into their fabric.[34]

Already in 1891 Robecchi-Bricchetti reported the existence of striped cloth of vivid colors, the most popular of which were yellow, blue, and red. He also mentions the production of a shorter, finer type of cloth than the traditional *futa* which had red, yellow, and black bands at the ends and was adorned with fringe. Sorrentino describes the cloth produced in Shingaani as being "cottons of various well harmonized colors." The imported thread for this cloth came from the Persian Gulf, Kutch, and especially from Bombay.[35] In 1895 there were 138 bales of cotton yarn worth M.T. $13,701 imported by the ports of the Benaadir; a decade later the dimensions of this business had mushroomed so that in 1905-1906 some 2,300 *frasilas* (36,846 kg) of yarn worth M.T. $49,986.85 was imported, ranking fifth in the Italian colony after *merikan,* coffee, other kinds of cloth, and sugar.[36] Most of this yarn was colored. It was manufactured in Germany and Great Britain now and "together with that prepared by hand by the women of the place, serves for making of the aforementioned Benaadir or Mogadiscio cloth," which because of its bright colors was especially favored by Benaadir women.[37]

Because of their "chemical and aniline colors, which by their vivacity outshine the simple vegetable-based colors which were characteristic of the Benaadir cloth," Chiesi echoed earlier observers in predicting the demise of these colored Benaadir cloths in the face of imported American and German colored and printed cloths. He also noted by way of substantiation that the number of weavers in Muqdisho and Baraawe had declined to no more than three hundred.[38] In fact, Baraawe was on its way to becoming a negligible factor in this handicraft industry, only Marka maintaining itself with Muqdisho as a significant historical center of production past the early colonial period, although by 1907 there were barely more than one hundred looms in operation there.[39] Only in the interior, writes Chiesi, where German cloths had not yet penetrated, was *futa Benaadir* still regarded with appreciation.

It was the interior market, as it happens, and the acuity of its patrons, which saved *futa Benaadir.* Twenty years after Chiesi wrote, the Italians undertook a systematic survey of the newly acquired (as of 5 July 1924) Upper Juuba region, the territory which extends from the right bank of the Juuba River to the present borders with Kenya and Ethiopia. One of the main concerns, as with all colonial regimes, was to determine the nature of the market which had thus been gained. It was discovered by Zoli that while *merikan* and various other cloths were still extremely popular, the origin of these cloths had shifted as a consequence of the First World War from the United States and Great Britain to India and Japan. Zoli also observed that the typical inhabitant of the interior "is very suspicious when purchasing cottons, he prefers those which he considers stronger to the touch, he unfailingly selects those with less sizing and pays close attention to the smell of the sizing, a smell which, if too sharp, disagreeably impresses him." The buyer also was susceptible to the influence of certain well-known trade marks, Zoli noted, and as the tarred paper in which imported cloths were wrapped also imparted an unpleasant odor, this was always discarded before offering them for sale up-country. At the time of his report, the most fashionable imported cloths in Upper Juuba were *kaniki, danga,* various brightly colored percales and kerchiefs printed with five or seven rosettes in combinations of black-yellow-red and red-yellow-white.[40] The question of fashion and established taste is an important one, as anyone who has lived in an African market town will know, and it appears that the "fantastic colored cloths" of the Benaadir which were "lively for local needs" had already solidly established themselves before the First World War. According to Stefanini, "each has its own types: a certain green, for example, is characteristic of Merca, and seems not to be found in the fabrics of other make."[41] In Upper Juuba in the mid-1920s, the most popular varieties of *futa Benaadir* were called *belandiro, bengalo,* and *gambalo,* which may have been the famous Marka green cloth (*gambolo*) or a Muqdisho variation in gold and red which went by the same name (in Soomaali: *shaal dhangalow*).[42] Zoli also remarked that *futa Benaadir* was then woven primarily with Indian yarn, which had recaptured the local market from the dominant European yarns of the pre-war era. The material itself was manufactured in stripes of vividly contrasting colors and in the traditional dimensions of *futa Benaadir.* Particularly revealing are his comments about the colors and sizing used in producing the local cloth:

> The colors are vegetable and extremely fast. The sizing is applied by hand and consists of a paste made of sorghum meal. Today *futa* from Germany are reaching the market which are similar to those of the Benaadir, but much less esteemed by the natives because the colors fade easily. These *futa* imitate the originals very nicely and at a glance remain misleading if the smell of the sizing does not reveal the origin of the *futa* manufactured in Europe.[43]

The careful attention which Soomaalis paid to the sizing used in cotton textiles was a well established habit. Half a century before, Hunter wrote that at Aden, "Somalis and Arabs prefer Bombay man-

ufactured cotton goods. They believe that the starch, etc., used in sizing Manchester goods destroys the fabric; bales, when left unopened
for a few months, are often found to be mildewed, or covered with
large patches."[44] Certainly, fashion was important, but on the basis of
this evidence it appears that established taste for the feel and smell of
futa Benaadir was the critical element in preserving a vital domestic
market for locally produced cotton textiles.

During this period of rapid major readjustment in the Benaadir
weaving industry, a small amount of plain white cloth was still produced in the coastal towns, although the economics of its survival are
unknown.[45] A considerable volume of plain white cloth continued to
be woven from domestically grown cotton for local consumption in
the freed slave villages of the lower Shabeele, where Pàntano counted
139 looms in ten villages and mentioned the existence of many others
in two other villages.[46] The quality of these cottons was less fine than
those of the Benaadir towns and they appear not to have competed
directly with *futa Benaadir*. Rather, the continued production of plain
white cloth seems to have enabled these poor agricultural communities to resist the penetration of *merikan* and, therefore, to remain just
that little bit less entangled in the colonial capitalist economy.[47]

This option was not available for the weavers of Muqdisho and, to
a lesser extent, of Marka, who depended exclusively on weaving for
their livelihood. To survive successfully they had both to maintain
their up-country market and to exploit whatever possibilities for overseas exportation that presented themselves. Before the First World
War this export market had become quite reduced. In 1895 only 5,872
pieces of *futa Benaadir* worth M.T. $4,419 were sent overseas, the
value of exports declining in the following year to M.T. $3,277.25
(88.4% of which were from Muqdisho). A decade later exports were
up marginally to 6,440 pieces worth M.T. $8,759, but in 1909-1910
they fallen to 3,721 pieces. Marka continued to export a very few
pieces during this period, only 229 in 1907, for example, so presumably most of these figures represent the production of Muqdisho
weavers.[48] In the second decade of this century, the units of measure
and currency changed, so it is difficult to calculate precisely the vol-

ume of *futa Benaadir* exports on the basis of present evidence.

That said, what is quite apparent is that the First World War, which seems to have been an important factor affecting the up-country market, as we have seen, gave a tremendous temporary boost to overseas exports of *futa Benaadir,* as well. In 1913 exports were worth a total of Italian *lira* (Lit.) 60,275 [U.S. $11,633.08]. Five years later the value of exports was about the same at Lit. 64,385.19 [U.S. $12,426.34] for a total of 5,324 bales of indeterminate composition. In 1919 and 1920, however, the volume of exports exploded to 32,585 bales worth Lit. 154,453.62 [U.S. $29,809.55] and 31,098 bales worth a wildly inflated Lit. 809,676.60 [U.S. $156,267.58].[49] How this affected production and the up-country trade can only be guessed at for the moment, but it must have represented a great boost to the local textile industry and windfall war profits for local merchant capitalists.

At the very least this flurry of activity seems to have caused the recruitment of a number of new workers to the weaving industry. I have no figures for Muqdisho, but we were told that the father of Shaykh Suufi apprenticed himself to a weaver after he had failed in business at about this time. Certainly, there was a great increase in the number of weavers at Jelib-Marka, an isolated peninsula about fifteen kilometers north of Marka which today is the other major center of production besides Muqdisho. In the first decade of this century Pàntano and Carletti noted only that there were a number of looms to be seen in this "industrious and prosperous" community of about 900 persons, but by the mid-1930s there were about 200 weavers working there, equal to the number at Marka and all other locations in that administrative district. Barile estimated the monthly production of this flourishing community of weavers at 3,500 *futa* of several different varieties and qualities "which are sold in all the centers of the colony because in no other place is the skill of these weavers surpassed."[50] In Muqdisho at this time the dominant colors used in making *futa Benaadir* were yellow, red, and dark blue. Production was still carried out by individual weavers working in the open air and side streets of the old city, although Corni illustrates a well constructed, raffia-roofed open workshop with five looms. The Italian administration is also remembered as having levied an annual license fee of Lit. 2 for weavers.[51]

If the 1930s were a fairly successful period for the Benaadir weaving industry, this reflects the peculiar economic history of the Italian colony, which witnessed several years of "unprecedented prosperity" around the time of the Fascist war against Ethiopia.[52] But the Second World War did not provide the same sort of stimulus to *futa Benaadir* production as had its predecessor. Indeed, the decade of the 1940s was generally bleak for the economy of southern Somalia under British military occupation. In the 1950s, though, more than 1,000 Soomaalis and their families were still engaged in weaving *futa Benaadir*, "which is in constant demand in the markets of neighboring countries," according to a World Bank mission.[53]

Soon after the newly unified Republic of Somalia gained its independence in July 1960, the Government requested the International Labor Office to send out an expert on handicrafts and small-scale industries to help it in its long range planning. According to this individual, Mario P. Grassi, although *futa Benaadir* was essential for a Soomaali couple who were getting married, it was rarely worn on an everyday basis, particularly in the cities and by women, who were adopting European dresses.[54] The cloth was primarily produced in Muqdisho and Jelib-Marka. In Muqdisho there were about sixty weavers active, "while the families assist them in preparing the yarn. Yarn is given to the weavers by local merchants who pay them a fixed amount per futa made." At Jelib-Marka over 1,500 people were engaged in cloth production, though he does not specify the number of weavers. Production was organized under the direction of twenty-two chiefs "who give them the yarn and pay them for each working day."

Grassi then remarks that "the working conditions of these weavers are bad. Working in an open court-yard, their only protection against the sun and rain is a poor construction of wooden sticks and newspapers." When it rained the pits in which the men sat to weave became filled with water "and there is no work for several days – and no pay either." He believed this to work a particular hardship on those peo-

ple for whom weaving was a full-time occupation. But the difficult circumstances of the weavers were not only physical. As Grassi points
out, "The weavers have always been at the mercy of unscrupulous
merchants who take advantage of their poverty." Not only was the
income for their work unsteady, it was also below the conservatively
computed average salary of workers in this sector of the Soomaali
economy (So.Sh.3.17 per day or So.Sh.952 per year).[55] According to
information that he gathered from merchants who dealt with the
weavers, the price paid for two standard length *futa* was So.Sh.32. Of
this sum, however, So.Sh.25 was deducted for the anticipated cost of
the yarn, so that only So.Sh.7 remained to the weavers for work that
normally took him three days, although this may be a miscalculation
on Grassi's part.[56] The finished product was then sold in the market
by the merchant for So.Sh.50-60, "thus leaving an exorbitant profit
with the merchant who has already profited on the yarn."

Conditions were somewhat better in Jelib-Marka, where wages
were paid by the chiefs at the rate of So.Sh.4-6 per day. "The Chiefs
collect the 'futa' which they sell to merchants in Mogadiscio who supply them with new yarn in lieu of cash." Any attempt to circumvent
these merchants, he suggests, would close off the market to them for
their cloths. "Dependence on merchants is thus heavy as no yarn can
be bought without 'futa' (because of lack of money), and no futa is
accepted if yarn is not purchased."[57] He concludes his discussion on
the conditions of work in the traditional textile industry by explaining that

> the appearance of the merchant—even if an
> exploiter—is sometimes welcomed because many
> weavers do not have the money nor the credit to buy
> yarn in order to produce for the market, thus losing
> the possibility of work. . . . In general, workers do not
> complain about the low pay but more about working
> conditions; they consider the security of being able to
> sell their product very important.

This is the first substantive evidence that we have about the really desperate working conditions and extreme exploitation suffered by the Benaadir weavers in the 20th century. We cannot, of course, project these conditions back any farther, I suspect, than the post-Second World War period, though the elements of debt bondage to the local merchant capitalists can perhaps be traced back into the late 19th century or early colonial period. But there can be little doubt that by the early 1960s, at the latest, the handloom weavers were among the most abjectly exploited workers in the entire Soomaali economy. This impression is borne out by two later reports, one by the (then) current Soomaali regime (of Maxamed Siyaad Barre) and the other again by the I.L.O.

The first of these recounts the achievements of the traditional weavers since being reorganized into cooperative societies with government financial and administrative assistance. This new development was made possible by a law passed in October 1973. The report asks:

> What were the conditions of these specialist workers before the Revolution? They were very poor and had to struggle each day to survive; in fact they had not even the money to buy the raw materials for their work and had therefore to submit to an undesirable relationship with rich merchants who sold them the raw materials, speculating on the poverty and misery of these people by charging them prices that were many times more than the normal market prices. The material was sold on credit and repaid with the finished products at under-cost price. The situation in which these people lived was much like the relationship between slave and master. They had to work in open places, under the scorching sun. Entire families had to work in order to finish the work on time. When the rain season came the fabric workers couldn't work and their small earnings were thus continually consumed just to keep themselves alive. There was no way out.

Cooperatives, as had been recommended by the 1963 I.L.O. report, were seen as the solution to this vicious circle of exploitation of household production through the medium of merchant capital. According to the official version, however, the merchant capitalists of Muqdisho did not surrender their advantage without a struggle when the Muqdisho cooperative was formed in 1974. "One night, all the raw cotton in Mogadishu disappeared, seeing no other measure of solution, the government threatened the merchants with legal prosecution." Only when the Ministry of Commerce began to import the yarn required by the weavers and to assure them guaranteed markets for their product, were the merchant capitalists defeated.[58]

One of the immediately tangible results for members of the weavers' cooperative in Muqdisho was the physical improvement of working conditions in the airy concrete building where they were located near the market in Xamarweyn when I conducted my research in 1980. The fact remains, however, that in 1976 the Benaadir weavers were still numbered among the three major poverty groups in the entire country. By that time six weavers' cooperative societies had been organized and there were some 800 weavers active in the industry. In 1973, when the consumer price index in Muqdisho was only 114 on a base of 100 for 1966, the average monthly wages of textile workers (figured on the basis of a nominal wage for unpaid family labor) was So.Sh.46, far lower than those for any other group of workers in either the public or private sector.[59] In stressing the importance of the informal sector from an employment perspective, the I.L.O. report also provides us with a clue as to why the weavers were willing to endure an existence as objectively miserable as that depicted in these post-independence accounts:

> It is this sector that provides refuge to those who cannot make their both ends meet in the agriculture, pastoral or large industrial sectors and that it is a bulwark against open unemployment in urban areas. The flexibility of this sector to absorb people and their initiative to find some work for themselves to live hon-

ourably, even though miserably, should not be stifled
by any irrational or hasty Government policy.[60]

The ability to survive and to work, no matter how oppressive the
conditions, arguably gave dignity and a sense of worth to a highly
skilled group of artisans and their families in an historical context
which offered them no viable alternative other than casual wage
labor.[61] Although by the middle of the 20th century they were no less
wage slaves than other segments of the Soomaali urban and rural
proletariat, because of their ancient skills they still maintained control of at least some of the factors of production involved in the manufacture of cotton textiles. Not least of these was the knowledge
which was still imparted from master weaver to apprentice. This was
no small triumph, especially in generally impoverished Somalia.

*   *   *   *   *

When I wrote this chapter in the early 1980s I observed that it would
probably not be entirely inappropriate to repeat earlier concerns that
the weavers of *futa Benaadir* faced an uncertain future. *Futa Benaadir*
was no longer an inexpensive alternative to imported cloths, and as a
prestige textile it faced competition from Tanzanian *kitenge* and similar stuffs.[62] I also expressed more optimistically than I would have—
had I known at the time what I know now—that its ability to endure
for more than seven centuries, and particularly to make the radical
adjustments that historical circumstances had forced upon it over the
past century, suggested strongly that it would continue to survive.
How little did any of us know that Somalia would collapse in a spiral
of internecine violence from which economic recovery—of which it is
highly unlikely that *futa Benaadir* will be a part—now seems a dis-
tressingly remote possibility.

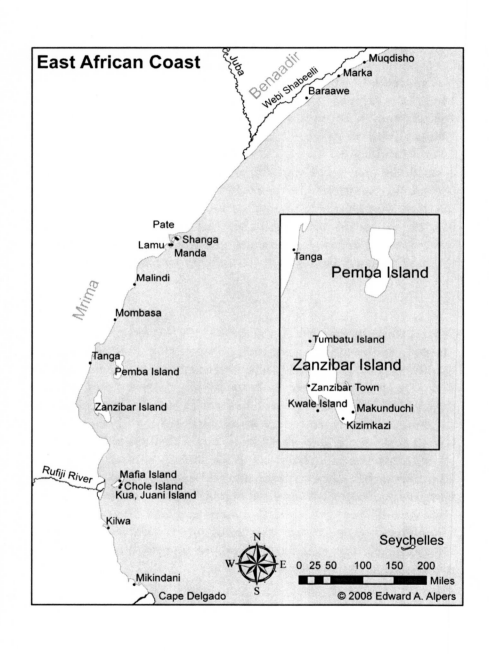

East African Coast

Benaadir

Juba

Webi Shabeelli

Muqdisho
Marka
Baraawe

Mrima

Pate
Lamu · Shanga
Manda

Malindi

Mombasa

Tanga
Pemba Island

Zanzibar Island

Rufiji River

Mafia Island
Chole Island
Kua, Juani Island

Kilwa

Mikindani
Cape Delgado

Tanga

Pemba Island

Tumbatu Island

Zanzibar Island

Zanzibar Town
Kwale Island · Makunduchi
Kizimkazi

Seychelles

N
W E
S

0 25 50   100   150   200
Miles

© 2008 Edward A. Alpers

"Ordinary Household Chores": Ritual and Power in a Nineteenth-Century Swahili Women's Spirit Possession Cult*

This paper concerns a women's spirit possession cult that was described at Zanzibar in 1869 by an Alsatian Catholic missionary.[1] It is
my contention that the ritual which he observed encapsulates certain
fundamental aspects of the historical experience of Zanzibari women
at that time and, moreover, that the ritual explicitly declares what it is
about—the domestication of women.

Attempting to understand this cult, which was dedicated to a spirit named *kitimiri*, and to place it in its specific historical context has
caused me to think through much more critically than ever before
what we know both about Swahili society and about Swahili women
during this period. On the one hand, we know a great deal about
Zanzibar and the coast in the nineteenth century with reference to the
intensified penetration of merchant capital and the expansion of the
colonial Busaidi Omani state. Subjects like the slave trade, slavery,
expanded commodity production, and Islam have all been studied

* Reprinted from *International Journal of African Historical Studies*, 17, 4 (1984), pp. 677-702.

carefully. On the other hand, the same cannot be said about either women or spirit possession. Fortunately, the pioneering work of Margaret Strobel enables us to appreciate the history of women in coastal society from the end of the nineteenth century,[2] while a variety of studies on spirit possession among the peoples of coastal East Africa and a growing literature on spirit possession in the wider Muslim world opens up other possibilities for understanding this phenomenon in historical and comparative perspective. At the same time, I have attempted to situate my discussion in the broader methodological and theoretical debate about gender relations, the sexual division of labor, and the character of women's subordination in history. It is thereby my hope that this contribution will be accessible to readers interested in African history, Islamic history, and women's studies.

Zanzibar in the 1860s and the Deteriorating Situation of Women

This is not the place to reconstruct in detail the nineteenth-century history of Zanzibar, but it is important to emphasize the real need for care not to overgeneralize or to assume too much when attempting to analyze specific socio-historical phenomena. Swahili society, in particular, is characterized by local variations on a general theme of Afro-Islamic culture, so that what one knows about Lamu or Bagamoyo may not hold true for Pemba at any point in time. As a starting point, then, I want to focus attention on what I think was happening at Zanzibar—specifically in the town itself and its immediate environs—in the years preceding Père Horner's description of the *kitimiri* spirit possession cult in 1869. Horner does not, in fact, tell us how and where he made his observations on the cult, but in the absence of other evidence we must assume that his knowledge came from practice in and around Zanzibar Town, as that is where the mission was located.

In 1869 Zanzibar was a society in the midst of an enormous process of transformation in which the pre-existing relations of production of the indigenous Hadimu and Tumbatu people were subordinated to slavery. In the western part of the island, where land alienation for Arab plantations was concentrated, Hadimu farmers had been either pushed to the less fertile eastern and southern extremes of the island, or allowed to remain in scattered communities within the Arab colony. During these decades, and especially after 1840, Hadimu men were subject to increasing demands for corvée labor as part of their subordination to the Busaidi state.[3] We have no evidence for how these developments affected the organization of production among the Hadimu and Zanzibar Tumbatu, but the combination of resettlement or incorporation and increased demand for public labor by these men probably expanded the responsibility of women in production for use—that is, in the production of food—and crystallized the role of women in the domestic domain.[4] Such political intervention into the sphere of production was not entirely unprecedented, as both the Hadimu and the Tumbatu maintained indigenous overlords, but the degree of state exploitation of male labor was certainly transformed under Busaidi rule during this period. Furthermore, it can be argued that the exploitation of male labor for public works such as the building of "Stone Town," roads, the clearing of land for Sayyid Said ibn Sultan's plantations, and the harvesting of cloves, gave that labor social value in the context of the Omani state and thereby emphasized its importance, even while subordinating Hadimu and Tumbatu men to the state. The consequences of such a process would thus have been to further dichotomize male and female socio-economic roles and to exacerbate gender relations.[5]

The great commercial expansion of Zanzibar during this period also created a context in which male activities were increasingly accorded greater social value than were those of women. Everything connected with the ivory and slave trades depended on male labor, whether slave or free, including porterage, maritime transportation and maintenance, dockside labor, marketing and storage. The same was true for the marketing of mainland commodities such as gum copal, sesame, and other products.[6] Part of this process intimately involved the rise of an urban center at Zanzibar Town, which grew from a small Hadimu town with a few Arab residents at the beginning of the century to a large, multi-ethnic town of perhaps 25,000 people at mid-century and continued to expand thereafter. Representative indices of urban growth which are perhaps more accurate than population estimates are the increase in the number of wards (*mitaa*) in "Stone Town" from three in 1835 to eighteen in 1857, the growth of Ng'ambo in the 1840s as the working class section of the city, and the tenfold increase in the number of mosques between the early 1830s and the 1860s.[7]

Ramachandran Menon argues persuasively that the rise of the town was wholly dependent on the exploitation of the countryside by slave labor:

> From the 1830s the country was the life-blood of the town. As the bread-basket, it took care of the material reproduction of the Arabs in town. As a source of income, it enabled the Arabs to accumulate wealth and retire to a life of luxury and ease, either in their town or country residences. The country was the scene of exploitation, and the town the home of the exploiters.[8]

In the town itself, class divisions and relations of exploitation were also expressed spatially in the existence of "Stone Town" and Ng'ambo. "Ngambo's [sic] function was essentially to serve the needs of stone town," concludes Menon, whose analysis of the labor force makes it quite clear that most urban public occupations were restricted to males. He also suggests that by the 1870s it is possible to group both slave and free labor together as "the nascent urban proletariat."[9] The public participation of women in all of this was limited to the menial tasks of semi-skilled labor, such as house construction, where women are reported as being engaged in the plastering of walls and roofs.[10]

In both countryside and town, then, I would suggest that the nineteenth-century transformation of Zanzibar both trivialized the socio-economic role of Swahili women and increased their subordination to Swahili men. While I am not addressing myself to the problem of origins here, I believe that the specific historical process that I have provisionally reconstructed bears out the general conceptual points that have been made both by Karen Sacks, regarding the relationship between gender hierarchy, exploitation, class stratification, and the state, and by Eleanor Leacock, regarding the part played by exchange, colonization, and urban-rural relations in similarly encouraging sexual asymmetry.[11]

If this hypothesis is correct, then we should also be able to find certain superstructural elements which support such a contention. Randall Pouwels demonstrates that until the reign of Seyyid Barghash ibn Said (1870-1888) there was no conscious attempt by the Busaidi to manipulate the ideological realm in support of the state, but he also provides abundant evidence of a variety of social responses to this transformation that undoubtedly had considerable impact before then.[12] Before about the middle of the nineteenth century, he suggests, "civilization" was intimately linked to local concepts of Islam and was embodied linguistically by the word *uungwana*. This concept was quite distinct from any notion of "Arabness."

> "Civilization" and Arabness, in fact, seem to have become associated only after the mid-nineteenth century when the Busaidi dynasty in Zanzibar began to have a cultural, as well as a political, impact on coastal communities. It was sometime after the 1860s and 70s then, that "civilization" was characterized less and less by *uungwana* and its implications concerning parochial concepts of Islam, and was gradually replaced by the word *ustaarabu*—in other words—to be like an Arab.[13]

It would seem, then, that the two decades leading up to 1869 represent a critical period of transition between two conflicting concepts of what it meant to be civilized on the coast of East Africa. Cultural ambiguities and uncertainties would have been commonplace and nowhere more advanced than in Zanzibar Town, which was in the process of becoming "an intellectual center of great importance."[14] What I am trying to avoid here is a static view of Islam and the notion of a fixed place occupied by women in the Islam of East Africa.[15] Indeed, it is clear from Pouwels's remarkable work that Islam itself was changing as part of a larger process of cultural reorientation during the nineteenth century. It must therefore be assumed that the position of women was equally mutable and varied. The question remains to verify this assertion and to establish its details.

It must first be admitted that without much more primary research we are very limited in what we can say about this fundamental problem. Nevertheless, there are indications that gender relations were more equitable in Hadimu and Tumbatu society on Zanzibar before the mid-nineteenth century than subsequently. Trimingham notes, for example, that "in certain mosques of the waHadimu and waTumbatu . . . women are allowed to worship, screened off from the men by a curtain running across the back or down the center," while "some of the ruined mosques have an annex or section which may have been used by women," including one built during the reign of Seyyid Majid ibn Sultan (1856-1870) at Bububu, north of Zanzibar Town.[16] Similarly, among both the Hadimu and Tumbatu family land rights (*kiambo*) could be and were inherited by women, while the community position of guardian of the soil (*muyale* or *mviale*) could also be occupied by women.[17] Finally, the highest political office among both the Hadimu and Tumbatu was twice occupied by a woman.[18] Though scarcely compelling evidence, taken together these examples suggest that Hadimu and Tumbatu women enjoyed potential and sometimes realized public roles in the religious, economic, and political life of Zanzibar before the effective imposition of Busaidi colonial rule. This is not to say that gender relations up to that era were egalitarian or that sexual parallellism reigned, but simply to point out that sexual asymmetry may have been both less extreme and less institutionalized than it became during the later nineteenth century.[19]

What basis is there for constructing such a hypothesis? Even before the conscious ideological transformations that were effected by Seyyid Barghash, important changes were being instituted in Islamic practice at Zanzibar which Pouwels characterizes as "the rise of absolute transcendence." As the court of Seyyid Said (1806-1856) at Zanzibar assumed an unprecedented grandeur after 1840 and was built upon by his son and successor, Majid, a new generation of Hadrami *sharifs* and Comorian and Benaadiri *'ulama* introduced new concepts of Shafi'i Islam which emphasized literacy and a cosmopolitan Indian Ocean tradition of education over local, orally-based Islamic traditions. No doubt this new orthodoxy was preached in the increasingly large number of mosques in Zanzibar Town. In time these changes became institutionalized and a beginning may be seen in the appointment after 1837 of the renowned popular religious leader, Shaikh Muhyi ad-Din al-Qatani al-Wa'il (1794-1869), as Shafi'i *qadi* in the courts of both Seyyids Said and Majid.[20] What this meant for women was primarily a closer adherence to the Sharia than had previously prevailed and the weakening, though certainly not the obliteration, of the authority of customary law.[21]

To sum up, from the 1830s to the 1860s Zanzibar witnessed the transformation of its social relations of production, the emergence of a colonial state and a pre-capitalist class society, and the rise of a less parochial form of Islam, all of which combined to subject Hadimu and Tumbatu women to a steady loss of status and, perhaps, sense of worth in their society.

Spirit Possession Cults and Women's Responses to the Transformation of Zanzibar Society

Although the reconstruction that I have offered should help us generally to appreciate why Swahili women at Zanzibar in 1869, the date of Horner's description of *kitimiri*, might have been susceptible to participation in some form of compensatory women's activity, it in no way explains anything in particular. To do this requires a closer and somewhat circuitous examination of the specific nexus of popular religion in mid-nineteenth-century Zanzibar.

The first thing to clarify is that we have absolutely no idea as to the origin or antiquity of spirit possession cults in Swahili society. It does seem possible that notions of spirit illness in the East African coastal hinterland spread inland from the Swahili from the 1870s,[22] but we can do no more than assume that this concept and associated cult activity obtained among the Swahili at the beginning of the nineteenth century. If we accept this postulate, the focus of our analysis should be the nature of cosmological response to exogenous change among Swahili women at Zanzibar. In this context, therefore, it is important to underscore Mary Douglas's point

> that rituals are not fixed from time immemorial. They are not unchanging hard cores of some mystic cosmology. . . . People are living in the middle of their cosmology, down in amongst it; they are energetically manipulating it, evading its implications in their own lives if they can, but using it for hitting each other and forcing one another to conform to something they have in mind. . . . [Rituals] are extremely plastic.[23]

The earliest reference to spirit possession at Zanzibar that I have identified dates from the late 1840s, in other words, from around the beginning of regular European presence at Zanzibar. Noting the general belief in evil spirits, an American voyager from that once spirit-ridden town of Salem, Massachusetts, observed that over every doorway in the town was a passage from the Quran written on a piece of paper or carved in wood as protection. He also recorded that "To relieve the sufferings of demoniacs, goats and black fowls are killed upon the seashore, with exorcising ceremonies; after which a miniature boat is launched, in which his satanic majesty is supposed to take passage."[24] Echoes of this practice are found in the *nyange* spirit exorcism dance peculiar to the Hadimu community of Makunduchi, on the southeast coast of Zanzibar, which was recorded by Ingrams in the 1920s; in the custom of making offerings to the general category of sea spirits "by floating little boats out to sea," which was reported by Caplan from Mafia Island in the 1960s; and in the unique reiteration of this feature in the Zanzibar-derived *mrewa* spirit exorcism, which was observed by Lambek on Mayotte, one of the Comoro Islands, in 1976.[25] A more specific identification is suggested by an emic source, Mtoro bin Bakari of Bagamoyo, who wrote at the end of the nineteenth century. Mtoro concludes his description of the *tari* spirit exorcism – which also incorporates the slaughter of a goat – with a paragraph concerning the launching of a miniature dhow made from fibrous material of a coconut or raffia palm. "This dhow is fitted with mast and sail and loaded with food, bananas, a little cane, a little sugar, and a piece of bread. When the release [of the spirit] is complete, the dhow is left in the sea to carry the spirit back to its home in the sea."[26] In view of this evidence, I think it quite possible that what Osgood described with reasonable accuracy in the late 1840s was the conclusion of an exorcism of the *tari* spirit.

What do we know about this spirit and how can that help us to locate it in this analysis? First, *tari* is identified unambiguously as a sea spirit, and sea spirits, as opposed to land spirits, are everywhere associated with Arabs in Swahili culture. This may not always have been so, but by the nineteenth century, it was certainly true. The very word for sea spirit, *jinni*, is derived from the Arabic *djinn*. Krapf first recorded this association in his 1882 dictionary,[27] but it is Craster, writing of Pemba in 1913, who makes the dichotomy absolutely clear. After distinguishing between the two tribes (*kabila*) of devils *(shetani*; Arabic *shaytan)*, namely *jini* and *kibwengu*, the native spirits of Pemba, he comments that "the Geni came to Pemba with the Arabs, and are generally to be found near the sea-coast."[28] Returning full circle to the *tari* spirit, Sacleux records in his monumental dictionary that "if a sick person speaks Arabic, even a single word of it, the person is always told [by the spirit-doctor] s/he is possessed by the *tari* spirit."[29]

Although Horner's detailed description concerns only the *kitimiri* spirit possession cult, he also noted the existence of *tari* in 1869 and identified it as a sea spirit. Furthermore, Mtoro bin Bakari leaves no doubt that both *kitimiri* and *tari* were considered to be Arab spirits.[30] Before turning to my analysis of *kitimiri* and addressing the question of women's participation in these spirit possession cults, let me suggest why I think that the *tari* spirit might have become popular as early as mid-century at Zanzibar, as it bears upon all that I will subsequently argue.

The essential definition of *tari* (Arabic *tarr*) is "tambourine," which was apparently the most characteristic Arab musical instrument in East Africa and was played at many weddings and *maulidi* celebrations of the Prophet Muhammad's birthday and of circumcisions.[31] Notably, among the religiously important Hadrami Arabs at Zanzibar, the *tarr* was played at *maulidi* and all solemn occasions.[32] Indeed, Hadrami were ubiquitous throughout the Indian Ocean and played an especially important role as popularizers of certain Islamic practices from the bottom rung of East African Muslim coastal society (as opposed to the mass of non-Muslim up-country slaves who were constantly being absorbed in it), in direct opposition to the indigenous elite tradition of *uungwana*.[33] Squeezed between two conflicting elite cultural paradigms – *uungwana* and *ustaarabu* – it is possible that, because of their despised social position on the coast, Hadrami religious practices were both attractive and accessible to relatively disadvantaged or deprived Swahili who did not share willingly or were denied participation in the dominant cultural norms. If this hypothesis can be sustained, it would make sense that one of its characteristic material manifestations, the *tari*, was seized upon by Swahili and incorporated into popular concepts of spirit illness as a possessing *jini*. As Monica Wilson has observed about the highly selective and idiosyncratic nature of symbolic incorporation in ritual change,

> What particular symbols are retained, or borrowed, or transformed depends on what catches the imagination. A poet's associations always lie within the frame of his [or her] experience as a member of a particular society within a given culture, but inside that frame his [or her] imagination rules; the symbols used in rit-

uals are poetic or dramatic forms accepted by a community, through time.[34]

To this point I have said nothing about who among the Swahili were actually possessed by these spirits. All later descriptions leave no doubt that the main group of possessed individuals consisted of adult females, although some men were also subject to spirit possession. We are fortunate, however, to possess two very different indigenous pieces of evidence that are contemporary to Horner's account of *kitimiri* and which make it quite plain that women were the main victims of spirit possession at Zanzibar in the 1860s, too.

The first is a poetic diatribe against spirit possession and the male ritual experts (*fundi*) or doctors (*waganga*) who lead their female clients away from the true path of the faith. It was composed by the venerable Shaikh Muhyi ad-Din, and among the nine spirits that he specifically denounces in the name of religious orthodoxy are *kitimiri* and *tari*. This quatrain, which Lyndon Harries entitles "The Judge and the Sorcerer's Client," but which in an abbreviated version is called *Wapungaji* or "Against Exorcists," vilifies the *waganga* for pretending to possess medical knowledge and for taking money from the women whom they pretend to treat, while also charging them with enjoying sexual relations with their patients.[35] Shaikh Muhyi ad-Din also draws a sharp contrast between the true knowledge of literary education and the false knowledge of custom. This theme, in particular, is emphasized in the final two stanzas:

> If you want my blessing/ O created beings who listen/ prevent them with chains/ the whole lot of these children/ and whosoever believes in God/ keeps himself without reproach/ and whoseoever denies this/ he is no Muslim but an infidel.
>
> What necessity have you/ to believe in things like these?/ (you) who know the Quran/ with more than its hundred chapters/ a matter which is impossible/ (why) do you believe in it/ and so go in for trouble/ by night and day?[36]

Both the expressed tension between the new orthodoxy of the dominant Arab society of Zanzibar, with its commitment to absolute
transcendence, and the older, town Islam of *uungwana,* with its historical roots in local tradition, and that between Swahili men and
women are critical elements which will redound in my discussion of
the *kitimiri* spirit possession cult.

The second contemporary source that bears witness to the predo-
minance of female participation in these cults serves as an invaluable
methodological check against drawing too facile conclusions about
the dissemination of specific possession spirits and the nature of cult
organization. It consists of a long description of possession by
Salima binti Said, the daughter of Said ibn Sultan and a Circassian
slave wife (*suria*), who was forced to flee Zanzibar in 1866 when she
was in her early twenties after becoming pregnant during the course
of an affair with a German merchant.[37] It is especially interesting for
what it reveals about spirit possession among women, both free and
slave, at the very apex of Zanzibar society, where purdah was most
carefully guarded.[38]

Salima's account begins with the observation that children were
especially prone to possession, a phenomenon which may have been
limited to those of the upper class, as it finds little echo in later
accounts of Swahili spirit possession, though Mtoro bin Bakari was
thought by his parents to have been possessed as a child by a certain
land spirit.[39] She then continues:

> Grown-up people are also frequently possessed—
> men but rarely, but many women, and of the
> Abyssinian women, nearly one-half. Convulsive
> attacks, want of appetite, and general apathy, the
> desire to remain shut up in dark rooms, and such
> propensities, are taken as sure signs. A person thought
> to be possessed, is treated with a tremendous amount
> of respect, or rather—fear!
>
> A special examination takes place to find out
> whether a person be really possessed. For this cere-

mony a party is invited, of which all the guests must be acknowledged habitations of the evil one. These pitiable victims form a kind of secret society, in which they keep their movements quite dark.

The newly attacked woman sits down in a dark room, wrapped so completely in her schele (Arabic *shela*, a large black veil worn over the head by Arab women out of doors), that she cannot be touched by the slightest ray of light. She is then, in the true sense of the word, smoked out, a vase containing strong incense being held close to her nostrils. The company round her begin to sing a strange song, wagging their heads all the time to and fro. Some Abyssinian concoction, composed of corn and dates, which tastes rather pleasant, is a beverage necessary for the occasion. I have been told that all these combined influences put the victim into a state of second sight; she first talks incoherently, until at last she raves with foam at the mouth. Then is the time that the spirit has taken possession of her. The company present enter into conversation with this spirit, and request to be informed what it wants; for it must be understood that the sick are not plagued by evil spirits alone—there are also good spirits, that may have taken a special fancy to a person, wishing to protect her in life. Sometimes it occurs that two spirits, a good and a bad one, contest for the same person, and during this exorcism they are sure to manifest themselves. It is said that frightful scenes sometimes ensue on such occasions, which none but the very bravest can face out.

Frequently an expert woman will drive out an evil spirit; with a good one a kind of agreement is made, allowing it to pay visits to its victim at times, when it would be well received, on condition that it predicts what may befall the possessed one, as well as her relations.

> Possessed people are in the habit of drinking the
> blood of immolated animals, such as fowls and goats;
> they devour eggs and meat raw. Of course the poor
> people who have undergone such an examination suf-
> fer from its effects for many a day afterwards.[40]

Salima binti Said's testimony may, in fact, be unique for all of the
East African coast, as it appears to be a description not of a Swahili
spirit possession cult, but rather an account of the Ethiopian-derived
zaar spirit possession. The *zaar* cult is today an important nexus of
women's cultural activity in Egypt, northern Sudan, and Somalia, but
it is not known in East Africa.[41] It seems to have been spread from its
Ethiopian cultural context to those areas, as well as to Mecca and
Oman, by so-called Abyssinian female slaves during the nineteenth
century, which witnessed renewed expansion of the Ethiopian slave
trade.[42] In all of those regions *zaar* possession cults have maintained
the important feature of female cult leaders, called *shaikha,* which
was also noted by Salima.[43] We have already noted, however, that
among the Swahili ritual leadership of spirit possession cults was in
most cases controlled by men. This important structural difference,
which relates directly to the issue of ritual and power, may explain
why *zaar* possession was not accessible to Swahili women and apparently remained restricted to the women of the Arab ruling, class at
Zanzibar.[44]

The *Kitimiri* Spirit Possession Cult and
Islamic Practice at Zanzibar

Let us now turn to Horner's description of the ceremonies associated
with the identification and exorcism of the *kitimiri* spirit, which he
specifically identifies as possessing women. First of all, his account is
far more detailed than that for any other specific spirit (*pepo*) among
the Swahili-speaking people, but in its detail it is confirmed by all
subsequent accounts. He points out at the beginning of his narrative
that the ritual experts (*mafundi*) of the women's spirit possession cults

were Hadimu men (p. 24). He also observes that the dance of the *kitimiri* spirit is called *Mwana maua* or "Mistress of the Flowers." Indeed, two pages earlier in his letter he refers to *Mwana maua* as a "divinity . . . whose exceptional beauty is set off by the whiteness of her skin, while her husband is always presented in the form of an old monkey."

This spirit is also reported by Steere and by Krapf (citing Steere), who defines the name as "a sprite represented by a white woman with an ugly black husband."[45] By the 1920s this spirit, among others, was not well known in Zanzibar. "I asked about them all," states Ingrams, "but though several of the names were recognized, my informants said they did not now exist."[46] *Mwana maua* is mentioned, however, by Topan at Mombasa in the 1960s in the context of his discussion of the danger represented by female possessing spirits, although he does not provide further details as to its specific character. For this we are again indebted to Sacleux, who records a variant on this name and defines it as an evil spirit "which people say is to be found sometimes on the flowers of the pandanus," or screw pine, a botanical order which is found chiefly in Indonesia. Indeed, these flowers figure prominently in Horner's description of the *kitimiri* exorcism. Sacleux also attributes *Mwana maua* to a southern dialect of Swahili and seems to suggest that both it and the *kitimiri* spirit exorcism dance were especially bothersome at Lamu, on the northern Kenya coast, though he does not actually link them together.[47] If his southern attribution has any significance for the derivation of this spirit, it may be worth noting that Horner's reference follows immediately on a description of another spirit which was known among the Yao, who inhabited the southern interior of East Africa.

The Yao constituted one of the main ethnic groups among the slave population of Zanzibar and Strobel has demonstrated the important cultural influence that they exercised at Mombasa in the popularization of *makungwi* associations among women.[48] Whether or not it was of Yao origin, however, the association of *Mwana maua* with *kitimiri* suggests strongly that, despite *kitimiri* being reckoned as an Arab spirit from the sea, the actual content of the spirit exorcism, as we shall now see, integrated several different cultural elements and was by no means exclusively reflective of Arab culture.

Horner begins his account of *kitimiri* by describing how a possessing spirit was identified after other forms of secular medical treatment had failed to relieve an individual's illness. In this case he describes how the *mganga* to whom the patient was directed "takes some sand, throws it on a board, and traces some figures on it," which are then examined carefully for indication of possession. This use of a specifically Islamic form of divination, *ramli* or geomancy, which is included in Mtoro bin Bakari's much briefer description of *kitimiri* exorcism at the end of the nineteenth century, was by no means general to Swahili spirit diagnosis. Indeed, Pouwels comments that *ramli,* which was part of the new written tradition of Islam in East Africa, was unavailable to most Swahili townfolk in the 1850s, though it was absorbed by coastal Islamic teachers (*walimu*) during the 1870s. Thus, its employment in the divination (which is correctly identified by Horner as *tezamia*) for *kitimiri* at Zanzibar in 1869 suggests, not unreasonably, that this synthesis was more advanced at Zanzibar than in the towns of the littoral.[49] One can suggest, as does Caplan, that "the very choice of diviner determines to some extent the type of explanation,"[50] since Horner notes that the diviner "ordinarily finds that the demon is *kitimiri* who has a great number of ritual experts." Finally, the *mganga* consults the figures traced in the sand again and names the specific fundi who must be consulted for the appropriate exorcism, giving the example of "Kondo, son of Mzee Kondo Tumbatu" (p. 25). This name is close enough to the naming of "Kongo's sons, you understand/Asmani and Saidi," in Muhyi ad-Din's poem against exorcists that I wonder if Horner was not making a garbled reference to this prominent Zanzibar family of ritual experts.[51]

Horner's long presentation of the actual exorcism begins with the fumigation of the patient for a period of seven days, which is consistent with all later descriptions of Swahili spirit exorcism dances (*ngoma za pepo*). He recounts a fascinating interrogation of the spirit during which negotiations are carried out concerning what must be sacrificed in order to appease the spirit. Basically, the fundi haggles with the spirit in order to temper its exorbitant demands, stating that the patient is poor and must wait until the rich harvest, after which she can make some pottery and straw mats to sell and earn the money necessary for the *ngoma,* sacrifice, and turban. The patient then recovers sufficiently until the appointed time of the *ngoma* is at hand. This initial treatment would appear to correspond to the minor form of exorcism called *kusemea* ("to talk to") which Gray reported among the Segeju in the 1960s.[52]

Finally, when the patient is ready for her major exorcism, she pays the fundi a fee of two silver *piastres* or Spanish dollars, which were then equal to eleven French *francs,* besides those things required for the *ngoma*. These included a goat; three pieces of cloth, one of which was for the turban, the other two being for the fundi; three measures (probably of one *kibaba* each, equivalent to about one pint or one-and-a-half pounds of grain) of flour for the sacrificial cake; seven small cups; one faïence bowl; seven pieces of sugar cane; seven flowers of white water-lily; a little honey and arrowroot; a piece of sandalwood; a white mat; two measures of rice for the table of the fundi and four measures for those persons who are invited to the sacrifice. It should be immediately apparent that it cost a significant amount of money to stage an *ngoma ya pepo,* considering that daily wages for an adult in Zanzibar averaged only somewhere between ten to twenty Indian pice (128 pice = one piastre). At the very least it would seem to have cost about a month's wages to earn the amount of money necessary to finance such an undertaking.[53] This is a pattern which has persisted into the twentieth century, although excessive expenditure was not apparently everywhere the rule.[54]

Once payment was made, the fundi called together those women who were already initiates (*wari*) in this spirit possession cult. They prepared the patient for the ceremony by shaving her head, washing her, and by dusting her body with sandalwood powder and rubbing it with rose petals. Her head was decorated with various figures drawn in a paste of sawdust and then she was dressed in white clothing. She also wore a pair of wooden clogs (probably *msuruaki*). The *wari* then prepared the sacrificial plate of food for the spirit and in doing so observed a careful hierarchy of age in which the eldest *mwari* always took precedence. The platter was built around sets of seven pieces of each kind of food and flower, including seven clusters of sweet smelling pandanus flowers. During these preparations the *wari,* all of whom wore white turbans, sang songs of their cult which, unfortunately, Horner did not record. Finally, they decorated their own faces with daubs of red, white, and black, and each one carried a zebra or donkey tail whisk in her hand. Here we have another clear example of the mixing of Muslim symbolism in the magical numerology of seven and African color symbolism, while the clothing and bodily preparation of the new *mwari* also resonate with Arab modes of personal adornment, particularly the donning of a turban.[55] Indeed, the fact that the turban was not only a man's article of clothing, but also a widely recognized symbol of political authority in the nineteenth century, might reflect an unconscious, ritual attempt to identify with the power of men at a time of declining influence for women in public affairs at Zanzibar.

At this point, the eldest *mwari* cries out, "Taireni," to which the fundi responds, "Taiti, tai," which marks the beginning of the actual ceremony of exorcism (*kupunga pepo*).[56] The patient is assisted into the middle of the room by two other *wari,* again led by the eldest, who makes her sit down and stand up seven times. Once she is seated the dance itself is begun by a repetition of the *taireni* formula and the fundi's ringing of a small iron bell seven times back and forth. The dance proceeds to drumming and eventually the patient and the fundi are surrounded by a circle of the adepts. As they dance, the fundi calls out, "Mwana maua, she is calling you, rise up so that I may see you."[57] As the pace of the dance increases, the surrounding *wari* cry, "Hey, hey, stranger! Hey, hey, let's inspect the stranger closely! Hey, hey:" ("*io, io, mgeni, io, io! achoungoulieni mgeni, io, io!*"). After a long silence the *mwari* becomes motionless and in the silence that falls the fundi intones, "we pray to God" ("*Touombe Monggou*"), which is then repeated many times by the choir. The fundi next puts on a crown made up of sweet basil flowers and sweet smelling pandanus flower clusters wrapped in leaves and repeats his prayer.

After a long silence the initiate says, "Greetings to you" ("*Salut à vous*"), three times. Although he does not say so, it is very likely that these words are said in Swahiliized Arabic, "*Salamu aleikum*," as Mtoro bin Bakari reports for the *tari* exorcism.[58] This done, the fundi then makes up a white turban and places it on the head of the *mwari*, after which the senior adept dresses her further with either a necklace of silver chain or white beads and with bracelets and anklets on her left arm and leg.

At this point in the ceremony most of the foods are eaten by the assembled group and at the end the goat is slaughtered, its blood collected, and the fundi annoints the patient with the blood. The fundi then drinks some of the blood and gives the remainder to the *wari* for them to drink. This is a fundamental aspect of all descriptions of Swahili spirit exorcism and is clearly of African origin. Finally, the fundi addresses the patient, or as Horner very correctly points out, "the spirit who possesses her," stating that it has been honored with sacrifice, dance, and a turban, and beseeching it to reveal its name so that it can be properly exorcised.

The *pepo* replies, "I am goungoni daughter of goungoni. My family lives at Mahri, descends from Mana Vamoana and our ancestors come from the island of Pemba" (p. 19). This formulation is consistent with the naming of specific spirits belonging to one of the larger "tribes" of spirits, but it also raises some very interesting problems. On the first point, Horner's account adds a dimension concerning names of spirits that has not previously been noted. Topan notes that "A spirit's name usually contains four pieces of information. He states his own name, his father's name, the type of 'work' he does, and, finally, his original residence, i.e. the spirit-dwelling he originally came from."[59] The formula recorded by Horner does not include information about the spirit's "work," but conforms more closely to Lambek's observation of the *patros* spirits of Mayotte that these names "provide a series of truncated genealogies and residence patterns" which are an important aspect of their personality.[60]

The next important point raised by the identity of Horner's *pepo* is that it is female. Skene observes that "the only *pepo* who appear to have sex distinction" are the *kiarabu* ones, so that this distinction would seem also to have been true for Arab spirits in nineteenth-century Zanzibar. Skene adds, however, that "if a male *pepo* seizes a man, or a female *pepo a* woman, there is believed to be little hope of the recovery of the patient, whose fate is practically sealed. If on the other hand a *pepo* of one sex seizes a human being of the opposite sex, then the recovery of the patient is assured." The danger here, according to Topan, is that female spirits are dangerously jealous, which presumably reflects something about characteristic Swahili marital tensions.[61] As the patient in Horner's description recovers, however, and at the spirit's naming "all the women present who are kin with the spirit of the new initiate are believed possessed" (p. 29), there would seem to be a contradiction here. This contradiction can be resolved, I believe, by further examination of the full genealogy of this particular spirit.

The spirit Gongoni binti Gongoni (to recast it in its Swahili format) is said to be descended from Mwana wa Mwana (Mana Vamoana), who was the last female *sheha* or "queen" of the Tumbatu people and whose marriage to the Mwenyi Mkuu or "king" of the Hadimu, Hasan bin Ahmed, who died in 1845, is remembered in legend to have excused the Tumbatu from paying taxes to the Omani.[62] According to Lambek, among the Malagasy-speakers of Mayotte "virtually all the *patros* that actually possess people are male," though a few female spirits which replicate the other, Sakalava-derived form of *trumba* possession are also known. He reasons:

> I suppose this is because notions of power and public responsibility are more clearly recognizable in the activities of males in an Islamic society. Gender is not a means by which the various spirit classes contrast with one another. However, the *trumba*—which are Malagasy and non-Islamic—do include women among their powerful elders.[63]

Indeed, the northwestern Sakalava who carried this form of spirit possession to Mayotte share female monarchs with other Malagasy and incorporate them in their ruling class ideology.[64] By analogy, the public responsibility exercised by Mwana wa Mwana can be considered to have placed her in the same light as the powerful female spirits of Mayotte. Looked at in this light, female possession by this particular female spirit in 1869 among the Swahili of Zanzibar would not have represented a danger to those possessed, but rather could have symbolized the rapidly declining public position of women under Omani hegemony.

Two final points about the spirit of Gongoni binti Gongoni also deserve comment. First, like so many spirits among the Swahili, this one comes from Pemba, whose people enjoyed "a great reputation as magicians throughout East Africa." Indeed, Gray records that several of the leading Segeju *waganga* had travelled to Pemba for "advanced studies."[65] The spread of these possessing spirits from Pemba and the prominence of that island in this coastal complex certainly deserve further research. Second, the indication of Mahri as the home of the spirit provides a fascinating clue to its Arabness, since the Mahra dominate the country between Oman, on the east, and the Hadramaut proper, on the west, in southern Arabia.[66] What we have here, then, is a female spirit whose mixed origins link it to Pemba, the Tumbatu ruling house, and southern Arabia.

Following the naming of the spirit, according to Horner, the fundi orders it to participate without complaint in the daily domestic drudgery of the patient ("*il faut que tu partages ses occupations sans te rébuter de rien*"). At once the drumming recommences and the fundi leads the *mwari* in a dance which mimics "ordinary household chores" ("*les travaux ordinaires du ménage*"). The patient mimes in dance the measuring, pounding, and washing of rice, washing the dishes, stirring up the fire, drawing water from a well and then carrying it back to the house. When all of this is completed, the fundi directs her to embrace her husband and her children in the midst of these dances, which carry on until dawn. The context of Horner's language does not make it entirely clear whether the patient merely acts out this display of wifely and maternal affection in dance, or actually embraces her husband and children as she dances in trance, but the purport of this male-directed ritualization of domesticity is unambiguous. More to the point, it is not the patient who embraces them, but the spirit who does so, thereby entering into a domestic relationship with the patient's real family, especially with her spouse, as I shall suggest in my conclusion.

The next day, Horner continues, the ceremonies draw to a conclusion with a general feast for all of the clients of the cult and a general dance in which anyone in the community may participate. While he explicitly denounces "these deplorable ceremonies," Horner recognizes the significance of "the gathering as a society of individuals who belong to the same possessing spirit. The possessed *wari* form among themselves a sort of corporation or society of mutual assistance." He then adds several illustrations of how this sort of guild (*chama* in Swahili) works. "If a possessed woman falls ill, all the possessed [in her society] visit her, bringing help and presents to her. In the case of fire all club together to rebuild the house of their associate." Finally, Horner indicates that the funeral of a fundi of a spirit possession cult is celebrated with the drumming and dancing of the exorcism itself, and that a small tomb is built for him at which communal sacrifices of various trinkets are made. He notes, too, that there was such a tomb somewhere in the country outside of Zanzibar Town (p. 29). The remainder of his account, concerning his own speculations on the origins of this cult and his belief that its symbols mimic the ceremonials of the Roman Catholic Church, need not detain us. But before turning to my own tentative conclusions about the meaning and significance of the *kitimiri* spirit possession cult, we need to consider carefully that of the spirit's name itself, which implies a powerful guardian spirit. Like *tari*, this knowledge should also give us some indication as to the reasons for its popularization in this socio-cultural mode of expression.

Kitimiri (Arabic *kitmir*) is the name of the dog who guards the Seven Sleepers of the cave in the 18th sura of the Quran, which is consequently known as the *Surat al-kahf*, "sura of the cave."[67] The dog appears initially in verse 18 of the 18th sura:

> Thou wouldst have deemed them
> Awake, whilst they were asleep
> And we turned them
> On their right and on
> Their left sides: their dog
> Stretching forth his two fore-legs
> On the threshold: if thou
> Hadst come up to them,
> Thou wouldst have certainly
> Turned back from them in flight,
> And wouldst certainly have been
> Filled with terror of them.

It is also mentioned in verse 22, which deals with the impossibility of establishing the true number of the Sleepers, which is known only to God, but among whom the dog is clearly numbered as being blessed.[68] In fact, however, the name *kitmir* never appears in the Quran and is known only through popular tradition and subsequent Quranic commentary dating back at least to the late medieval period.[69] Some of these stories concern the exact identity of *kitmir*, or its color, but all assert its blessedness. In particular, *kitmir* is said to have spoken with the voice of Allah directly to the young men who were fleeing to the cave. After being unsuccessfully driven away by them, according to Kaab al-Ahbar, the dog said. "Ye people. What do you want from me? Do not fear me, for I love the lovers of Allah. Sleep to guard you?" Thus, in both the Quran and Quranic commentary, it is the role of *kitmir* as guardian of the faithful that is stressed.[70]

The entire *surat al-kahf,* only part of which (v. 9-22) actually concerns the Seven Sleepers, is permeated by a strong apocalyptic eschatological message which is reinforced in the subsequent verses on Gog and Magog, who are well known in popular Swahili tradition as Juju and Majuju.[71] Its lessons are the relativity of Time, the unreality of the position of the oppressor and the oppressed on earth, the truth of the final Resurrection and the restoration of true values, and the potency of prayer and faith in attaining that restoration. Louis Massignon has called it a "troubling text" which raises important fundamental folk issues relating to the Final Judgment, including the rupture of the wall of the Community of Believers (*'Umma*), a message which may have found a receptive male audience in a Zanzibar where *uungwana* was being subordinated to *ustaarabu*.[72] In the abstract, one can imagine how a figure such as *kitmir* might have appealed no less to Muslim women in Zanzibar, but we must establish more clearly their exposure to both *kitmir* and the *Surat al-kahf* before we can make such a connection historically.

The key here lies in universal official Islamic practice and in the spread of popular Islamic magic to Zanzibar in the nineteenth century. The *Surat al-kahf* occupies a unique place in Islam because it alone is apparently recited in every mosque at every Friday midday prayer by the faithful. According to Massignon, it is recited "for prophylactic motives which render it increasingly 'antipathetic' to 'enlightened' Muslims, but which an immemorial tradition thus reveals."[73] Unfortunately, I can find no reference in the available literature to its recitation at Zanzibar, but this could presumably be ascertained by fieldwork there. We do know that in East Africa amulets are made which use the *Surat al-kahf*.[74] Indeed, elsewhere in the Muslim world this weekly recitation has caused the Seven Sleepers text to become translated into a unique popular cult that has penetrated the folk traditions of areas as widely scattered as Algeria and Kirghiz.[75]

For Zanzibar, there are a number of suggestive inferences which can be drawn from our general knowledge of the magical significance of the Seven Sleepers and *kitmir*. In his important discussion of East African Islam in 1910, Carl Becker includes a brief commentary on local magical practice which he partly apologizes for by affirming in conclusion that "what Doutté has shown to be the case in North Africa in his excellent fashion, is confirmed point by point by our East African researches."[76] Doutté, for his part, specifically mentions the names of the Seven Sleepers "and the name of their dog Kitmir" as magic names, and also notes the use of the *Surat al-kahf* in connection with a specific magic square.[77] Another example of popular magical use which may well have extended to Zanzibar is the custom of hanging up leaves on the door frames of houses with the names of the Seven Sleepers inscribed on them for the purpose of divine blessing (*baraka*) or averting evil. Here, it seems, the name of *kitmir* played a special part. "Among the Turks of East Turkistan, as in Indonesia it was still customary in recent years to inscribe letters which it was desired to protect from loss, with the name *kitmir* instead of 'registered,'" a practice which was also followed in East Africa in the 1930s.[78] Finally, and again recalling the Hadrami impact on popular belief for which I have already argued, Massignon reports that commercial vessels, such as those at Aden, inscribed the names of the Seven Sleepers on the poop.[79]

Though the evidence is mostly indirect, I am confident in hypothesizing that in the rapidly changing economic, political, social, and cultural climate of mid-nineteenth-century Zanzibar, popular knowledge of the magical powers of the Seven Sleepers and *kitmir* was sufficiently accessible to Swahili women to have given rise to belief in *kitimiri* as a guardian possessing spirit. Like the symbol of *tari,* that of *kitimiri* clearly dramatized for Swahili women the momentous changes that were affecting their world. To cite Wilson again, "Ritual draws sanctity from antiquity, but it must be felt relevant to the celebrant's world or it becomes an empty shell."[80]

Some Conclusions

Although no one is more aware than I of how problematic is my reconstruction of the *kitimiri* cult, I think that the general picture that I have drawn of the worsening position of Swahili women during this era can withstand challenge. Moreover, the validity of such an interpretation finds support in theoretical and comparative studies of the distinction between the public and domestic roles available to men and women. While I reject Michelle Rosaldo's subscription to a notion of "universal male dominance," her important suggestion of an exploratory model relating "recurrent aspects of psychology and cultural and social organization to an opposition between 'domestic' orientation of women and the extra-domestic or 'public' ties that, in most societies, are primarily available to men," certainly seems appropriate to the case of Busaidi Zanzibar.[81] But in view of the changes in the relations of production taking place on Zanzibar in the nineteenth century, with its increasing resort to slave and wage labor, I think that my interpretation agrees even more with Sacks's important discussion of women in class societies, which focuses on the dichotomy between "women in domestic work for family use, men in social production for exchange." Indeed, Sacks's observation that "the effect of state legal systems and other aspects of ideology developed mainly by ruling classes has been to convert differences between men and women in terms of their roles in production into differential worth," corresponds well with the case of Zanzibar.[82]

The importance of a newly formalized, literary-based ruling class ideology in Busaidi Zanzibar cannot be underestimated. Though Islamic for centuries, Hadimu society on Zanzibar seems clearly to have been characterized before the nineteenth century by superstructural elements based on custom and tradition, a notion that fits well with Pouwels's analysis of town Islam on the East African coast during the eighteenth century. The legal and religious changes of the following century, as we have seen, followed rapidly from the changes in relations of production on Zanzibar and replaced custom with a literary tradition that was associated with the new state and its ruling class. As Lois Beck and Nikki Keddie remark, "What is special about Islam in regard to women is the degree to which matters relating to women's status have either been legislated by the Quran . . . or by subsequent legislation derived from interpretations of the Quran and the traditional sayings of the Prophet." Custom, in short, is replaced by the *shari'a*.[83] In Zanzibar, I suggest, these changes worked to the particular detriment of women (though Hadimu and Tumbatu men were perhaps also adversely affected) and may well have increased the popularity of spirit possession cults as an expression of their declining social recognition of public worth.

Clearly, this last conceit is a hypothesis to be tested, but the forced domestication of the possessing spirit by the male *mganga* in Horner's description of the *kitimiri* exorcism suggests the reduction of a powerful descendant of Mwana wa Mwana to the position of a submissive domestic worker, the role occupied by all of the cult members. This vivid symbolic representation of the constraints of domestic labor, which stands at the very center of the *kitimiri* cult, is especially important in view of our lack of historical data on women's work and the conceptual problems of analyses which ignore domestic labor.[84] Furthermore, the establishment of bonds of affection between the spirit and the *mwari*'s husband, in particular, is indicative of this change in status.

One question which needs to be addressed is the meaning of female solidarity in the context of the *kitimiri* and similar spirit possession cults in nineteenth-century Zanzibar. I.M. Lewis has argued forcefully that spirit possession among women and dispossessed men often represents protest against the dominant men who rule society.[85] I believe that this is a legitimate way of regarding *kitimiri*, but I also think that Lewis's subsequent qualification of spirit possession as "the voice of protest, even if sometimes it appears to be muffled," is perhaps more apt.[86] What we need to discover eventually, of course, but do not yet know, is what other avenues of protest, if any, were available to these women in nineteenth-century Zanzibar.

No matter how much mutual support women afforded each other in their spirit possession cult guilds, the fact remains that it was men who were in control of the esoteric knowledge which was essential to the functioning of the cults. It could be argued, too, that the domestication of the possessing spirit indicates that the women of the cult not only accepted their domestic role in society, but that they even insisted that their spirits accept that same role. If so, as Janet Bujra has argued, then women's solidarity in such an historical context, "far from challenging their oppression, actually reinforces it."[87] Moreover, the collective action of these women cannot be considered as a form of sisterhood, as Sacks defines the term, because they are in no way struggling to control productive means. In fact, what they are affecting through the medium of spirit possession and the cult organization, with its requirement of lavish gifts to placate the spirits, is the redistribution of commodities and social value.[88] Yet even here there is a heavy price to pay. As Roger Gomm cogently posits:

> It can be argued with some truth that spirit posses-
> sion attacks may redress the disadvantages of a lowly
> and deprived status, but at the same time the way in
> which this amelioration is obtained ensures that
> deviants conform to a mystifying theory which is an
> essential element in the control system which main-
> tains them as lowly and deprived persons. . . . The
> privileges they receive may frequently be regarded as
> rewards for colluding in their own oppression.[89]

Finally, Topan adds his voice to this consensus by his conclusion that this kind of cult "reflects a Muslim norm of male 'superiority' that is already prevalent in the Swahili community as a whole." To be sure, "women themselves acquiesce in the status quo by conforming to the norms of the cult (as they do of the community), thereby confining themselves to the roles expected of them."[90]

Another aspect of this phenomenon concerns determining explanations for women's possession in this society. Horner tells us nothing about such women except to indicate that they are defined as being ill. From comparative studies of female possession one can suggest a variety of possible causes, of course, most of them reflecting female powerlessness and very probably applicable to Swahili women in Zanzibar at this time.[91] In particular, case studies of *zaar* possession in Northeast Africa emphasize themes of initial virilocal marriage, the husband's intended marriage to a second wife, barrenness, and similar themes reflecting male-female tensions within the domestic and marital context as being of particular significance.[92] Salima binti Said's description of female spirit possession, which is contemporary to Horner's *kitimiri* text, suggests a kind of female ennui which can be associated with these general causes, but derives from a different class context. The only convincing indication that such fac-

tors can be directly linked historically to *kitimiri* is a secondary definition of this word in a recent dictionary as a "charm to ensure easy
childbirth."[93] This is not much on which to base an interpretation, but
it does fit into a wider comparative framework which includes later
examples of spirit possession among the Swahili.[94]

Lambek's fascinating work on Mayotte suggests some important
ideas for further investigation concerning the way in which spirit possession serves as a system of communication between spouses in a
comparable social context. In his analysis, possession "changes the
conjugal relationship," since "the husband has demonstrated the
degree of his concern for his wife and for fulfilling the obligations of
his role as husband," which in this situation are mainly financial. He
does not argue, it must be noted, that the marital relationship is
improved, only that it is "thickened" and new dimensions added to it.[95]

Lambek also raises another important cultural element which
deserves consideration in trying to determine the incidence of possession. He is not convinced that spirit possession correlates with depri-
vation and suggests instead that "susceptibility to possession is
acquired in the process of growing up female in a domestic environment in which possession among other members of the family is
not uncommon."[96] That this environment also probably existed at
Zanzibar is indicated by Dale's observation that "those possessed have
been familiar from childhood with the ritual, and know what is expected of them."[97] Lambek's qualification notwithstanding, it seems
to me that "growing up female in a domestic environment" by definition involves the learned acquisition of deprived status which I have
argued was a feature of nineteenth-century Zanzibar society.

I think that it can also he suggested that spirit possession was to
some extent determined by wealth. Certainly, initiation into a guild
has not been inexpensive at any time in Swahili history, though it may
not always have been restricted to the relatively wealthy families in
society, as Gray argues for the Segeju.[98] I wonder, however, whether
there might not have been some correlation between high status and
spirit possession guild activity, as Lucie Saunders concludes from her
study of *zaar* in Egypt.[99]

One aspect of cult activity which cannot be overlooked historically is the pure entertainment value that these *ngoma* provided for their participants and for the entire community. Unambivalently echoing Wilson's conclusion about ritual and symbols, Gray points out, as a number of other scholars have similarly observed of *zaar,* that the spirit possession dance "furnishes the village with its major form of public entertainment and recreation, and for the participants it offers a means of dramatic and artistic expression." Indeed, this partly accounts for "the vigor and popularity of the cult and for its persistence in the face of some disapproval on the part of the highest religious authorities in the society."[100]

Finally, and again recalling Wilson, we must understand spirit possession and the *kitimiri* cult in the wider cultural setting of rapid historical change. Steven Feierman observes that "the concepts of spirit illness [among the Shambaa of northeastern Tanzania] . . . described the tensions of life in a period of intensified contact with the outside world."[101] The same point has been made rather differently by Beattie and Middleton writing about spirit mediums, as by Pamela Constantinides discussing urbanization and *zaar* possession.[102] Once more, the case is perhaps made most eloquently by Lambek, who believes that "spirits operate, in a sense, on the cutting edge of history. They adapt by micro-changes to the macro-changes in which they exist, pulling in bits and pieces from the future and the past to create new oppositions."[103] His complete analysis is more sophisticated than the evidence for mid-nineteenth century Zanzibar will admit, but his general conclusion is certainly applicable to what we know about *kitimiri,* and even *tari,* which both seem to draw upon all the available cultural information and traditions which were then struggling to find a place in the transformed Zanzibar society of which Swahili women were an integral part.[104]

PART III

The Mozambique Channel

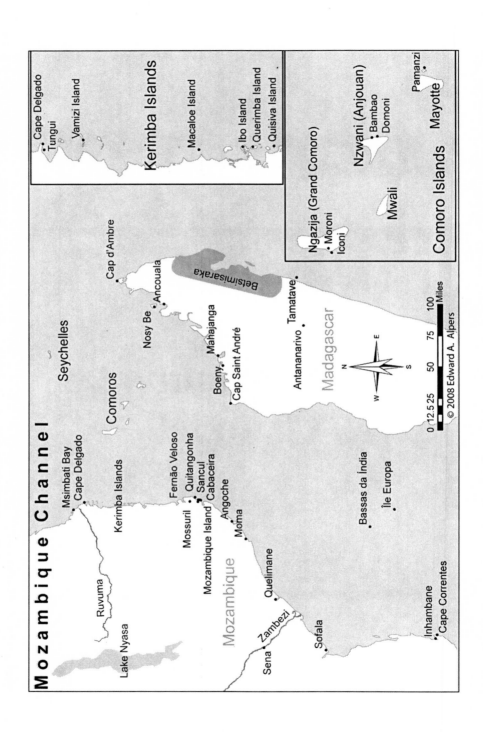

CHAPTER 7

Madagascar and Mozambique in the Nineteenth Century: The Era of the Sakalava Raids (1800-1820)*

Important historical links have existed between Madagascar and Mozambique for many centuries, but no single episode stands out more vividly than the Sakalava raids against the East African coast, which Deschamps has called "one of the most astonishingly daring exploits in Malagasy history."[1] The two earliest scholarly reconstructions of the raids, both of which were published in 1845, drew upon a variety of French and British sources and have continued to exercise a major influence on subsequent interpretations, all of which have focused on them from a Malagasy or Comorian perspective.[2] They have not, however, been able to utilize the contemporary Portuguese documentation which was generated primarily as a consequence of the devastating expeditions launched against the northern Mozambican coast in the second decade of the century, but also as a result of well established commercial connections with the Comoro Islands, Madagascar, and the Swahili coast to the north of Cape Delgado.[3] In this paper I shall look more carefully at the Sakalava

* Reprinted from *Omaly sy Anio*, 5-6 (1977), pp. 37-53.

raids from a coastal perspective by utilizing these sources in an attempt to establish more clearly when they occurred; the nature and extent of their impact on the coast; and, most importantly, what we can learn about their motivation, organization, and demise.

The earliest documented attack from Madagascar on East Africa occurred late in 1800 and has traditionally been attributed to the Sakalava.[4] On closer inspection, however, the details are rather less precise. According to the Portuguese Governor of the Kerimba Islands:

> On 29 November three boats of people from São Lourenço Island arrived at Vamizi Island [the northernmost of the archipelago with a significant Portuguese population] with nearly sixty people to await the monsoon so that they could return to their land, having been put out of the lands of Tungui [immediately south of Cape Delgado] by the chief of that place, and finding themselves with nothing to eat and nothing with which to buy food, they went first to one of our settlements in that jurisdiction to frighten the inhabitants in order to rob food, whereupon seeing before long that our people were intimidated they were encouraged to continue on to two other settlements, where they burned the houses and seized some Negroes.

Absolutely no resistance was organized by the Portuguese commander at Vamizi, though he could call upon some two hundred men, which the Governor deemed especially miserable in view of the fact that the attacking party consisted of only twenty men, as the others were dispersed fishing.[5]

Clearly, there is no mention of the Sakalava here and although a few captives were taken in these skirmishes one cannot confidently assert that the object of the men from Madagascar was to capture slaves. Those few Africans who were taken captive appear to have been an afterthought according to this source. The vague wording regarding their ouster from the Swahili community of Tungui also raises more questions than it provides answers. Perhaps these were not, after all, Sakalava? Certainly no particular notice was taken of their boats, which suggests to me that they were not sailing in *lakandrafitra,* the characteristic outrigger canoes of the Sakalava and Betsimisaraka raiders. Finally, to compound the uncertainty, there is a passing reference by the same Governor to the arrival at Ibo, the Portuguese administrative headquarters for the Kerimba Islands, of the King of Mayotte with three boats and 150 armed men from Madagascar with whom he was intending to fight another "king"— presumably, but not clearly, one based on the African coast.[6] Might not his quarrel have been with the Muslim ruler of Tungui and the three boats of pillagers around Vamizi the survivors of his ill-fated expedition? Further speculation is fruitless at this point, but the possibilities raised by this initial incident deserve bearing in mind as we turn next to the decade of conflict between the Portuguese, Swahili, and Sakalava.

Well before the first major Sakalava attack against the Portuguese possessions in the Kerimba Islands, the Portuguese had already come to know and fear them as a consequence of two humiliating encounters at sea. In the first, a Portuguese merchant vessel, the *Boa Mãe,* was sacked by "Sakalava, or Malgaches, Negroes from the north of the Island of Madagascar," in 1805 while standing at anchor in the harbour of Domoni, Anjouan Island (Nzwani). Thinking that they were friendly, the crew of the *Boa Mãe* did not prevent the ship from being encircled by some twenty-five canoes of about twenty or more men each. Once their true purpose was recognized resistance was offered, but in the ensuing combat almost the entire crew was killed.[7] Determined to punish the Sakalava, on 19 January 1806 the Portuguese military schooner, *Emboscada,* sailed from Mozambique with a crew of seventy bound for Madagascar. After touching at Anjouan the *Emboscada* apparently proceeded on towards Cap d'Ambre, near where it was rendered helpless in a dead calm and surrounded by the Malagasy fleet. The entire crew was put to death and the ship taken to port at Ancouala, on the far northwest coast of Madagascar, where it was demolished in order to recover its hardware. No better index of Portuguese insecurity in Mozambique at this time exists than the fact they took seriously the rumor that during these maritime attacks the Sakalava "committed their usual barbarities (they say that they eat human flesh and drink salt water)."[8]

From September 1808 until 4 January 1809 a major force of Sakalava terrorized the entire Mozambican coast from Ushanga, just north of the Lurio River mouth, up to Tungui. Those Portuguese residents of the mainland who did not seek refuge in the stout fortress at Ibo fled into the interior, abandoning houses and plantations to the invaders. Hardest hit of the Portuguese settlements was Querimba Island, immediately south of Ibo Island, while a total of some 800 persons, "including titled land owners, Moors, and slaves," were taken captive.[9] The effects of this devastation were echoed across the next few years by the inhabitants of the islands, who regularly sought relief from their impoverished condition in appeals to the Portuguese administration at Mozambique Island.[10] Normal trading relations between the islands and Madagascar also yielded unexpected rewards during this period. Late in 1810 a mulatto woman from Querimba Island who had been captured by the Sakalava was ransomed by a Muslim Makua trader—the brother of Chief Mutuga, whose town was located at the mouth of the Tari River, just north of Pemba Bay, and was the center of Swahili trade at that time – who purchased her and several others at an unspecified Sakalava port while doing business at Bombetoka Bay. This particular woman was actually returned to Ibo by a Prince of Ngazija [Grande Comore], who had come directly from Bombetoka and who also carried word from the Makua trader that there were other female captives from the islands in Sakalava country, including the *prazo* holder of Vamizi Island, Catarina Pais de Morais, the granddaughter of the most powerful Portuguese settler on the entire mainland of northern Mozambique during the last quarter of the eighteenth century.[11] Yet for all this disruption, the principal object of the Sakalava expedition of 1808-1809 was Tungui, against which they employed all the hostilities that they could possibly carry out, penetrating a considerable distance into the hinterland. But the Sakalava paid dearly for their time in East Africa and according to escaped prisoners such a large number died from smallpox that they had to abandon some *lakas* (the number of which is never given in the Portuguese documentation for this expedition) and burn others because they did not have enough men to sail them home.[12]

For the next several years there were constant rumors reaching the Portuguese at Ibo of an impending attack against the Kerimba Islands by the Sakalava. In 1811 the Sultan of Anjouan warned of an attack on Mozambique, noting that the Sakalava had guides with them who knew Mozambique and the mainland well and reporting that he had heard of French accompanying the Sakalava.[13] A year later vague reports from Madagascar suggested renewed aggression and by 1814 reports from the Sultan of Anjouan and his ambassador, Bwana Kombo, more concretely did the same.[14] By 1815 rumor had become reality again.

In August of that year "different Moors from the Island of Mada-gascar" advised the Portuguese at Mozambique "that the Sakalava had managed to gather together there as many as forty Lacas (the name which is given to their boats) with two thousand and more well armed men, and that they are proposing to come to attack this capi-tal and the adjacent mainland." The Governor-General claims to have taken measures to resist their attack and advised of his precau-tions they altered their plans "and after having committed sufficient aggressions on the northern coast, fell upon the wretched Cape Delgado Islands." This time, however, the Portuguese were much bet-ter prepared to deal with the situation and instead of awaiting an attack on Ibo they met the Sakalava in battle on 9 November 1815 while the latter were encamped on Querimba Island.[15] Nor was this the end of their troubles. According to the victorious Governor of the Kerimba Islands, the Sakalava "were devastated in the vicinity of Vamizi by a Moor named Bwana Hasan, Governor of Tungui, and although I do not know where they went from here until they reached that island, in all the ports where they cast anchor they always suffered some losses [sempre ião de menos]."[16]

Despite the demise of this particular expedition, most inhabitants of the Kerimba Islands jurisdiction still lived in fear of Sakalava raiders and were unwilling to renovate their mainland holdings. In awarding the commission of Governor of the islands to José Antonio Caldas in 1816, the Governor-General of the colony cautioned him regarding the critical circumstances which confronted him.

> The inhabitants scattered about in different parts of the hinterland, seeking to abandon their homes with the panicky terror of the Sakalava, this is the principal object in which you should take care, encouraging them to return to their houses and refusing licenses which would allow them to return to this capital of Mozambique, as many intend.[17]

Within a few months the fears of the inhabitants of the Kerimba Islands were amply confirmed by the largest and most fascinating expedition launched against the coast of East Africa from Madagascar.

In March 1816 word filtered down through the Swahili network from Mikindani, just south of Kilwa, that a force of 150 *lakas* was being readied to attack the coast at the beginning of the southern monsoon.[18] Six months later they struck. In October a Sakalava fleet of seventy-one *lakas* led by a Prince Sicandar of Anjouan raided Arimba Island, the first port of the islands to the south, and then sailed north to Querimba Island and ultimately to Ibo. Later in the month they engaged in a battle lasting two days with the Portuguese, who successfully resisted the attackers with few injuries. In the aftermath Governor Caldas negotiated with them in a attempt to forestall further hostilities. During the discussions he was told by Prince Sicandar that the expedition was not directed against them, but against the Shaikh of Sancul, whose town was situated immediately south of Mozambique Island, on Point Bajone. Sicandar alleged that this shaikh had captured the wife and son of a certain "Moor" and that ill winds had forced them off course. This explanation Governor-General Abreu e Meneses believed to be entirely fictitious, although it is interesting to note that in the 1970s Pierre Vérin encountered living traditions of the Sakalava raids while visiting Point Bajone.[19] Whatever the case may have been, the important fact for the Portuguese was the departure north of Sicandar's fleet.

What was welcome for Ibo, however, proved to be the undoing of Vamizi and Tungui, where the Sakalava under Sicandar soon followed on the heels of a massive fleet of a reported five hundred *lakas* commanted by a "Moor" named Nassiri, which had already devastated Vamizi and headed up the coast towards Kilwa, Mafia, and Zanzibar.[20] Here they were considerably less successful. According to a letter written from Sultan Yusuf bin Hasan of Kilwa to the Governor-General of Mozambique at this time, the Sultan informed him of having thrown the Sakalava who had been there out of Kilwa in less than three days. This defeat is confirmed both by the comment of Fortuné Albrand, who visited the island in 1819, that "Kilwa was attacked not long ago by the Sakalava. These pirates have been received vigorously and forced to re-embark with loss," and by the *Ancient History of Kilwa Kisiwani*.[21] It is our loss that none of these sources mentions Nassiri or any other leader, but in view of everything else that we know this defeat must have been at his expense.

Sicandar's party did not leave the area around Cape Delgado until late in January 1817 and between his men and those of Nassiri much damage was done and many prisoners taken. According to the ruler of Tungui, Hasan, who now styled himself "King" since his salary from the Portuguese had been suspended, the Sakalava of Nassiri captured more than three hundred people, while those of Sicandar seized another thirty or more. Among those taken were a number of Portuguese, whom Governor Caldas charged had only themselves to blame, since they had ignored his orders to seek refuge in the fortress at Ibo.[22] So while the Portuguese at Ibo had proved conclusively by 1816 that they could successfully resist the Sakalava, they remained impotent to deal with them beyond the walls of their fortress. Indeed, a series of reports and petitions in 1817 leaves no doubt as to the miserable state of the entire Portuguese establishment in the Kerimba

Islands.[23]

Later in that year the Kilwa coast was again visited by a Sakalava fleet, this one consisting of only thirty-eight *lakas,* which earlier passed Cape Delgado without incident, although twelve took port at Vamizi. Two also touched briefly at tiny Quisiva Island, a little ways offshore from Arimba, as a result of which a Portuguese counter-offensive was launched by sea. Eight days of seeking the Sakalava in every inlet between Ibo and Arimba produced not a single *laka,* and by the end of November word had arrived from Tungui that the Sakalava "had been unsuccessful there."[24] For once the rumor proved to be understated. Sometime at the end of 1817 or early in 1818 the Sakalava finally met their match in the coastal waters of East Africa, when an armada of eighteen boats was dispatched from Zanzibar to avenge the capture of more than one thousand men and women at Kilwa and, particularly, at Kua, Juani, and Chole, both tiny islands in the Mafia island cluster. After sixteen days of pursuit, thirty *lakas* were encountered in Msimbati Bay, immediately north of the Ruvuma River mouth. One hundred of the Sakalava were armed with firearms, while the remainder possessed only spears. In port to port combat many Sakalava were killed and some injured, while the Zanzibar forces suffered only two deaths and thirty wounded. Before they were wiped out the Sakalava sued for peace and after some dis-agreement among themselves surrendered all of the captives and booty taken in their raiding and swore an oath never again to make war against the Omani and Portuguese coasts of East Africa.[25]

Indeed, this was last Sakalava expedition to reach the coast of East Africa, although rumors of attack persisted and preparations contin-ued to be made for the next two years. Some time late in 1818 Sultan Alawi of Anjouan sent his son and eventual successor, Abdallah, as ambassador to Mozambique, "to inform us that the common enemy of this coast—the Sakalava—had readied a grand armada of *lakas* to venture out from their port at the beginning of the southern mon-soon, but that their destination was not known."[26] Strengthening of the fortifications at Ibo was proposed early in 1819 and in July a ru-mor had reached Mozambique that "the enemies of the State, the

Sakalava," were on the coast near Moma, to the south of Angoche, although this was earlier than all of their previous attacks on East Africa and seems doubtful in view of the wind regime. By September, however, a boat had come directly to Ibo from Mayotte "which brought the certain news that the Sakalava were not coming this year," although the Bishop of Mozambique remarked three years later that in 1819 a fleet of more than one hundred *lakas* with thousands of men had been almost totally annihilated by a typhoon in the Mozambique Channel.[27] But it was neither respect for Portuguese military preparation or Omani naval prowess nor fear of the natural elements which ultimately put an end to the Sakalava threat; rather it was the pressure of Merina expansion, as both Deschamps and Vérin have emphasized.[28]

According to an undated letter which probably was written in the middle of 1820 by Bwana Kombo, who by then was serving as Portuguese consul at Anjouan, the Comoro Islands were at peace, although the Sakalava had gathered "many boats" to sally forth against both the islands and the African coast. But "they began to fight with each other, namely, Balambo [Amboalambo, the Sakalava name for the Merina] against Sakalava, as a result of which the voyage that they wanted to make was broken up. . . . After the Sakalava and Balambos had fought others joined to make war against the islands and Mozambique in May or June."[29] But they, too, were diverted from this end by the apparent resumption of hostilities with the Merina. In October 1820 a letter from the Wazir (Governor) of Bombetoka [i.e. Mahajanga] informed the Portuguese that "there is a war between twelve [possibly a misreading for two?] chiefs and the Sakalava, who find themselves roundly defeated and without forces; and in this matter you and the other lands can rest at ease that they are free from the Sakalava."[30] The final note regarding the demise of the Sakalava raiders so far as the Portuguese were concerned came two years later, when the Bishop of Mozambique noted briefly that the Sakalava had been defeated at home by their neighbors and the British.[31]

From a Mozambican perspective all that really mattered was the certain end to the raids from Madagascar. It remains, however, to sort out more precisely what factors might have been at play in motivating, sustaining, and ending the expeditions. For this task I am more dependent upon secondary sources and my own less certain knowledge of Malagasy history, but let us go back over these same events and see what possibilities emerge.

First, what motivated the raids? Both Kent and Vérin unequivocally state that the principal reason for the raids was to acquire slaves. Each emphasizes the Sakalava demand for both slave labor and slaves for trade, and the inability of the Sakalava to obtain them internally by the end of the eighteenth century, while Vérin places rather more emphasis on the role of the Betsimisaraka and the Antalaotse and thereby on the external slave trade.[32] It is also clear that although the raids on the Comoro Islands were initially and principally organized by the Zana-Malata led Betsimisaraka, they were referred to exclusively in East Africa as Sakalava raids. To my knowledge the only contemporary observer who made this distinction was the astute British ambassador to the kingdom of Ethiopia, Henry Salt:

> This foe consisted of a nation of pirates on the north-east point of Madagascar, called by the Portuguese Sekelaves, but whose real name I have reason to believe is Marati* [i.e. Zana-Malata], which for many years back has been known to infest the Comoro Islands.
>
> *This I learned from the Arabian traders. The Sekelaves, I was informed by Captain Fisher and others who visited that part of the island, are subjects of the Queen of Pembetoc, residing on the north-western side of Madagascar.[33]

This peculiarity of nomenclature does not mean that no Betsimisaraka ever participated in the raids on East Africa, but it does suggest strongly that the less numerous Sakalava component of the larger expeditions against the Comoros—a point which is made

explicitly by Epidariste Colin at the beginning of the nineteenth century and is repeated by Froberville—was generally responsible for
those launched across the Mozambique Channel.[34] If this is a correct
deduction, why should it have been so?

Quite apart from geography, which I do not consider a factor here,
since all of the raiders departed from the far northwest coast,
whichever side of the island they called home, I believe that the key
to understanding may lie in the complex Muslim economic network
that linked the entire East African littoral and its offshore islands.
Vérin has already pointed the way towards this conclusion, but I
think that the Portuguese documentation adds considerable weight to
what he has already written.[35] The earliest possible implication of
Muslim (variously Arab, Swahili, Antalaotse, or "Moor") complicity
in the raids is suggested by the ambiguous details of the small 1800
attack on Arimba, which I have already indicated might have involved
the Sultan of Mayotte. Perhaps, too, the especially harsh treatment
received by Tungui in the great raid of 1808-1809 may point in this
direction. By the 1820s, however, a theory had emerged that specifically pointed to people of Bombetoka Bay, both Antalaotse and
Sakalava, as the driving force behind the raids on East Africa. How
did this interpretation take shape?

In 1845 Guillain correctly observed that the maritime raids began
during the reign of the Sakalava Queen of Boeny, Ravahiny (c. 1770-
1809). "They were not, it is true," Guillain adds, "ordered by her; but
her subjects took part in them."[36] Furthermore, Fressanges, who is
cited by Guillain, noted at the beginning of the nineteenth century
that Mozambique slaves reaching the east coast of Madagascar were
transshipped by Arab *chelingues* (small boats of about twenty to
twenty-five tons burden) from the Muslim trading town of
Mosangaie or Moudzangaïe, the forerunner of Majunga (modern
Mahajanga) in Bombetoka Bay, and the commercial prosperity of
that place is attributed by many subsequent writers to Ravahiny's
patronage of the Antalaotse.[37] But it does not follow that either she or
the Muslim merchants of her kingdom were involved in the raids.
Quite the contrary. In 1805 the Queen of Bombetoka – clearly

Ravahiny – warned the Governor-General of Mozambique that a fleet of six hundred Sakalava boats "called *chalengas*" were preparing to raid the Kerimba Islands, information which together with the loss of the *Boa Mãe* and a direct appeal for aid from the Sultan of Anjouan led to the dispatching of the ill-fated *Emboscada* in 1806. It would be interesting to know if there were really Muslim vessels incorporated into this fleet, but this nautical reference is unique in the Portuguese documentation.[38]

Only in 1812, after the death of Ravahiny and the subsequent fragmentation and decline of Sakalava, especially Boeny, power in western Madagascar, does Bombetoka Bay directly, and apparently incorrectly, become identified as a center for raids on the coast of East Africa. In that year both the captain and the surgeon of HMS *Nisus*, which sailed from the Cape of Good Hope to Mozambique and Anjouan in response to a request for assistance from both the Portuguese and the Sultan of Anjouan, gathered information on the organization of the raids on East Africa.[39] Captain Beaver was told after some hesitation by the Governor-General of Mozambique "that the Malagassi generally come over every year [which was not true] to the no. of four or five thousand men, in about a hundred canoes; that they always assembled at Bombetouk, whence they stood, with a leading breeze, over to Mayotte," and thence to their ultimate destination for that year. Surgeon Prior, for his part, generally confirms this source but adds to it the important qualifying testimony of a French ship's captain who was at Mozambique in August 1812 during the visit of the *Nisus* and who told Prior that in one of his seventeen voyages to Madagascar, "while *near* Bombatoke [my emphasis], he saw nearly the whole surface of the bay covered by canoes, and more than 40,000 people, men, women, and children, assembled preparatory to an expedition." Ten years later Boteler was led to believe, that the Arabs of Bombetoka incited the Malagasy to make these raids.[40]

This seems patently incorrect. The persistence of friendly commercial relations between Mozambique and the Muslim traders of Bombetoka Bay argues against any officially sanctioned participation

in raids, actual or contemplated, at least during the lifetime of Queen
Ravahiny of Boeny. In 1804 Colin described an Arab controlled trade
in slaves from Mozambique in exchange for rice from Bombetoka [i.e.
Mosangaie]. A year later a "Moor" is reported to have carried a cargo
of slaves from Macaloe Island, which at that time was still inhabited,
to Madagascar, although two years later an unidentified boat from
there was refused permission to trade at Ibo.[41] The ransoming of
Portuguese subjects of the Kerimba Islands at Madagascar in 1810,
however, indicates positively that good relations were maintained
with Bombetoka throughout these years, and the presence there of a
Grand Comoro prince who was friendly to the Portuguese seems
unlikely if it were at all deeply involved in the raids. Finally, there is a
tantalizing entry in the official port log book of Mozambique at the
beginning of 1811 which lists approval of a license for a "Massane
Bunu carrier from the Queen Vaine [Ravahiny] of Bom-Bottoque," to
buy forty slaves.[42]

   This official Portuguese recognition of the Muslim slave trade to
Madagascar, a business which flourished illicitly to the very end of
the nineteenth century after Portuguese legal abolition in 1836, suggests additionally that neither the political nor the commercial masters of Boeny were at all inclined to undercut a mutually profitable
relationship with Mozambique by participating in a series of short-
lived piratical ventures. Perhaps it is worth pursuing the possibility
that the main Sakalava component of the raids on East Africa was
composed of the so-called "petits Saclaves," including the Antankara
and Tsimihety who were ruled by Sakalava Volafotsy princes. They
were bitter rivals of the Sakalava kingdom of Boeny during this period and might possibly have looked upon these expeditions as an
extension of their commercial harassment of Boeny trade to the east
coast along the Sofia River valley.[43]

   With the raid of 1816-1817 the complexity of the issue deepens.
First, there is the clear identification of the leaders of both Sakalava
fleets, Sicandar and Nassiri, as Muslims. According to Guinet, in
about 1860 he was informed by a Malagasy from the north of the
island that "it was generally an Antalaotra who took general direc-

tion of the entire flotilla ...." This was apparently done because of
their superior navigational ability, but the Portuguese documentation
suggests a much stronger Muslim leadership role for at least some of
these expeditions.[44] Second, there is the tale about the real object of
Sicandar's expedition being to settle a score with the Shaikh of Sancul and the tradition noted by Vérin in that same area expressing fear
of the Sakalava. Third, there is the garbled and clearly mythic tradition recorded by Freeman-Grenville at Kua, Juani, which links a
vengeful Muslim builder, the Sakalava, and Ibo together in explaining the great raid on that settlement in 1816.

To be sure, none of this is more than suggestive, but it speaks to a
highly mobile system in which there was plenty of room for personal
grievances to emerge and perhaps to be settled by violence. It also
implies a system which could support both an officially sanctioned
trade that tolerated (in the case of Boeny) and sometimes required (in
the case of Anjouan) formal relations with Europeans in order to
maintain a command of specific niches within that system.[45] By the
same token, ambitious individuals who were excluded from formal
authority within such a system could always be moved to seize by
force what they could not otherwise claim legitimately in peace.
Indeed, a hint of just that also exists in a casual paraphrasing of oral
tradition existing in the Comoro Islands in the 1930s about the raids:

> People say that the invaders were Betsimisaraka
> and that they pushed their expeditions up to the East
> African coast to Kisimani Mafia and to Ibo and that
> they were piloted by some people from the Comoros,
> Zanzibar and the coast of Africa who would only
> have been common law prisoners driven out from
> their country.[46]

Finally, if the characteristic division of Swahili communities into
competing moieties holds true also for those of the Comoro Islands
and northwestern Madagascar, then this sort of conflict would have
been normal.[47]

The political history of both Anjouan and Mayotte at this time bears witness to this process. Here were two small, weak, and ravaged polities which could barely withstand the continual assaults launched against them from Madagascar. Successive sultans of Anjouan had solicited European assistance and protection, but none succeeded before the usurper Alawi, who after failing to overthrow his infant nephew, Ahmad, in about 1797, fled to Zanzibar before returning after 1804 to dethrone him for good.[48] Perhaps Sicandar was a disgruntled scion of Ahmad's house who sought retribution against Alawi by attacking his Portuguese and Swahili allies? It seems an idea worth exploring, particularly in the collection of oral traditions. As for Mayotte, its history is rife with dethronings and political assassinations in the eighteenth and early decades of the nineteenth century, which at the very least provides a possible context for the pursuit of a rival on the East African coast in 1800. Possibilities such as these seem all the more attractive when we consider the elaborate connections between the seizure of Mayotte in 1832 by the deposed Boeny king, Andriantsoli—the Islamized grandson of Ravahiny who by the early 1820s had linked his fortunes more intimately with the Antalaotse than with his non-Muslim Sakalava subjects—and the preexisting rivalries which plagued its politics.[49]

If resolution of the research questions raised by this paper is to be effected it will involve further investigation of both archival and oral sources. There may well be further sources to be found in the French archives of the period, in those housed in Mauritius, La Réunion, and Madagascar. It seems likely, too, that additional British sources exist in the British Museum and the India Office Library, although many of these repositories have been carefully searched by scholars such as Jean Valette. Nor have the Mozambican archives ever been examined with this topic in mind. The same may be true of the Comorian archives, although here I am less certain. In particular it is vitally important that we obtain accurate, scholarly translations of the various Swahili, Arabic, and Malagasy documents in Arabic script that are known to exist in the Portuguese archives, as well as those available in public or private hands in Madagascar, the Comoro

Islands, and Mozambique. Finally, we need to follow up the leads of Guinet in 1860, Fontoynont and Raomandahy in the 1930s, and Vérin in the 1970s and pursue these questions in the field. For on present evidence, so far as East Africa is concerned, the Sakalava raids may have been rooted more immediately in the political and economic rivalries of the Muslim trading network linking Madagascar to the continent than in the wider setting of the slave trade of the western Indian Ocean.

CHAPTER 8

A Complex Relationship: Mozambique and the Comoro Islands in the Nineteenth and Twentieth Centuries*

Introduction

The Comoros have historically played a vital role in the commercial and religious history of the southwest Indian Ocean and as a human bridge between the African continent and Madagascar. In this paper I explore three aspects of this relationship that have hitherto been relatively ignored.[1]

The first topic examines the web of trading and political connections between the Comoros, Madagascar, and Mozambique. While much attention has been focused on the slave trade of this commercial circuit in the 19th century, we must not overlook the thriving, complex exchange of foodstuffs that was equally part of the same regional network. Both of these are well attested to in Portuguese sources and reveal how normal this traffic would have been regarded by the inhabitants of the coastal areas and islands of the northern half of the Mozambique Channel. These connections provided the foundation for the second and third issues that I will discuss in my paper.

* Reprinted from *Cahiers d'Études Africaines*, 161 (2001), pp. 73-95.

The second aspect of this relationship focuses on the African diaspora in the Indian Ocean world. One of the features of the Indian Ocean diaspora that distinguishes it from the Atlantic world is the forced overseas migration of African labor to other parts of the African continent, including the offshore islands. There are or until recently were identifiable relocated populations from East Central Africa and the Tanzanian hinterland (mainly of "Nyasa," Yao, Makua, Ngindo, and Zigua background) as far afield as southern Somalia, the Kenya coast, Pemba, Zanzibar, the Comoros, and western Madagascar. I am interested in how these populations were absorbed into their host societies, the ways in which they maintained and transformed their own cultural identities, and the influences that they carried with them into these new historical situations. The Comoros are an integral part of this aspect of the diaspora, one that merits closer examination.

The third element concerns the history of Islam in northern Mozambique, which is intimately tied to the Comoros. This connection derives partly from the new commitment to Islamic education that marked the close of the nineteenth century in the face of aggressive European colonialism, but there is good evidence from earlier in the century for an especially tight Islamic network linking the dominant political lineage at Angoche to the Comoros. The critical moment, however, dates to the introduction of the Shadhiliyya Yashruti and the Qadiriyya *turuq* [sufi orders], both of which had strong Comorian connections, at Mozambique Island a century ago. Moreover, even during the later colonial period Portuguese authorities looked to the Comoros for adjudication of problems within the Muslim community of Mozambique.

In what follows I attempt a preliminary reconstruction of each of these histories from the sources available to me and to identify future questions for research that arise from this initial effort. Above all, I hope to be able to stimulate new research involving collaboration with and among Comorian and other regional scholars on these important historical questions.

Trade and Politics: Mozambique and the Comoros
in the Nineteenth Century

There can be no meaningful appreciation of the history and culture of the Comoros in isolation from the human currents of the Mozambique Channel and the wider world of the western Indian Ocean. Towards the end of the eighteenth century these were severely disrupted and then transformed, first by the beginning of several decades of intermittent warfare by Malagasy maritime raiders against both the islands and the African littoral and, second, by the growth of slavery and slave trading throughout the sub-region.[2] One consequence of the threat of Malagasy raids was the regular exchange of intelligence through Muslim emissaries in the first decade of the new century between the Portuguese authorities at Mozambique Island, the Sultan of Nzwani [Anjouan], and the Queen of Bombetoka, the important trading entrepôt that was the predecessor of modern Mahajanga.[3] Although the era of Malagasy raids effectively ended in 1820, a sense of shared political vulnerability and convergence of commercial interests fostered the maintenance of official correspondence between the rulers of the Portuguese colony and the island sultanates for the next decade.[4] Indeed, virtually all of this correspondence relates either to matters of political intrigue and rivalries on the islands or to trading in provisions. Much of it involves letters between Portuguese officials at Mozambique Island and the Sultan of Nzwani or his representatives; only a few concern either Ngazija or Mwali, while none are recorded from or to Mayotte.[5] Portuguese records of ships entering the port of Mozambique Island, on the other hand, record arrivals of ships from all four islands. For example, an early letter from the Sultan of Mwali to the Governor-General of Mozambique was precipitated by war between that island and Nzwani, its effective overlord, in 1828. A year later, the Sultan's assertion that the forces of Nzwani had suffered many more losses than had his own was confirmed by a letter from the Sultan of Nzwani to the same Portuguese official that claims some 400-500 deaths from this conflict. In addition, the Sultan of Nzwani sought to trade with the Portuguese, asking in particular for "some old slaves or small boys for my agriculture."[6] Many of these letters consist of professions of friendship, including offers of one party or the other to provide hospitality and services for the facilitation of trade between Mozambique and the Comoros.

Although the slave trade inevitably attracted most attention from European observers, it would be a mistake to consider that this was the only trade carried on between the Comoros and Mozambique. The islands supplied Mozambique with rice, sorghum, finger millet, some oats, beans, mung or green gram, coconuts, coconut oil, ghee, honey, goats, cattle, and *sambo* (from *ntsamabu* in ShiNgazija; *Cyclas circinalis*), a form of sago that was used only for feeding slaves.[7] We know from Portuguese accounts that these provisions were carried to Mozambique aboard vessels belonging to shipowners from the islands. Although most of these records refer only to ships making port at Mozambique Island, some are reported to have touched at the Kerimba Islands, as well.[8] A French visitor at Mwali in 1828 notes that ships from this island annually traded to both Mozambique Island and Quelimane.[9] This body of evidence also includes one instance of a Portuguese vessel bringing foodstuffs from the Comoros to Mozambique Island and one case of a local Indian trader seeking a license to trade for *sambo* at Ngazija.[10]

Depending on local politics, however, relations were not always cordial; for example, traders from the Comoros were sometimes regarded as a threat to local agriculture by Portuguese officials because of the low price of their provisions. According to one source, Comorian vessels had not been admitted to the Portuguese roadstead before 1821-1822, when traders from Mwali first gained access, while the Governor-General in 1830 strongly opposed the role of Comorian trade at the Portuguese colonial capital.[11] In fact, it seems that European traders were no more welcome at Mwali than were Comorians at Mozambique. In 1828, when the French traveler Leguevel de Lacombe was captured at Mwali, he discovered that Sultan Husayn, brother of the Sultan of Nzwani, hated all Europeans because one trader had sailed away without payment for the full cargo of goods he had taken on at Mwali, despite the fact that he had previously accommodated them with supplies of provisions and "slaves that my subjects went to buy for them on the coast of Africa."[12] Indeed, in 1831 tensions increased as a consequence of the capture of a Portuguese ship by Arab pirates. A letter from the Sultan of Nzwani to the Portuguese Governor-General in April of that year requests that the latter make peace with the Sultan of Quitangonha, an independent Swahili chiefdom immediately to the north of Mozambique Island, and regrets the Arab seizure of this Portuguese ship. Hoping to re-establish "the former friendship" that existed between Nzwani and the Portuguese, he specifically comments on the differences that existed between the Arabs and the people of Nzwani, "(among whom there exists only a community of belief)."[13] A month later, the Sultan of Ngazija, Amad Bun Sahid Sualee [Ahmed b. Said Ali b. Soali, better known as Mwinyi Mkuu (1792-1875)], afforded protection to some of the Portuguese subjects whose vessel had been attacked at sea. According to his letter to the Portuguese Governor-General, the ship had been seized by one Abdallah b. Muhammad b. Suleiman Marzuqui, four of its crew killed, and the remainder carried to the port of Quitanda [Kitanda, Itsandra], which lay beyond his authority on Ngazija as Sultan of Bambao. The survivers fled to the Sultan's port, which although it is not named would have been Moroni, from which he sought to repatriate them to Mozambique.[14] Whatever tensions and disruption to trade were produced by this incident, reality soon intervened. During a crisis precipitated in 1831 by the culmination of the extended period of devastating famine in southeastern Africa, the Portuguese establishment at Mozambique Island depended for its very existence on the importation of food-stuffs. Accordingly, in June the Governor-General of Mozambique wrote a series of desperate letters to one of the rulers of Madagascar, the governor of Bombetoka, and to the rulers of Nzwani and Ngazija, requesting them "to send their *pangaios* (small sailing vessels) with provisions and cattle to Mozambique." By September the Governor-General could report that the crisis had passed and that Mozambique enjoyed "very good understanding with the kings of

Ngazija and Nzwani" among other regional potentates.[15]

Nor did the commercial and political connections stop there. The Governor of Mwali in 1828 was a refugee from Sofala, an ancient center of Muslim commercial and religious activity on the southern coast of Mozambique, where his brother had defeated him in a local power struggle. So while he spoke neither French nor Malagasy, he is reported to have understood Portuguese.[16] Similarly, the Portuguese were entangled diplomatically in the political restructuring precipitated in northwestern Madagascar and the Comoro Islands following the death of Radama, the Merina defeat of the Sakalava kingdom of Boeny, and the Malagasy invasions of Mwali and Mayotte.[17] But by 1832 Portugal's fortunes were in steep decline in eastern Africa and the role they had played as potential counterbalance to competing forces in the Comoros was rapidly eclipsed by France, England, and Zanzibar under Sayyid Said ibn Sultan (r. 1804-1856). Although no one has searched the Mozambican and Portuguese archives for subsequent references to correspondence and traffic between the Portuguese at Mozambique and the Comoros, it seems unlikely that the regular exchanges of "official" letters during the first three decades of the nineteenth century were sustained after the early 1830s. A decade later, however, we know that at least two claimants to leadership at Nzwani, Said Hamza El Masela and Sultan Alawi M'titi, withdrew strategically to Mozambique when their political fortunes at home waned.[18] Occasional exchanges of official correspondence must certainly have occurred subsequently, although the only one that I have seen dates to mid-1861 and was addressed by the Governor-General of Mozambique to Said Omar El Masela, the ambitious Prince of Nzwani who spent at least some time at Mozambique where he learned to speak a little Portuguese.[19] Similarly, we have scant knowledge of the trade in provisions from the Comoros to Mozambique for these decades.[20]

By contrast, we know quite a bit about the slave trade and the exportation of so-called "free" labor or "*libres engagés*" from Mozambique to the Comoros, western Madagascar, and beyond to the Seychelles and Mascarene Islands that were stimulated by the rise of plantation economies in those places.[21] Nancy Hafkin quotes some fascinating correspondence addressed to Molidi Vulai, the Captain-Major of Sancul, a mainland port to the south of Mozambique Island under nominal Portuguese suzerainty that was captured in 1879 as part of the Portuguese anti-slave trade campaign. Among them a letter from Sultan Abdallah III of Nzwani reveals the problems facing individuals who engaged in slave trading at this time, not least because of the French occupation of Mayotte in 1843. Others indicate difficulties in settling accounts without reliable agents in each place of business. Most illuminating is a letter from Sultan Said Bakr of Ngazija written from Moroni to Molidi Vulai on 5 January 1878:

> My agent Modohama just arrived here, having left three slaves there with Ambar. I ask you to keep an eye on them. We do not know each other except through letters, but I hope that you will watch over this collection. Your brother's young nephew is on Mohilla and Allah willing when he finishes his studies I will send him home to Mozambique. I repeat that I would like you to watch over my accounts. My father Sultan Ahmed passed away [in 1875].

As Hafkin astutely observes, "Despite the fact that the two had never met, a sense of Swahili kinship and mutual reciprocity emerges from their correspondence." Moreover, she continues, although this group of letters is apparently unique, "the trade patterns it represents were common" as were the linkages among Muslim elites throughout the southwestern Indian Ocean.[22]

At the end of the century, before the Portuguese wars of conquest finally brought their East African territories under effective colonial rule, Mozambique continued to provide refuge for political refugees from the Comoros, as the French steadily imposed their own colonial domination over the islands. Thus, in early 1898, the deposed regent of Mwali, Mahmoud bin Said, and a handful of followers sailed away to the Mozambique coast, where they made land at Sito, just south of the Arimba peninsula on Mussongoma Bay, eventually sailing north to Ibo before finally reaching Zanzibar aboard a German steamship.[23] But if by this time the commercial and political links between the Comoros and Mozambique had reached their limit, the religious ties had already begun to take on renewed vigor.

The African Diaspora in the Comoros

Before taking up the history of the Islamic network that spans the Mozambique Channel, let me turn to the fate and impact of those Africans who were sent as forced emmigrants, whether in bondage or as contract laborers, to the Comoros in the nineteenth century. It is not my intention to reconstruct the history of slavery in the Comoros during the nineteenth century. Gill Shepherd provides a useful overview of this subject that draws upon the most important published sources and touches upon the major issues involving slavery during this period. In general, she makes no distinctions among different ethnic groups within the slave populations of the islands, but in two instances she does include details that address the socio-cultural position of slaves from Mozambique. In her analysis of slavery and hierarchy, Shepherd observes that

> Locally-born, fully-Islamised and culturally-integrated slaves, the *wazalia*, despised the *wamakwa*, the Makua tribesmen newly arrived from Mozambique. These were the only slaves for whom the blunt term "slave" was used—*mrumwa* (pl. *warumwa*)—with its literal meaning of "used person."

She notes further that urban-based, acculturated slaves had little social intercourse with rural, agricultural slaves, a pattern that is familiar from many other slave-owning societies.[24] In addition, African-born slaves were easily identifiable "with their filed teeth and tatoos," a description that would fit many Makua and Makonde at this time and well into the twentieth century. Not surprisingly, new slaves did their best to assimilate by adopting local habits of dress, customs, and above all, Islam.[25] Furthermore, since at Nzwani the term *makwa* was clearly pejorative, it is not surprising that those to whom it was applied did their best to claim other identities.[26] Nor should we wonder that Makua chafed under the burden of excessive tax collection by the Nzwani ruling class.[27] In 1856, rural Makua joined a larger body of Sakalava led by Bakari Koussou in a revolt against the French at Mayotte. In seeking to quell the rebellion, the French approached several notable community leaders, including one Namkopo, "a Mozambican chief greatly respected among this element of the population."[28] Half a century later, in 1902, the chief spokesman for the disaffected workers who unsuccessfully challenged the authority of the autocratic Léon Humblot on Mwali, was a Makua overseer named Catchou.[29] Clearly, these scattered examples of rural rebellion reflect the objective class position of these workers, but class and ethnicity were closely intertwined in the Comoros. Nevertheless, not all Makua were despised agricultural slaves. For example, two of the wives of Andriantsoli, the Sakalava Sultan of Boeny on Mayotte in the 1830s, were Makua. In 1899, during the brief tenure of Henri Pobéguin as French Resident for Ngazija [Grande Comore], a Makua named Cazambo briefly served as chief for the Société Humblot police force.[30] So at least some Mozambican slaves were incorporated into the changing ruling elites of the Comoros or had some possibilities for upward mobility during this era.[31] One wonders whether any oral traditions exist that would help us reconstruct the histories of these individuals or others like them who have escaped notice in the European documentation.

One gauge of the demographic impact on the Comoros of the importation of unfree African labor during the nineteenth century comes from the sporadic population censuses on Mayotte after the French occupation in 1843. In that year, of an estimated population of 3,000 half were reckoned to be slaves, among whom many were undoubtedly mainland Africans. When Charles Guillain classified the population after emancipation in 1846, he counted 843 Makua (16.0%), 513 Makonde (9.7%), and 372 Mozambiques (7.1%) among the total of 5268 individuals. Whatever the ethnographic accuracy of Guillain's Makua and Makonde enumeration, his third category probably reflected slaves shipped from the ports of Quelimane and, perhaps, Inhambane. The real value of his careful attention to origins, however, is to disaggregate the entirely artificial ethnonym of "Mozambiques." His figures are also valuable because they indicate that not all slaves, whom he totaled at 2733 (51.8%) were from these new African immigrant groups, who represented 63.2% of the slave population and 32.8% of the total island population.[32] In 1852, Philibert Bonfils engineered a detailed census that also included information on ethnicity, although without Guillain's specific attention to African origins. In a total population of 6,191 organized into 131 villages, a total of 2,036 (32.9%) individuals were identified as Mozambiques (Makoas); in the two villages on the islet of Pamanzi, 157 of 707 souls (22.2%) were Mozambiques.[33] The virtually unchanged total percentage of slaves from Mozambique in these two censuses suggests that Guillain's internal distinctions between Makua, Makonde, and Mozambiques accurately reflects the ports of origin from which slaves were shipped from the northern Mozambique coast to the Comoros: namely, the central littoral that included Angoche, Sancul, and Quitangonha; the Cape Delgado/Kerimba Islands zone; and Quelimane. The next census for Mayotte dates to 1866 and includes a total of 3,716 Africans (31.7%) in a total population of 11,731. Of particular interest in this census is the demographic division by sex, which notes that men constituted 76.0% (2,824) of the African population in a society where men comprised 58.0% of the total population. This should not surprise us in what was by then a vigorous plantation economy where male agricultural labor was at a premium. Even more striking, however, are the 1867 figures for contract laborers working at Mayotte, of whom Mozambiques constituted the overwhelming majority, 2,245 (74.8%) out of 3,002, with Mozambican men outnumbering women by 1,951 to 294, or 86.9% of all Mozambican *engagés*. Gevrey also notes approvingly that "after having ended their contract, the majority renew, remain on the island, and augment the labor force."[34] Despite the fact that he lumps all Africans together as Mozambiques in discussing Mayotte, Gevrey observes that although all slaves introduced from both the African coast and Madagascar are subsumed under the name of "Cafres" in the Comoros, the majority belong to three ethnic groups, "Makoua, Montchaoua and M'Chambara." The Makua identification is clear; that of Montchaoua can confidently be identified as the Yao, the important trading people of northwestern Mozambique and southern Malawi, and probably indicates shipment from Quelimane by this time; that of M'Chambara, however, is obscure, although my suspicion is that it may have been a name given to people coming down to Quelimane from the lower Tchiri valley.[35]

Although one cannot assume that what obtained at Mayotte also prevailed demographically on the other islands, at the end of the century Heudebert remarked upon the presence of "Makua, Makonde and the people of Nyasa," who certainly reflect both slave and "free labor" exports from Quelimane, among the African population of Ngazija.[36] And if the skewed gender balance of the African population at Mayotte roughly approximates that for the Comoros as a group, this would have had a significant impact on the transmission and retention of cultural traits by these diaspora populations, as also on the cultural impact of these groups on island societies. In addition, residential patterns that maintained social distance between urban and rural Comorians must be taken into account when seeking signs of African origins, as Shepherd suggests and others have equally noted.[37] According to Gevrey, "Their customs vary with the duration of their residence; for a while they retain their customs and the language of their country, but nearly all end by adopting the religion and habits of the Arabs."[38] Not surprisingly, little remains of clear Mozambican origin in the languages of the Comoros. According to Sacleux's research, only a dozen words of eMakhuwa have found a home in the Comorian lexicon, although his work suggests that there have been more retentions from Bantu languages of the Upper Zambezi around Sena.[39] If this observation can be verified, it may reflect the fact that the last major group of African migrants to the Comoros embarked from Quelimane, despite the fact that the generic name for Mozambique slaves became Makua, for the people who dominated the earliest nineteenth-century wave of forced labor migrants. Nevertheless, considering the evidence for the survival of eMakhuwa-speaking communities and for the retention of eMakhuwa folklore in western Madagascar and on Nosy-Bé well into the twentieth century, it is surprising that so little of this language has been recorded for the Comoros. According to Gueunier, in fact, at the end of the nineteenth century Pobéguin compiled a comparative lexicon of 250 words for a variety of languages spoken in the Comoros, among them "makoua."[40] So it may be that eMakhuwa survivals were more significant a century ago than they would appear to be from Sacleux's oddly compiled dictionary, since Sacleux never visited the Comoros.[41]

Other examples of diaspora culture refer to music and dance. At Antananarivo in the early 1820s, Leguevel de Lacombe noted that the "bobre africain," a widespread form of musical bow with a calabash resonator at its base and an instrument that he recognized from Mauritius and Réunion, "had been imported to Madagascar by the numerous Cafre and Mozambican slaves that the Arabs had brought there," a comment that would seem to be verified for the Comoros by Capmartin and Colin's observation in 1810 that Africans there played an instrument called the "violon Mozambique."[42] Gevrey provides further testimony to the African origins of this widely disseminated percussive stringed instrument.[43] These last two sources also specifically identify the *tam-tam* as a drum of African origin. According to Bensignor and Elyas, during the nineteenth century new styles of music were introduced to the Comoros through the slave trade and contract labor from Africa. These new musical styles were often gender specific, women performing *deba*, *lelemama*, *wadaha*, and *bora*, men dancing *mshogoro*, *shigoma*, *zifafa*, and *sambe*. They note that the dance known as *ikwadou* is said to have been performed in the past by slaves, while today it is to the Comoros what *maloya* is to Réunion, "with its sense of reclaiming the past, its function of gathering ordinary people together and building solidarity."[44] It will take further ethnomusicological research to determine the specific origins of these musical and dance genres, at least one of which - *lelemama* - clearly has wider regional provenance with connections to Manyema slave origins in eastern Congo through Zanzibar.[45]

Closely related to music and dance is spirit possession. Most of the modern literature for the Comoros on this topic focuses on Mayotte and on Malagasy-speakers. At the beginning of our century, however, one writer ended his discussion of Malagasy *tromba* spirit possession at Mayotte with the additional note that "The Makoa tromba is called 'mouzouka' or 'doungoumara'." This is confusing, at best, since both *mzuka* and *dungumaro* were widely dispersed Swahili possessing spirits in this century, but at least it points the way to further research among Makua descendant communities.[46] No less interesting for its reflection of wider Western Indian Ocean cultural exchange is the identification of African possessing spirits today on Ngazija as *somali* and their dichotomous opposition to Muslim spirits, called *rauhan*, both as distinct from authoctonous possessing spirits bearing island-specific names and the Malagasy *trumba*. As Blanchy et al note, "They represent the two polar values in the social hierarchy: Arab Muslim and African pagan, white and black." Moreover, unlike those uncontrollable forces represented by indigenous spirits, *rauhan* and *somali* "are of external origin."[47] Here the interesting research question is to determine when this category of spirit entered the cosmology of Ngazija and whether it replaced an earlier category, such as, for the sake of argument, *mozambique*.

The Islamic Connection

The history of Islam in both the Comoros and Mozambique dates back many centuries, but both experienced a significant revival in the ardor of their belief and practice from the second half of the nineteenth century as part of the wider reform currents sweeping the world of Islam and the Muslim response to the forcible imposition of European colonial rule in Africa and the islands. In particular, the penetration and expansion of Islam throughout the coastal hinterland and far interior of northern Mozambique effectively dates primarily from this period. Although the first phase of this process of religious revitalization and conversion can be traced to the activities of individual *walimu* and *mashaykh*, the second phase and more extensive phase was primarily the work of two major *turuq*, the Shadhiliyya Yashruti and the Qadiriyya, several different branches of which took the lead in Mozambique. The groundwork for the introduction of the *turuq* was laid, however, in the commercial networks and personal relationships arising therefrom linking coastal Muslims in northern Mozambique to their co-religionists in the Comoros and Zanzibar.[48]

Although literacy in Arabic and advanced Islamic learning were strictly limited by class in the Muslim communities of northern Mozambique, even before the era of the *turuq* they were not isolated from the wider world of Islam. By the early decades of the nineteenth century the Comoros had already established an important regional reputation as a center of learning, a reputation that was further enhanced by the close connections that evolved between the Comorian *'ulama* and their counterparts in the rising Busaidi state of Zanzibar from the mid-1830s on.[49] For educated Muslims in northern Mozambique, the *walimu* of the Comoros acquired a special place of honor and important families sent their sons to study with these men when they could. In 1830, for example, a son of the Shaykh of Quitangonha was sent to study in the Comoros.[50] The most important community linking Mozambique and the Comoros through Islam was Angoche, which by the beginning of the twentieth century was a major center for Islamic activity. According to oral traditions regarding the life history of Musa Momadi Sabo, who later gained considerable economic and political notoriety as Musa Quanto, in his youth he traveled up-country along the northern bank of the Zambezi River to its confluence with the Lugenda River on a proselytizing mission with a relative who was a *sharif* and a *haji*. Upon returning to the coast, he circulated through the well-established Islamic commercial network of the southwest Indian Ocean to Mozambique Island, Zanzibar, the Comoros, and northwestern Madagascar before sailing home to Angoche in the mid-1850s to make his mature reputation.[51]

Although the sources do not indicate the identity of Musa Quanto's kinsman, who was apparently the real force behind this religious peregrination, my guess is that he was probably Comorian. In fact, descendants of Comorian ancestors inhabit the entire coast from Angoche north to Mozambique Island. Furthermore, there is some additional indirect evidence to support this hypothesis in the oral traditions that identify a man from the Comoros named Hassan who married into one of the leading clan families at Angoche, the Murreiane, even though this story would seem to be entangled in more generalized regional stories of Shirazi origins.[52] Still another case of the close linkages between these coastal settlements and the Comoros dates to 1878, when the son of the *Shaykh* of Sancul - the nephew of Captain-Major Molidi Vulai—was sent to study at Mwali, as we have seen above.[53] More generally, on the mainland opposite Mozambique Island members of the Murrapahine lineage of the Lucasse clan around Mossuril recognized similar Comorian links. According to Melo Branquinho, "They do not know how to give a good explanation for the family and clan ties to Iconi canton in the Comoros, of which many are natives who come to these lands." In one place he notes that they were descendants of Molidi Vulai, but later in his massive intelligence report he states that a chief named Murrapahine, who ruled the territory of Lunga during Molidi Vulai's time, was their progenitor, and that he in turn was descended on his father's side from "a native of Grand Comoro [Ngazija], of the Morone [sic] clan, and on his mother's side from the Muanacha clan of Sangade."[54] Each of these examples speaks to the intimate family and religious connections between coastal Mozambique and the Comoros, especially Ngazija, during the nineteenth century, a subject that cries out for further research by scholars on both sides of the Mozambique Channel.

In contrast to this neglected theme, there is no need to reiterate the well known career of Shaykh Muhammad Ma'ruf b. Shaykh Ahmed b. Abi Bakr (1853-1905), a *sharif* who was born into a Hadrami family at Moroni. Shaykh Ma'ruf championed the Shadhiliyya Yashruti in the Comoros, where it had been introduced by 'Abdallah Darwish, and in northwestern Madagascar. He preached its message to all who would listen, even though this often put him in conflict with leaders of the dominant Alawiyya *tariqa*. Fleeing to Zanzibar as a consequence of political persecution in about 1886, Shaykh Ma'ruf returned to Ngazija following the exile of his political nemesis, Sultan Said Ali b. Said Omar, by the French in September 1893. In 1896 the Yashrutiyya was apparently brought independently to Mozambique Island by a trader from Moroni named Shaykh Amur ['Amir] b. Jimba, who was based at Zanzibar and also conducted business at Madagascar. The following year, perhaps ordered there by 'Abdallah Darwish, Shaykh Ma'ruf himself is said to have visited Mozambique Island for a month and granted *ijazat* [diplomas] to two men, Muhamade Amade Gulamo and Nemane b. Haji Ali Twalibo (also known as Nemane Haji Galibo) whom he left as co-leaders of the Shadhiliyya Yashruti. We do not know why Shaykh Ma'ruf passed over Shaykh Amur, but a contest for authority ensued in which the latter emerged as the dominant force in the *tariqa* at Mozambique Island. In 1898 Shaykh Ma'ruf entrusted his brother, Sayyid 'Ali b. Sheikh with the responsibility of resolving what must have been an unseemly struggle for power in this new outpost of his branch of the Yashrutiyya. Sayyid 'Ali issued three additional *ijazat* as *khalifas* to Ussufo Jamal Amur, Issufo Cassimo, and Sayyid Junhar b. Saide Amade. He also negotiated an agreement whereby Shaykh Amur would remain as head of the Yashrutiyya until his death, at which time leadership would pass back to Shaykh Anlauê b. Saide Abu Bakari, who was *khalifa* of the *tariqa* in the Comoros. Apparently this arrangement resolved the internal struggles of the Yashrutiyya at Mozambique Island for the next quarter-century, when Haji Muhamade Amade Gulamo, one of the two original *khalifas* appointed by Shaykh Ma'ruf in 1897, succeeded Shaykh Anlauê as *khalifa* in 1921. Internal competition soon resurfaced, however, and in 1924-1925 a new branch of the *tariqa*, the Shadhiliyya E'Madhania, was created by direct intervention from the center of the order at Medina. A decade later, in 1936, a third and final branch of the Yashrutiyya broke off to become the Shadhiliyya Itifaque.[55]

Notwithstanding these divisions, in the late 1960s, the Yashrutiyya was still connected spiritually to the Comoros.[56]

The Comoros were also a powerful external point of reference for those Mozambican Muslims who became adherents of the Qadiriyya *tariqa*. Thus, although the Qadiriyya was introduced at Mozambique Island from Zanzibar in 1904 or 1906, the *shaykh* whose mission it was to propagate the *tariqa*, Issa b. Ahmed, "was a native of Moroni canton . . . having completed his Quran studies in the Comoros and, much later, in Zanzibar." Given the many connections between Ngazija and the Mozambique coast, his decision to carry this *tariqa* to Mozambique Island cannot have been entirely coincidental. In any event, Shaykh Issa remained at Mozambique Island as leader of the Qadiriyya Sadate until he returned to Zanzibar, where he died, in August 1925, so that although his successor as *shaykh*, Khalifa Momade Arune, was a native of Cabaceira Pequena on the mainland opposite Mozambique Island, he would certainly have been well aware of the prominence of the Comoros in the life of his *shaykh*.[57] A quarter century later, the *khalifa* of the Qadiriyya Sadate was Sayyid Momade Sayyid Habibo, better known as Baguir or Bacre, the nephew of the recently deceased *shaykh* of the order. In the 1960s Baguir was regarded with suspicion by the Portuguese because of his well developed connections to the extensive network of Islamic leaders in eastern Africa. In 1950, Baguir left Mozambique Island to study in Zanzibar in the company of Shaykh Xará Abahassane b. Ahmed, a native of Zanzibar whose father was a Comorian, who had come to visit in the Portuguese territory; in Zanzibar he studied for three years with Shaykh Saide Omar b. Abdalia, also a native Zanzibar of Comorian descent. After studying for a further four years in the Hadramaut, with which the Arab families of the Comoros had multiple ties, Baguir returned to Mozambique Island, where he was regarded as heir apparent to leadership of the Qadiriyya Sadate. Indeed, until the Revolution of 1964, Zanzibar was widely regarded as the center of Islamic learning in East Africa, overshadowing other regional places for study, such as the Gazila Islamic Center in the Comoros, which Portuguese authorities claimed was "considered in official documents as the third most important Islamic center in East Africa." Following the Revolution, however, the spiritual line to the headquarters of the *tariqa* in Baghdad now ran through the Comoros, rather than Zanzibar.[58] Thus, with Zanzibar incorporated into a secular Tanzania and Islam fragmented in Madagascar, at the time of Melo Branquinho's report in 1969, he could state confidently that "The Comorians constitute the most important Islamic element in steady growth."[59] No better mnemonic reminder of this living presence is the name given to one of the four single-headed hand drums used at Mozambique and Angoche in *tufo*, an Islamic musical genre in which men do the drumming and women do the dancing: Ngazija.[60]

Elsewhere in the Portuguese colony, by 1931 there were enough Comorians resident in the new colonial capital of Lourenço Marques (today Maputo), far from the historic commercial and religious circuit of the northern Mozambique Channel, to give rise to the formation of an Associação Maometana Comoreana (Association Mahometane Comoréene). According to the official statutes of this association, it was designed to promote the education and recreation of its members for their "moral, intellectual and physical development." Membership was open to "all adult Muslim individuals of 18 years of age, natives of the Comoro Islands, Madagascar, and Zanzibar, and those born in other places, but children of parents who are natives of those places and themselves Muslims."[61] The activities of this organization and its members are still another topic that requires further research.

The last aspect of the complex relationship between Comorian and Mozambican Muslims that I want to discuss dates to the period of the armed liberation struggle waged by Frelimo for the independence of Mozambique and the Portuguese response in seeking to win the hearts and minds of Mozambican Muslims against what they feared was a common, atheistic enemy.[62] By 1971 Portuguese intelligence services had initiated a multifaceted psychological warfare offensive that was designed to win the support of the Muslim leadership of Mozambique, in particular that of the *turuq*, who were regarded as a traditional, conservative force, against Frelimo. In August 1972 the Portuguese organized a carefully orchestrated gathering of twenty-one Islamic leaders, including those of all eight *turuq* (five Qadiriyya and three Shadhiliyya), at Mozambique Island to launch the officially published Portuguese translation of al-Bukhari's *Hadith*, one of the key texts of Islam. Part of the propaganda generated by this very public event was the publication of a letter to Sayyid Omar b. Ahmed b. Abu Bakr b. Sumait al-Alawi, Mufti of the Comoro Islands, from Shaykh Momade Said Mujabo, a key figure in the Portuguese psychological counter-offensive at Mozambique Island who was not affiliated with any particular *tariqa*, in which he declares his joy at this expression of Portuguese suppport for Islam. In addition to their potential role as a conservative force against the secular, radical nationalism of Frelimo, the Portuguese also considered the *turuq* to be a more reasonable form of Islam than that of the new generation of radical Islamic reformers who were beginning to make their presence felt in the southern urban centers of the colony, especially Lourenço Marques. At about this time, the "Wahhabis," as they were dubbed by Portuguese intelligence services, had launched an attack against the unorthodox character of the traditional Islam practiced by members of the eight *turuq* that dominated Mozambican Islam, focusing their criticism on the way in which funerals were conducted and, especially, on the peaceful resolution that had been effected by the mediation of Shaykh Momade Said Mujabo between those who prayed silently and those who expressed their piety by shouting. Fearing this threat to one of their staunchest new Muslim allies, the Portuguese called officially upon the Comorian Mufti, Sayyid Omar b. Ahmed, to resolve this dispute about *bid'ah* [innovation] between the eight Mozambican *turuq* and their "Wahhabi" critics. His decision in favor of the traditionalists brought about their enthusiastic endorsement of the Portuguese translation of the *Hadith*, the statement of which is included as a preface to the final Government publication in 1972. What is missing in this reconstruction based on official Portuguese sources is any idea of how this Comorian intervention in the religious politics of Mozambique was regarded by the

Mozambican Muslim leadership and how it figures into the rapidly evolving and conflicted politics of French decolonization and nationalism in the Comoros. More generally, although there has been some work done on the Islamic learned networks of northern East Africa, with extensions down to the Comoros, nothing of this sort has yet been attempted for the networks of the Mozambique Channel. It should be.[63]

Since achieving independence by quite different routes less than a month apart in June and July 1975, both Mozambique and the Comoros have experienced many difficulties and challenges. While I have no specific information on the survival or attrition of the historic connections between these two Muslim communities, it would be interesting to know how these may have affected the alleged logistics support provided by South Africa through the Comoros during Renamo's war against Frelimo during the 1980s.[64] Finally, considering the increasing acceptance and official recognition of Islam as a major national religion in democratic Mozambique, which has recently become an official member of the Organization of the Islamic Conference, it seems likely that relations with the Federal Islamic Republic of the Comoros will endure into the future at the levels of state diplomacy, *turuq* organizational links, and family alliances. Out of this web of relationships I hope that we shall see increasing attention paid to the study of this shared history.

CHAPTER 9

Littoral Society in the Mozambique Channel*

Historians have for many years struggled to define the Indian Ocean world so as best to capture both its unity and its diversity. According to August Toussaint, writing more than four decades ago, "The only valid divisions in this connection are the natural ones based on the simplest elements that constitute the Indian Ocean." He enumerated these to include "the ocean itself," the African and Asian shores, and "the islands scattered over the ocean's expanse," for which as a Mauritian he suggested a special place of honor.[1] Nearly twenty years ago Michael Pearson argued persuasively that when thinking of the history of the Indian Ocean world we should consider the concept of littoral society, emphasizing the significance of the outward-looking character of those communities who faced the sea and the ways in which they connected to each other as much as their hinterlands.[2] Twenty years later, in the "Introduction" to his magisterial history of the Indian Ocean, Pearson continues to emphasize the importance of the littoral in the history of the Indian Ocean:

> Rather than look out at the oceans from the land, as
> so many earlier books have done, a history of an

*Reprinted from Himanshu Prabha Ray and Edward A. Alpers, eds., *Cross Currents and Community Networks: Encapsulating the History of the Indian Ocean World* (Delhi: Oxford University Press, 2007), pp. 123-141.

ocean has to reverse this angle and look from the sea
to the land, and most obviously to the coast. There
has to be attention to land areas bordering the ocean,
that is the littoral. A history of an ocean needs to be
amphibious, moving easily between land and sea.[3]

Adopting a complementary perspective, Kenneth McPherson characterized it as a series of over-lapping "core areas of cultural expression" that subsequently "formed links in the giant chain of human
activity which stretched across the littoral of the Indian Ocean." A
decade later, McPherson built upon this framework to present "the
interlocked world of the Indian Ocean" in his full-blown history of
the Indian Ocean world.[4] Also writing two decades ago, K.N. Chaudhuri refers to the Indian Ocean as "an area of social and cultural
diversity rooted in four different civilizations," although he famously
omits Africa from his register of civilizations. Despite this omission,
he makes the important observation that "the idea of a common geographical space defined by the exchange of ideas and material objects
was quite strong, not only in the minds of merchants but also in those
of political rulers and ordinary people."[5] More recently, Sugata Bose
has chosen to characterize the Indian Ocean as "an 'inter-regional
arena' rather than as a 'system.'" Later in the same essay he refers to
it as "an inter-regional arena of economy and culture."[6] Although
each historian phrases his conception of the Indian Ocean world differently and places different emphasis on those elements that he considers to be most significant to the larger history of this world region,
I believe one can see a good deal more agreement than disagreement
in their several positions. My purpose in this paper is not to take up
the larger issues raised by these historians of the Indian Ocean, but
rather to examine the salience of their ideas as applied to the history
of the Mozambique Channel, which I consider to be an important
region of the Indian Ocean world, located at the edge of the wider
arena, to adopt Bose's nomenclature.

    From early in the first millennium CE there are indications that the
Mozambique Channel was regularly traversed and crossed by peoples

of both African and Indonesian descent who combined to populate the great island of Madagascar. With the rise of Islam and the development of Swahili culture, a new element was added to this mix as trade and cultural exchange intensified. Portuguese intervention in the sixteenth century and the rising importance of Indian merchant traders in their wake created still other elements in the cosmopolitan mix. By the eighteenth and nineteenth centuries there had come into being a complex, multilingual littoral society that stretched along the coast of eastern Africa from Inhambane to Cape Delgado, across to western Madagascar and including the Comoro Islands. While this regional coastal society was significantly Islamic, it was by no means exclusively so; nor was it really Swahili. In this paper I propose to explore the components of this littoral society and to situate it in the larger context of Indian Ocean littoral society during this long period.

Physical Setting

Let us begin by seeing what we can make of Toussaint's natural boundaries definition with respect to the Mozambique Channel. According to the author of a nineteenth-century naval guide to the Mozambique Channel, "The Mozambique Channel is formed by the eastern coast of Africa to the West and by the island of Madagascar to the East."[7] Unlike the Red Sea or the Gulf, however, or even the Indian Ocean passages into the Indonesian archipelago and the South China Sea, the Mozambique Channel is open to the sea at both ends, so that it presents no clear definition at its extremities. If, at its southern entrance, it is completely open to the sea (with the exception of the dangerous, submerged volcanic islands of Bassas da Índia and Île Europa),[8] to the north it is partially roofed by the Comoro Islands, which also provide a bridge to the African coast. As we shall see, the Comoros played a critical role in the littoral society that developed around the northern boundaries of the Mozambique Channel. The channel measures some 900 nautical miles in length. In width, at its narrowest point, from Mozambique Island to the west coast of Madagascar at Cap Saint André, the Mozambique Channel measures

210 miles, expanding to more than 400 miles at its southern end at Cape Correntes.[9] While the Mozambique coast features a number of useful ports and safe harbors that are protected by the numerous islands that dot its coast, the western coast of Madagascar has relatively few such ports.[10] In addition, based on data that extend as far back as 1854, but are concentrated in the three decades after the mid-1950s, the U.S. Navy survey reports that most ships prefer to navigate "closer to the African coast than to the center of the channel or the Madagascar coast," mainly because of "the well-defined current along the western side of the channel."[11] It should be pointed out that this current flows southward so that before the innovation of steamships, sailing vessels approaching the Mozambique Channel from the south would have had to contend with this current if they held to the African coast, although there was a "countercurrent established in the eastern corridor of the channel with speed and direction much less constant due to varying flow around the ends of the island [Madagascar] and by numerous local conditions."[12] The currents were also reckoned to be "very variable in intensity, ordinarily being stronger during the southwestern monsoon."[13] Between Cap d'Ambre, at the northern tip of Madagascar, the Comoro Islands, and the northern coast of Mozambique around Querimba, the current runs west all year long, while just to the south of the islands it turns east.[14]

Seasonal winds are dominated by the northeast monsoon (October-April), which brings annual rains and reinforces the dominant southern current along the African coast, and the southwest monsoon (May-September), which signals the dry season. The closer one sails to the Mozambique coast, however, the more the monsoon winds are subject to local variation. According to Silva Costa, writing in 1878, although the transition from the southwest to the northeast monsoon was marked by good weather, "the worst weather in Mozambique is during the transition from the northeast to the southwest monsoon, which is marked by much rain and bad weather with the heaviest squalls." Accordingly, the stormiest months were usually January and February.[15] Finally, although most cyclones occur to the east of Madagascar, an average of one storm per 5 degree square affects the Mozambique Channel.[16] Silva Costa tells us that these were called *monomocáias* in Mozambique and usually occurred from mid-February until the beginning of April. Mozambique Island was particularly susceptible to these violent storms, which generally lasted between 24 and 36 hours. Evidence of the destructive nature of these cyclones at Mozambique Island can be seen from 1841 and 1843, when "ships were unfastened from their moorings and grounded," including a British vessel that beached on the reef beneath São Sebastião fortress, where it smashed to pieces and lost most of its crew. Again, on 1 April 1858, during an unanticipated *monomocáia*, "some *pangaios* [small coastal sailing craft, often translated as dhows], Moorish brigs, and a French war schooner that was on top of the reef of the fortress of São Sebatião, where it lost its rudder, were flung on the beach." Only the many rivers that reached the coast, the Bay of Fernão Veloso just north of Mozambique Island, and Ibo and the Kerimba Islands, which were usually not seriously affected by cyclones, provided safety from these devastating storms.[17] Such devastating seasonal storms continue to wreak havoc across the countries that border the Mozambique Channel, as in the case of Cyclone Hudah that caused extensive damage in both Madagascar and Mozambique in 2000.

The combination of currents and monsoons in the channel made navigation difficult, at least for the Europeans who left records about sailing its waters in the nineteenth century. For example, Frederick Barnard's account of his years with the British anti-slave trade patrol in the Mozambique Channel is full of commentary on the dangers of sailing those waters and of running aground on sandbars and reefs on either side of the channel.[18] Because of the prevailing currents, those who were headed for Madagascar could follow the northerly eastern current to their ports of call, whereas those who were bound for the Mozambique coast found it necessary to navigate towards the middle of the channel before heading towards the ports of northern Mozambique. This central route through the channel probably accounts for the history of landings that brought European ships coming from the south to the Comoros. In sum, the Mozambique Channel presented significant challenges that required serious maritime skills for the people who inhabited its shores and those outsiders who entered its waters.

The Indonesian Legacy

This is not the place to engage in a lengthy discussion of the Indonesian peopling of the great island of Madagascar. Suffice it to say that we know much less than we should about the details of this historical process, although the general outlines seem clear enough, if still open to scholarly dispute.[19] Essentially, most scholars agree that the previously uninhabited island was populated by a series of small-scale movements of people coming from the Indonesian archipelago, probably across the Bay of Bengal to Sri Lanka and the coastal regions of South India, around the rim of the western Indian Ocean to the Horn of Africa, down the coast of eastern Africa, and finally across to Madagascar. The most obvious and likely route from the mainland to Madagascar would have been the Comoros bridge, but for sailors as skilled as these Indonesians it is possible that some may have crossed the channel directly from the Mozambique coast. Indeed, it is possible that some enterprising Africans may have done likewise by either route. The dating for the remarkable population movement spans the period from about 300 to 1000 CE. Because of their route along the coast and the time it must have taken them to eventually reach Madagascar, these early Indonesians arrived there with a creolized form of their original language that included loan-words that can be traced to the Kaskazi (i.e. northern) communities of emerging Bantu speakers and suggest that a certain degree of Afro-Indonesian mixing had already occurred by the time of their initial arrival. Over time, several strata of what one scholar calls "the unceasing process of lexical borrowing from Coastal African languages" took place.[20] The Indonesians brought with them a number of important tropical food crops, such as Asian yams, taro, sugarcane, and bananas, as well as chickens, that were adopted and bred to local conditions by Bantu-speaking Africans.[21] Christopher Ehret suggests further that Indonesians may have introduced the pig to the peoples of the lower Zambezi.[22]

Another important cultural artifact for the development of littoral society that Indonesians introduced to the region was the outrigger canoe. Although most of the seaborne trade that occurred at the ports of the Mozambique Channel would have been carried aboard ships of Arab, Indian, or, during the height of the slave trade in the eighteenth and nineteenth centuries, European ships, the ordinary inhabitants of the littoral moved goods, fished, and communicated along the coasts in much smaller boats. Outrigger canoes were one form of transport that was found on both sides of the channel and in the Comoros, as well.[23] Thus, despite the significant linguistic differences between the Bantu-speakers of Mozambique and the Comoros and the Malagasy-speakers of Madagascar, all owed significantly to the Indonesians who pioneered the settlement of Madagascar during the first millennium CE.

The Islamic Factor

If the Indonesian migration down the coast of East Africa and across the Comoros to northwest Madagascar created the original matrix for littoral society in the Mozambique Channel, then it was the rise and expansion of Islam with its successive groups of (often dissident) Arab and Islamicized coastal Africans or Swahili who cemented it. Archaeological evidence, Arab accounts, and oral traditions all confirm the significance of this process and the constant movement back and forth that linked emerging settlements in the Mozambique Channel to those along the coast to the north of Cape Delgado (the border between modern Mozambique and Tanzania). Muslims first established coastal settlements on the offshore islands, inlets and bays of the northern coast dating from the tenth century CE, with increasing layers of settlement continuing right into the sixteenth century that witnessed the emergence of the Islamo-Malagasy communities known as Antalaotse (or Antalaotra).[24] For the Comoros, we have equally compelling archaeological evidence dating to the same period.[25] For Mozambique the evidence is neither as complete nor as compelling, and would seem to indicate that Afro-Arab settlement may have occurred slightly later than elsewhere in the northern reaches of the Mozambique Channel.[26] It should be pointed out, however, that there is some evidence to suggest that certain Muslim settlements on Madagascar derived directly from Mozambique.[27]

The discovery of gold emanating from the Zimbabwe plateau and the emergence of Sofala by the eleventh century CE as the port from which that gold was shipped both north to the Swahili coast and across the channel to Muslim settlements in northwest Madagascar, was perhaps the critical feature in cementing an Islamic commercial network in the Mozambique Channel and linking it to the wider world of the western Indian Ocean.[28] Certainly, by the time the Portuguese entered these waters there was a thriving commercial and religious network that linked coastal communities on both sides of the channel and in the Comoros through trade and, no doubt, engendered familial ties that were an essential feature of Indian Ocean trade during this and later eras. It is also evident that the Swahili language was a lingua franca among these communities during this period, as it continued to be right through the nineteenth century.[29]

Europeans Enter the Scene

Notwithstanding the weight of received historiography, the intrusion of the Portuguese into this region of the western Indian Ocean, however disruptive, did not lead to a radical transformation of commercial relations around the channel. To be sure, there were major changes that Portuguese intervention caused in the international gold and ivory trades, but within the region it was the Portuguese who found they had to adjust to local and regional realities. For example, the inability of the Portuguese to subdue the coast opposite their base at Mozambique Island, which produced none of its own food, meant that they sometimes had to look to Madagascar for provisions.[30] Thus, in 1613 one aspect of a Portuguese mission to Samamo, the ruler of Mazalagem or Boeny in Boina Bay, concerned the procurement of provisions. Indeed, as Vincent Belrose-Huyghues observes for this period, "it is not possible to study the Northwest coast of

Madagascar without being informed about what was happening on the other side of the Mozambique Channel."[31] In fact, his statement can be projected both backwards and forwards. To take only one example that echoes the Portuguese search for provisions at Boina in the early seventeenth century, there is extensive evidence of a vibrant exchange in foodstuffs from the Comoros and northwestern Madagascar, which supplied rice, sorghum, finger millet, beans, mung, a variety of sago used only for feeding slaves, coconuts and coconut oil, ghee, honey, goats and cattle to Mozambique Island in the nineteenth century.[32]

Consideration of the exchange of provisions raises some of the issues concerning the role of "peasants and fishermen" as well as the extent of coastal hinterlands that Pearson touches upon in his thoughtful essay on littoral society. Who, exactly, produced the food that the Portuguese and traders from Mozambique sought in places like Mazalagem and, later, Mahajanga and Nzwani? It certainly was not the people with whom they traded. In fact, as Paulo da Costa observed in 1613, the people of Boeny produced virtually none of their food, trading with people on the mainland of Madagascar for these needs, including all the livestock that they consumed.[33] Among historians of the region, only Benigna Zimba has attempted to understand the production of provisions for overseas trade in her examination of the role of women in the trade of southern Mozambique during the period 1785-1830.[34] Thus, as Pearson reminds us with reference to the flexibility of the land-sea frontier:

> A final answer must then stress the sea, but not separate it from the land. Our definition of the history of littoral societies is simply that it is a history focusing on people whose lives were connected with the sea, and who often traveled over salt water or were influenced by what occurred on it. The history of such people is not restricted to the sea. Influences on littoral society of which we must take note can come from far inland. It is always a matter of interaction between the affairs of land and sea.[35]

The Slave Trade

The same point could be made with reference to the slave trade that flourished in the Mozambique Channel from the seventeenth deep into the nineteenth century. The origins of this expanding traffic can be traced to the immigration of Swahili and Hadrami Arabs to the region and the exportation of labor from northwest Madagascar to the ports of the Swahili coast and Arabia that reached its heyday in the seventeenth and early eighteenth centuries. The Madagascar trade was supplemented during this period by Africans from the hinterland of southern Mozambique, particularly through the port of Sofala. From the middle of the eighteenth century, however, developments in both the interior of Madagascar (the rise of the Imerina empire) and along the Swahili coast (the steady consolidation of Busaidi rule at Zanzibar and eventually over the Swahili coast) caused a shift in the trade so that Madagascar became a significant importer of bonded African labor from Mozambique.[36] An early example of the interconnectedness of politics and the slave trade in the Mozambique Channel is the series of late eighteenth- and early nineteenth-century maritime slave raids by Malagasy (Betsimisaraka and Sakalava) in large outrigger canoes, each carrying 50 to 60 men, from both the eastern and western coasts of northern Madagascar onto the Comoro Islands and the East African coast from the Kerimba Islands to the Mafia Islands in modern Tanzania.[37] Where the trade involved the importation of slaves from Mozambique into the Comoros or western Madagascar, this forced migration of Bantu-speaking people from northern and central Mozambique left a human legacy of the interconnected economic systems that dominated the littoral society of the channel during this period.[38] Vivid testimony to this human legacy may be seen in the fact that Makoa and Masombika descendants of enslaved Africans in western Madagascar regard their homeland across the Mozambique Channel as *mrima* or *morima*, that is, the coast.[39] In the Comoros bonded Africans introduced new music and dances during the heyday of the slave trade, while indigenous forms of spirit possession in both the Comoros and Madagascar reflected their impact.[40] Where it concerned the transshipment of human cargoes from the ports of the Comoros and Mahajanga to the Seychelles and Mascarene Islands in the nineteenth century, it still involved all parties to the commerce in a tightly interwoven commercial nexus.[41] On the western side of the channel, the slave trade reached deep into the interior of East Central Africa, affecting many more people who lived far from the sea than those who inhabited its shores.

Karany and Banians

In the seventeenth century, another population element became prominent in the construction of littoral society in the Mozambique Channel. These were Muslim Indian (Karany in Madagascar) and Hindu (Vania or Banian) merchants who came to dominate the financing and much of the maritime carrying trade of the western Indian Ocean. These merchants rose to prominence by exploiting new opportunities in the region and as a consequence of their connections to larger banking firms and collective corporations in Gujarat and Maharashtra with networks extending to Muscat and the Swahili coast. In the ports of the Mozambique Channel they were especially noteworthy at Mozambique Island, Inhambane, and Mahajanga, which emerged as the successor coastal trading emporium to Boeny in the late eighteenth century.[42]

Islamic Networks

Despite differences in the legal tradition of Indian Sunni Muslim traders from their African and Malagasy co-religionists (the former being Hanafi and the latter Shafi), and the fact that some Indian Muslims were Shi'i rather than Sunni Muslims, Indian Muslims contributed another element to the emergence of an Islamic network across the Mozambique Channel in the nineteenth century. In fact, as early as the late 1750s, the Portuguese authorities at Inhambane reported that Indian Muslims had established religious schools for local Africans.[43] More significant still during the nineteenth century was the dominant role of Hadrami religious leaders based in the Comoros for the Muslim littoral communities of the Mozambique Channel. I have elsewhere discussed this network at greater length with respect to Mozambique and the Comoros, but it is quite apparent that it extended as well to Mahajanga in the nineteenth century.[44] The trade in provisions, including both livestock and agricultural produce, from the Comoros and Madagascar to Mozambique in exchange for human labor—all of it fueled by a wide variety of Indian and European trade goods and capital—created bonds of interdependency that were not only economic, but also social and religious. For example, Portuguese officials at Mozambique Island carried out an intermittent correspondence with the Sultans of Nzwani in the early decades of the nineteenth century that reflected the economic needs of both and the political rivalries of the latter. Portuguese archives and the records of other Europeans in the area provide a multitude of examples of similar situations across the Comoros and including Mahajanga, then Quitangonha, Sancul, Angoche, Quelimane, and Sofala on the Mozambique coast during the first third of the century.

In 1863, as the slave trade across the channel continued to thrive despite British attempts to suppress the trade, the Portuguese seized the family of Musa Quanto, the powerful ruler of Angoche, the most important Muslim slaving port that lay between the two northern Mozambique poles of Portuguese control, Mozambique Island and Quelimane, and sent them into slavery to Madagascar. Seeking to free them, Musa Quanto apparently traveled to Mahajanga, where he wrote to Queen Rasoherina of Imerina (r.1863-1867) to seek her assistance in redeeming his four children, his sister, and his wife.[45] A final example comes from the beginning of 1878, when Sultan Said Bakr of Ngazija, the largest of the Comoro Islands, wrote the following letter to Molidi Vulai, Sheikh of Sancul on the coast south of Mozambique Island:

> My agent Modohama just arrived here, having left three slaves there with Ambar. I ask you to keep an eye on them. We do not know each other except through letters, but I hope that you will watch over

this collection. Your brother's young nephew is on
Mohilla [Mwali] and Allah willing when he finishes
his studies I will send him home to Mozambique. I repeat that I would like you to watch over my accounts.
My father Sultan Ahmed passed away [in 1875].[46]

As Nancy Hafkin astutely observed a quarter century ago,
"Despite the fact that the two had never met, a sense of Swahili kinship and mutual reciprocity emerges from their correspondence."
Moreover, she continues, although this group of letters is apparently
unique, "the trade patterns it represents were common" as were the
linkages among Muslim elites within the region.[47]

These connections endured right to the end of the nineteenth cen-
tury, as official Portuguese records of maritime movement between
Mozambique Island, Ibo, the Comoros and Madagascar make clear.[48]
A rare, but revealing letter from the Sultan of Nzwani, who appar-
ently sought to enter the trade for himself, to the Governor of
Mozambique in 1884, accompanied his personal dhow:

I am going to try to open business at Mozambique
and therefore send some of my *sharif*—Mohsoun,
Sied Owmer and Abdallah—to acquaint [themselves
with] the merchants there [and] to know the price of
articles. I hope they will enjoy your kindness while
they stay in the colony. I send you a bag of sugar
which you will favor me by accepting, being production of my estate.[49]

Five years later the French Governor of Mayotte wrote to his
Portuguese counterpart at Mozambique seeking to recruit workers
for the French establishments on his island-colony, as well as at Nosy
Be and Réunion, as he had done the previous year from Ibo.[50]

Perhaps the most important modern elements in the network, the
Sufi *turuq*, emerged only at the very end of the nineteenth century
and were built squarely on the wider commercial and religious network that connected the Islamic communities of the Mozambique

Channel to the Swahili coast and, especially, to Zanzibar (and beyond them to the Hadramaut).[51] Without going into detail, suffice it to say that both the Shadhiliyya and Qadiriyya expanded to northwest Madagscar and Mozambique Island from Ngazija and that there existed a complex web of familial and religious connections between Ngazija and the coast of Mozambique from around Mozambique Island right down to Angoche. In addition to the presence of Muslims from northern Mozambique in the Comoros and at Mahajanga, a number of Muslim clans in northern Mozambique still claim Comorian progenitors.[52]

*   *   *   *   *

While this essay has only sketched the outline of a littoral society, I would argue that by the middle of the eighteenth century, at the very latest, there had emerged, as Pearson puts it, "such a thing as a littoral society" in the Mozambique Channel.[53] With its mixed population of Mozambique Africans, Malagasy, Comorians, Swahili, Antalaotse, Arabs, Indians, Portuguese, and mixtures thereof, not to mention Dutch, English, American and French traders who resided in their midst from time to time, it conforms to Pearson's statement that "Littoral society is more pluralistic than the inland, because of the diverse groups of foreign merchants in its ports."[54] Just as certainly, around the coasts of the channel as in Pearson's model, "more fish is eaten than is the case inland," although this quotidian economic activity is little noted in the historical record.[55] Similarly, as elsewhere in the Indian Ocean world, trade within the Mozambique Channel was regulated by the monsoons and mediated by prevailing currents. Moreover, as Pearson stipulates and as was surely the case in the Mozambique Channel, "In economic terms a littoral society both in trade and production is geared to much more distant and 'foreign' markets than is an inland area."[56] Finally, as he observes, "there are important cultural and religious differences," even though we know very little in detail historically about such practices except as they relate to Islam. Thus, as Pearson called for nearly twenty years ago, "What is needed is empirical research to flesh out these distinctive elements," in this case as they relate to the Mozambique Channel.[57]

NOTES

Notes to the Introduction

1. Michael Pearson, *The Indian Ocean* (London and New York: Routledge, 2003), p. 10. I have previously acknowledged the peripheral status of eastern Africa in Edward A. Alpers, "International Importance of the Region," Chapter 35.5 of "The East Coast and Indian Ocean Islands," in M.A. Al-Bakhit, L. Bazin, and S.M. Cissoko, eds., *History of Humanity-Scientific and Cultural Development*, IV: *From the Seventh to the Sixteenth Century* (London and New York: Routledge and Paris: [UNESCO], 2000), pp. 536-538.
2. Lodewijk J. Wagenaar, "Roundtable: Reviews of Michael Pearson, *The Indian Ocean*, with a Response by Michael Pearson," *International Journal of Maritime History*, 16, 1 (2004-2006), p. 189.
3. K.N. Chaudhuri, *Asia before Europe: Economy and Civilisation of the Indian Ocean from the Rise of Islam to 1750* (Cambridge: Cambridge University Press, 1990). In fairness to Chaudhuri, he does not completely ignore eastern Africa in his earlier *Trade and Civilisation in the Indian Ocean: An Economic History from the Rise of Islam to 1750* (Cambridge: Cambridge University Press, 1986).
4. Pearson, *The Indian Ocean*, p. 9; Peregrine Horden and Nicholas Purcell, *The Corrupting Sea: A Study of Mediterranean History* (Oxford: Blackwell, 2000). For a convenient restatement, see their "The Mediterranean and 'the New Thalassology,'" in AHR Forum, "Oceans of History," *The American Historical Review*, 111, 3 (2006), pp. 729-730.
5. Kären Wigen, "Introduction," AHR Forum, "Oceans of History," *The American Historical Review*, 111, 3 (2006), p. 720, emphasis in the original.
6. Ibid. and Horden and Purcell, "The Mediterranean and 'the New Thalassology,'" p. 733. For examples of two scholars who explicitly adopt a network framework, if not network theory, see Anne K. Bang, *Sufis and Scholars of the Sea: Family Networks in East Africa, 1860-1925* (London and New York: Routledge-Curzon, 2003), and Pedro Alberto da Silva Rupino Machado, "Gujarati Indian Networks in Mozambique, 1777-c.1830" (unpublished Ph.D. dissertation, School of Oriental and African Studies, University of London, 2005). In this volume I do not include my essays on the African diaspora in the Indian Ocean, which I plan to bring together under separate covers.

Notes to Chapter 1

1. This paper was originally presented at the annual meeting of the American Historical Association, Chicago, December 1974. The present version benefited significantly from the helpful suggestions of Michael N. Pearson, University of

New South Wales, and John Zarwan, then a doctoral candidate at Yale University, whose attention to detail and bibliographical assistance I greatly appreciate. The standard introduction to the Portuguese in the Indian Ocean remains C.R. Boxer, *The Portuguese Seaborne Empire, 1415-1825* (New York: Alfred A. Knopf, 1969), but see especially his "The Portuguese in the East (1500-1800)," in H.V. Livermore, ed., *Portugal and Brazil—An Introduction* (Oxford: Clarendon Press, 1953), pp. 185-247. For early economic affairs, see Vitorino Magalhães Godinho, *L'Économie de l'empire portugais aux XVe et XVIe siècles* (Paris: S.E.V.P.E.N., 1969). For a more recent study see Sanjay Subrahmanyam, *The Portuguese Empire in Asia, 1500-1700: a political and economic history* (London & New York: Longman, 1993). For Portugal's part in the wider commercial history of East Africa, see Edward A. Alpers, *Ivory and Slaves in East Central Africa: Changing Patterns of International Trade to the Later Nineteenth Century* (London: Heinemann and Berkeley: University of California Press, 1975). The subject of this chapter has recently been examined in great detail by Pedro Alberto da Silva Rupino Machado, "Gujarati Indian Merchant Networks in Mozambique, 1777-c.1830" (unpublished Ph.D. dissertation, School of Oriental and African Studies, University of London, 2005).

2. See, for example, Ralph Davis, *The Rise of the Atlantic Economies* (Ithaca: Cornell University Press, 1974); Frédéric Mauro, *Le Portugal et l'Atlantique au XVIe siècle, 1570-1670. Étude économique* (Paris: S.E.V.P.E.N., 1960); and Pierre Verger, *Flux et reflux de la traite des Esclaves entre le golfe de Bénin et Bahia de Todos os Santos du 17e au 19e siècles* (The Hague: Mouton, 1968). Two pioneering analyses of Indian Ocean trade which focus on sub-regions other than East Africa should be recognized as well. They are M.A.P. Meilink-Roelofsz, *Asian Trade and European Influence in the Indonesian Archipelago between 1500 and about 1630* (The Hague: Nijhoff, 1962) and Niels Steensgaard, *Carracks, Caravans and Companies: The Structural Crisis in the European-Asian Trade in the Early 17th Century*, Scandinavian Institute of Asian Studies Monograph Series No. 17 ([Lund], Studentlitteratur, 1973). More recent regional studies include Anthony Reid, *Southeast Asia in the Age of Commerce, 1450-1680*, 2 vols. (New Haven & London: Yale University Press, 1988 & 1993); Uma Das Gupta, compiler, *The World of the Indian Ocean Merchant 1500-1800: Collected Essays of Ashin Das Gupta* (New Delhi: Oxford University Press, 2001); and R.J. Barendse,. *The Arabian Seas: The Indian Ocean World of the Seventeenth Century* (Armonk, NY & London: M.E. Sharpe, 2002).

3. D. António da Silveira to King, post-18 July 1518, in *Documentos sobre os Portugueses em Moçambique e na África Central/Documents on the Portuguese in Mozambique and in Central Africa, 1497-1840*, V (Lisbon: Centro de Estudos Históricos de Ultramar and National Archives of Rhodesia and Nyasaland, 1966), p. 563.

4. H.A.R. Gibb, trs. and ed., *The Travels of Ibn Battuta, A.D. 1325-1354*, The Hakluyt Society, 2nd series, no. 117 (Cambridge: Cambridge University Press, 1962), II, pp. 373-374.

5. Jean Aubin, "Alburquerque et les negociations de Cambaye," in Jean Aubin, ed., *Mare Luso-Indicum. Études et documents sur l'histoire de l'Ocean Indien et des*

pays riverains a l'époque de la domination portugaise, Centre de Recherche d'Histoire et de Philologie de la IVe Section de l'École Pratique des Hautes Etudes, IV, Hautes Études Islamiques et Orientales d'Histoire Comparée, 2 (Geneva: Droz & Paris: Minard, 1971), I, p. 3.

6. This paragraph and my overall understanding of Gujarati affairs is heavily indebted to the important work of Michael N. Pearson, "Commerce and Compulsion: Gujarati Merchants and the Portuguese System in Western India, 1500-1600" (unpublished Ph. D. dissertation, University of Michigan, 1971). Here see especially pp. 33-34, 38-42. The quotation is from p. 42. A greatly revised book subsequently emerged from Pearson's dissertation, *Merchants and Rulers in Gujarat: The Response to the Portuguese in the Sixteenth Century* (Berkeley & London: University of California Press, 1976). Since this essay was written before the publication of the book, with one exception I have decided to retain my original references to the dissertation.

7. Aubin, "Albuquerque." For details of the first and second sieges of Diu by the Portuguese between 1529 and 1534 and 1546 and 1548, see Pearson, "Commerce and Compulsion," pp. 210-212. The rise and fall of trading emporia and their ultimate dependence on political and military factors is a characteristic feature of the Indian Ocean economic system, which seems never to have tolerated more than one or two major commercial centers in any of its principal sub-regions at any one time. For a careful examination of one such trading port in the context of changing power relations in the Persian Gulf, see Andrew Williamson, *Sohar and Omani Seafaring in the Indian Ocean* (Muscat: Petroleum Development [Oman], 1973), especially pp. 4, 21-28. I am grateful to the late B.G. Martin of Indiana University, Bloomington, first for drawing my attention to this source and then for generously providing me with a copy of it.

8. M.L. Dames, trans. and ed., *The Book of Duarte Barbosa,* The Hakluyt Society, 2nd series, no. 44 (London, 1918), I, pp. 129-130.

9. Pearson, "Commerce and Compulsion," pp. 27-28.

10. Armando Cortesão, trans. and ed., *The Suma Oriental of Tomé Pires,* The Hakluyt Society, 2nd series, no. 89 (London, 1944), I, p. 41; Pearson, "Commerce and Compulsion," pp. 44-46.

11. Pearson, "Commerce and Compulsion," pp. 25, 45, 47, n. 86. I am again indebted to John Zarwan, who was completing a dissertation on Indians in East Africa, for alerting me to the major controversy surrounding the Weber thesis in Indian studies. See John Zarwan, "Indian Businessmen in Kenya during the twentieth century: a case study" (unpublished Ph.D. dissertation, Yale University, 1977), which was completed after I published this article. Whether or not I successfully avoided it is altogether another matter. See Milton Singer, *When a Great Tradition Modernizes: An Anthropological Approach to Indian Civilization* (New York: Praeger, 1972), especially ch. 8; and M.D. Morris, "Values as an Obstacle to Economic Growth in South Asia: An Historical Survey," *Journal of Economic History,* 27, 4 (1967), pp. 588-607. Although I attempt to follow Indian specialists in these matters, I remain uneasy about the way in which they handle the whole question of caste. For a suggestive Marxist approach, see Claude Meillassoux, "Are There Castes in India?" *Economy and Society,* 11, 1 (1973), pp.

89-111. For a detailed analysis of caste in Gujarat that was published after this article first appeared, see A.M. Shah and I.P. Desai, *Division and Hierarchy: An Overview of caste in Gujarat* (Delhi: Hindustan Publishing Corporation, 1988); for a more recent, provocative discussion of the broader topic, see Nicholas Dirks, *Castes of Mind: Colonialism and the Making of Modern India* (Princeton: Princeton University Press, 2001).

12. *Tomé Pires*, I, pp. 41-42.
13. A.C. Burnell, ed., *The Voyage of John Huygen van Linschoten to the East Indies*, The Hakluyt Society, no. 70 (London, 1885), I, pp. 60, 252-253. The translation is that of the first English edition of 1598. In quoting van Linschoten I have incorporated Burnell's notes on the original Dutch text, which does not reflect the anti-Semitism of the English translator, who substitutes "all Jewes" for "all other Indians."
14. Jean Baptiste Tavernier, *Travels in India*, V. Ball, trans. (London & New York: Macmillan, 1889), II, pp. 183-184.
15. John Ovington, *A Voyage to Surat in the Year 1689*, H.G. Rawlinson, ed. (London: Oxford University Press, 1929), p. 165. See also B.G. Gokhale, "Capital Accumulation in XVIIth Century Western India," *Journal of the Asiatic Society of Bombay*, new series 39-40 (1964-1965), p. 54; Pearson, "Commerce and Compulsion," p. 302.
16. Pearson, "Political Participation in Mughal India," *Indian Economic and Social History Review*, 9, 2 (1972), p. 120. Pearson notes that the other Indian definitions of *mahajan* include "an individual banker, a money-lender, a merchant, or an unspecified 'great man'." These other definitions imply that only in Gujarat were there collective *mahajans*, but the wider meaning appears to be "Principal person, representing a collectivity in India. In Goa the term is used, in particular, with respect to the spokesman of the brotherhood of a pagoda." Sebastião Rodolfo Dalgado, *Glossario Luso-Asiático,* II (Coimbra: Imprensa da Universidade, 1921), p. 46.
17. *Tomé Pires*, I, pp. 42, 45.
18. Ibid., p. 43.
19. Ibid., p. 45.
20. Meilink-Roelofsz, *Asian Trade*, p. 42.
21. *Tomé Pires*, I, p. 46.
22. See R.B. Serjeant, *The Portuguese off the South Arabian Coast—Hadrami Chronicles* (Oxford: Clarendon Press, 1963), pp. 10, 32-33.
23. Prospero Peragallo, *Carta de El-Pei D. Manuel ao Rei Católico, 1505,* and *Manuscrito de Valentim Fernandes*, 22 May 1506, in *Documentos,* I (Lisbon: Centro de Estudos Históricos de Ultramar and National Archives of Rhodesia and Nyasaland, 1962), pp. 47, 531, *535;* also Pearson, "Commerce and Compulsion," pp. 20, 25.
24. *Duarte Barbosa,* I, pp. 6-8, 28, 31, 129, 154, the quotation being on pp. 22-23. See also *Valentim Fernandes,* 1506, in *Documentos*, I, p. 533.
25. Gervase Mathew, "The East African Coast until the Coming of the Portuguese," in Roland Oliver and Gervase Mathew, eds., *History of East Arica,* I (London: Oxford University Press, 1963), p. 123. Justus Strandes, *The Portuguese Period in*

East Africa, J.E Wallwork, trans., J.S. Kirkman, ed., Transactions of the Kenya History Society II (Nairobi: East African Literature Bureau, 1961 [1899]), p. 61, notes that Muhammad Ankoni "is variously referred to as a rich merchant, or as an elder, or also as a Treasury official." See G.S.P. Freeman-Grenville, *The Medieval History of the Coast of Tanganyika* (London: Oxford University Press, 1962), pp. 141, 202-203. On Daybol traders in the western Indian Ocean, see Serjeant, *Portuguese*, p. 34.

26. Strandes, *Portuguese Period*, p. 107.
27. See, for example, Meilink-Roelofsz, *Asian Trade*, pp. 61, 63. For a modern study of Armenian trade networks in the Indian Ocean see Sebouh Aslanian, "From the Indian Ocean to the Mediterranean: Circulation and the Global Trade Network of Armenian Merchants from New Julfa, Isfahan, 1605-1747" (unpublished Ph.D. dissertation, Columbia University, 2007).
28. Pearson, "Commerce and Compulsion," pp. 31, 212-214.
29. Ibid., p. 235; Pearson, "Political Participation," p. 118.
30. Pearson, "Commerce and Compulsion," p. 243 n. 87 (from p. 242).
31. Pearson, "Indigenous Dominance in a Colonial Economy: The Goa Rendas, 1600-1670," in Aubin, ed., *Mare Luso-Indicum*, Hautes Etudes Islamiques et Orientales d'Histoire Comparée, 5 (Geneva: Droz and Paris: Minard, 1972), II, p. 62. This article demonstrates convincingly how very dependent upon Indian collaboration, in this case that of the Saraswat Brahmins for the collection of official revenue by contract, the Portuguese had become during the seventeenth century. See also Pearson, "Wealth and Power: Indian Groups in the Portuguese Indian Economy," *South Asia* (Perth), 3 (1973), pp. 36-44.
32. See Boxer, *Portuguese Seaborne Empire*, ch. 14.
33. Pearson, "Commerce and Compulsion," pp. 226-233, 309-311.
34. For the economic history of Mughal India, see the outstanding work of Irfan Habib, especially *Agrarian Systems of Mughal India* (Bombay: Asia Publishing House, 1963); "Usury in Medieval India," *Comparative Studies in Society and History*, 6, 4 (1963-1964), pp. 393-423; "Potentialities of Capitalistic Development in the Economy of Mughal India," *Journal of Economic History*, 29, 1 (1969), pp. 32-78; and "The System of Bills of Exchange (*Hundis*) in the Mughal Empire," *Proceedings of the Indian History Congress,* 33rd Session (Delhi, 1972). The most recent historical synthesis of the Mughal Empire is John F. Richards, *The Mughal Empire*, The New Cambridge History of India, I.5 (Cambridge: Cambridge University Press, 1993), esp. ch. 9.
35. This is Pearson's argument in "Political Participation," 113-131, although he sees antecedents in sultanate Gujarat as well.
36. See, for example, Gokhale, "Capital Accumulation," pp. 51-60; and Ashin Das Gupta, "The Crisis at Surat, 1730-1732," *Bengal Past and Present*, 86 (1967), pp. 148-149, 158-159, notes 3-5.
37. Pearson, "Political Participation," pp.121-128.
38. Tapan Raychaudhuri, "European Commercial Activity and the Organization of India's Commerce and Industrial Production, 1500-1750," in B.N. Ganguli, ed., *Readings in Indian Economic History* (London: Asia Publishing House, 1964), p. 70; B.R. Grover, "An Integrated Pattern of Commercial Life in the Rural Society

of North India during the 17th-18th Centuries," *Indian Historical Records Commission*, Proceedings of the Thirty-Seventh Session (Delhi, 1966), pp. 121-153.

39. See above, n. 7, and Steensgaard, *Carracks*, for the fall of Hormuz.

40. For a detailed discussion of East African trade during this period, see Alpers, *Ivory and Slaves*, especially chs. 3-6.

41. Neville Chittick, "Kilwa: A Preliminary Report," *Azania*, 1 (1966), pp. 14-15, 20, 22, for archaeological evidence. For Muqdisho in the fourteenth century see *Travels of Ibn Batuta*, II, p. 374; in the nineteenth century, see J.M. Gray, "Zanzibar and the Coastal Belt, 1840-1884," in Oliver and Mathew, eds., *History of East Africa*, I, p. 225; Chapter 4 in this volume. *Duarte Barbosa*, I, p. 9, describes a fascinating combination of primary and secondary manufacturing of cotton cloth at Sofala which integrated imported Gujarati material with locally produced stuffs, and was a direct response to Portuguese imperial control of trade. "In this same Çofala now of late they make great store of cotton and weave it, and from it they make much white cloth, and as they know not how to dye it, or have not the needful dyes, they take the Cambaya cloths, blue or otherwise coloured, and unravel them and make them up again, so that it becomes a new' thing. With this thread and their own white they make much coloured cloth, and from it they gain much gold." This impressive innovation to a drastically altered economic situation cannot, however, have survived the decline of Sofala, which dates from the initial Portuguese penetration inland up the Zambezi River in about 1530. See also Peter Garlake, *Great Zimbabwe* (London: Thames and Hudson, 1973), pp. 116, 193-194, and figure 20: 2, 3. For the similar re-working of imported with local cloth at Muqdisho, see Chapter 5 in this volume.

42. For statistical evidence, such as it is, for both the cloths and beads of Cambay in the first decades of the sixteenth century, see Alexandre Lobato, *A Expansão Portuguesa em Moçambique de 1498 a 1530* (Lisbon: Agência Geral do Ultramar, 1960), III, *passim*.

43. Strandes, *Portuguese Period*, pp. 130-131, 138, 173-174, 344.

44. Pearson, "Commerce and Compulsion," p. 244.

45. Pearson, "Goa Rendas," pp. 67-68, 71, and "Commerce and Compulsion," p. 311.

46. Alpers, *Ivory and Slaves*, ch. 3. For a more recent study of the Company of Mazanes, see also Luís Frederico Dias Antunes, "The Trade Activities of the Banyans in Mozambique: Private Indian Dynamics in the Panel of the Portuguese State Economy (1686-1777)," in K.S. Mathew, ed., *Mariners, Merchants and Oceans: Studies in Maritime History* (New Delhi: Manohar, 1995), pp. 301-336.

47. Miguel de Noronha de Paiva Couceiro, *Diu e Eu* (Lisbon: Agência Geral do Ultramar, 1969), p. 118. Paiva Couceiro, the count of Paraty, served as governor of Diu from 1948 to 1950. In his memoirs he also notes the close ties between Diu and Mozambique which existed for other Hindu castes, including both Brahmins and various artisans. See pp. 71, 119, 122-123, 142-143. For their very few numbers at Mozambique Island in the 1940s, see Lobato, *Ilha de Moçambique* (Moçambique: Imprensa Nacional, 1945), pp. 126, 129. In 1940 the agency of Calachand Irachand and Company in Lourenço Marques was located on the

Rua da Gavea. See *Anuario de Moçambique—1940,* planned and coordinated by Sousa Ribeiro and the Repartição Tecnica de Estatística (Lourenço Marques: Imprensa Nacional de Moçambique, 1940), p. 606.

48. See n. 16 above for the prevailing Luso-Indian definition of *mazane* as the representative of a collectivity, which suggests that a company of *mazanes* included the representatives of all the major commercial *mahajans* in Diu. See Pearson, "Commerce and Compulsion," p. 311, where he notes that in 1653 Goridas Parekh was captain of the Hindu and Muslim Gujaratis of Diu.

49. Belchior Amaral, Castellan of Diu, to Viceroy of India (?), Diu, 15 June 1789, in A.B. de Bragança Pereira, ed., *Arquivo Portugûes Oriental,* nova edição (Bastorá: Tipografia Rangel, 1938), IV: 2:2, pp. 566-567.

50. For a late nineteenth-century map of Diu, with specifically demarcated residential neighborhoods for *vanias,* Shia Bohras, Parsees, Christians, and *mainatos,* a Luso-Asian term for a very low Hindu caste of washers, see ibid., p. 396. Definitions of *mainato* can be found in Dalgado, *Glossário,* II, pp. 12-13.

51. John R. Jenson, ed., *Journal and Letter Book of Nicholas Buckeridge 1651-1654* (Minneapolis: University of Minnesota Press, 1973), p. 65; Pearson, *Merchants and Rulers,* p. 113, and "Wealth and Power," pp. 41-42. For Portuguese trading vessels from Daman (two), Diu, Chaul, and Bassein at Pate in 1653, see Jenson, ed., *Buckeridge,* p. 75.

52. Strandes, *Portuguese Period,* p. 174. Buckeridge names the chief merchants at Pate in 1653 as "Longe Corge Sas Bonn; Congees, & Nog gees sonns hassan Matacca," the first two of which are clearly Indian, and therefore probably *vania,* while the latter was a man of the coast, Mataka being a common Bajuni name. Jenson, ed., *Buckeridee,* 69, and personal communication from Randall L. Pouwels.

53. Quoted in Boxer, "The Portuguese on the Swahili Coast, 1593-1729," in Boxer and Carlos de Azevedo, *Fort Jesus and the Portuguese in Mombasa 1593-1729* (London: Hollis & Carter, 1960), p. 53; for the sack of Ndia Kuu ("the foxhole"), see p. 48. For a more recent and more extended synthesis of this period, see Pearson, *Port Cities and Intruders: The Swahili Coast, India, and Portugal in the Early Modern Period* (Baltimore and London: The Johns Hopkins University Press, 1998).

54. Jean Mocquet, *Voyages en Afrique. Asie, Indes Orientales et Occidentales* (Rouen, 1630), p. 258; Tavernier, *Travels,* II, pp. 4-6. For a detailed discussion of Gujarati cloths during this period, see J. Irwin, "Indian Textile Trade in the Seventeenth Century: (I) Western India," *Journal of Indian Textile History,* 1 (1955), pp. 5-33. For an important recent analysis of Gujarati cloths a century later, see Machado, "Gujarati Indian Merchants Networks," ch. 4.

55. Petition of Gujarati *vanias,* acted upon at Goa, 2 March 1646, in Bragança Pereira, ed., *Arquivo Portugûes Oriental,* II: 2:2, p. 657; Lady Fawcett, trans., Sir Charles Fawcett and Sir Richard Burn, eds., *The Travels of the Abbé Carré in India and the Near East, 1672 to 1674,* The Hakluyt Society, 2nd series, 95 (London, 1947), I, p. 136.

56. This figure is extrapolated from W.H. Moreland, *India at the Death of Akbar— An Economic Study* (London: Macmillan, 1920), pp. 234-235.

57. Raychaudhuri, "European Economic Activity," p. 70; Paiva Couceiro, *Diu e Eu*, p. 124.
58. Lobato, *Evolução Administrativa e Económica de Moçambique, 1752-1763* (Lisbon: Agência Geral do Ultramar, 1957), p. 257; Boxer, *Portuguese Seaborne Empire*, pp. 77-78, 186-187. For *vania* financial support of the Jesuits at Diu in the first decade of the seventeenth century, see Bragança Pereira, ed., *Arquivo Português Oriental*, IV: 2:2, pp. 646-647. For Jesuit support of the Mazanes in 1733 over matters concerning the ivory trade of Mozambique, see ibid., p. 499.
59. Alpers, *Ivory and Slaves*, ch. 4.
60. Population data for the Indians of Mozambique come from Arquivo Histórico Ultramarino, Lisbon, Moçambique, Caixa [hereafter AHU, Moç., Cx.] 6, proposal of the Senado da Câmara to David Marques Pereira, Mozambique, 9 May 1758; AHU, Moç., Cx. 6, petition of Indian merchants to Pereira, Mozambique, 22 May 1758; António Alberto de Andrade, *Relações de Moçambique Setecentista* (Lisbon: Agência Geral do Ultramar, 1956), p. 126. Andrade notes that the owners of shops opened between 18 June 1764 and 18 May 1765 included twenty-two *vanias*, seven Muslims, and five goldsmiths. There are no clues as to which sect or sects the Muslims of Gujarat at Mozambique and Diu belonged during this period. The census also notes three *bangações* (sing., *bangaçal*), or warehouses, the owners of which are not specified. For definitions, see Dalgado, *Glossário Luso-Asiático*, I (Coimbra: Imprensa da Universidade, 1919), pp. 95-96.
61. AHU, Moç., Cx. 17, Vicente Caetano da Maia e Vasconcelos to Crown, Mozambique, 18 Aug. 1781; AHU, Moç., Cx. 17, *residência* of Fr. José de Vasconcelos de Almeida, 1781; AHU, Moç., Cx. 19, "Mappa das Cazas...q passuem nesta Villa Cap.ᵃˡ de Moçambique os Banianes existente nella ... em o Mez de Dezembro de 1782," which is also summarized in Fritz Hoppe, *A África Oriental Portuguesa no tempo do Marquês de Pombal (1750-1777)* (Lisbon: Agência Geral do Ultramar, 1970), pp. 182-183. For the Portuguese population, see ibid., p. 113.
62. Francisco Santana, ed., *Documentação Avulsa Moçambicana do Arquivo Histórico Ultramarino*, II (Lisbon: Centro de Estudos Históricos Ultramarinos, 1967), pp. 114-115 #208.
63. The entire table is reproduced in Bragança Pereira, ed., *Arquivo Português Oriental*, IV: 2:2, pp. 404-405. The percentages given in the text are only an approximation based on the available insufficient population data. It is worth noting that the population at Diu at the end of the eighteenth century was considerably reduced from the mid-seventeenth century, when it had reached its peak of prosperity. Various accounts from that period suggest a population of perhaps fifty thousand or more individuals. See Pearson, "Commerce and Compulsion," pp. 242-243, n. 87. See also the rise and decline of Sohar, as documented in Williamson, *Sohar*.
64. Andrade, *Relações*, pp. 126-127; Hoppe, *África*, p. 180. For the significance of riding in palanquins, a privilege usually reserved only for Portuguese, see Pearson, "Goa Rendas," p. 70. On the similar importance of being considered *homens do chapeu*, note that Europeans in India were generally called "the

hatwearers," or *topiwalas*, for which see *Travels of Abbé Carré*, I, p. 148.
65. Andrade, *Relações*, p. 100; Crown to Viceroy, Lisbon, 7 April 1723, in George McCall Theal, *Records of South-Eastern Africa* (London: Government of the Cape Colony, 1899), V, pp. 124-126; AHU, Cod. 1324, fl. 316, *portaria*, João Pereira da Silva Barba, Mozambique, 9 Aug. 1765.
66. AHU, Moç., Cx. 17, and AHU, Cod. 1345, (fl. 95-96, Maia e Vasconcelos to Crown, Mozambique, 18 Aug. 1781; AHU, Moç., Cx. 19, Baltasar Manuel de Pereira do Lago to Crown, Mozambique, 10 Aug. 1772; AHU, Moç., Cx. 19, Pedro Saldanha de Albuquerque to Secretary of State; Mozambique, 12 Aug. 1783, also in *Arquivo dos Colónias*, I (1917), p. 235; Bragança Pereira, ed., *Arquivo Português Oriental*, IV: 2: 2, pp. 506-509.
67. The full presentation of this interpretation is in Alpers, *Ivory and Slaves*, pp. 70-76.
68. National Archives of India, Panaji, Goa [NAIPG], Livro das Monções [LM] 97-B, fl. 610-611, Faquy Abedu buno mwenha Saveia of Kilwa to António Cardim Fróis (n.d., but clearly *c.* 1728-1729); NAIPG, LM 97-B, fl.614-615, Secu Vegy to Alvaro Caetano (n.d., but from the same period); Pearson, "Commerce and Compulsion," pp. 225, 310; Das Gupta, "Crisis at Surat," p. 159 n. 6.
69. Jenson, *Buckeridge*, p. 46; NAIPG, LM 95-B, fl. 585, Sultan Babucar Bun Sultano Umar Bun Dhau and his brother, Bana Mucu Bun Sultano Babucar Fumovay, King of Jagaya, to Viceroy, 10 Oct. 1728.
70. Abbé de Guyon, *A New history of the East Indies, ancient and modern* (London: R. and J. Dodsley, 1757), I, pp. 285-287; Das Gupta, "Crisis at Surat," pp. 149-162.
71. J.S. Mangat, *A History of the Asians in East Africa, c. 1886 to 1945* (Oxford: Clarendon Press, 1969), ch. 1; Abdul Sheriff, "The Rise of a commercial Empire: An Aspect of the Economic History of Zanzibar, 1770-1873" (unpublished Ph. D. dissertation, University of London, 1971), since superseded by his seminal *Slaves, Spices & Ivory in Zanzibar: Integration of an East African Commercial Empire into the World Economy, 1770-1873* (London: James Currey, 1987); Walter T. Brown, "A Pre-Colonial History of Bagamoyo: Aspects of the Growth of an East African Coastal Town" (unpublished Ph. D. dissertation, Boston University, 1971),

Notes to Chapter 2

1. See, e.g., John R. Hanson II, *Trade in Transition: Exports from the Third World. 1840-1900* (New York: Academic Press, 1980), especially pp. 61-63; L. Blusse. H.L. Wesseling, & G.D. Winius, eds., *History and Underdevelopment: Essays on Underdevelopment and European Expansion in Asia and Africa* (Leiden: Leiden Center for the history of European Expansion, 1980). Research for this paper was supported by two grants from the UCLA Council on International and Comparative Studies (now the UCLA International Institute), to which I am most grateful. I wish also to acknowledge the research assistance provided by Mary F. Milewski and P. Godfrey Okoth.
2. See, e.g., Walter Rodney, *How Europe Underdeveloped Africa* (Dar es Salaam:

Tanzania Publishing House & London: Bogle-L'Ouverture, 1972); Charles Issawi, *An Economic History of the Middle East and North Africa* (New York: Columbia University Press, 1982), p. xii; Morris D. Morris, Toru Matsui, Bipin Chandra, & T. Raychaudhuri, *Indian Economy in the Nineteenth Century: A Symposium* (Delhi: Indian Economic and Social History Association, 1969), p. 147.

3. In addition to the previous citation. see K.N. Chaudhuri. "Foreign Trade and Balance of Payments (1757-1947)," in Dharma Kumar & Maghnad Desai, eds., *The Cambridge Economic History of India*, II (Cambridge: Cambridge University Press, 1983), pp. 804-877, especially pp. 841, 850; B.M. Bhatia, *Famines in India: A Study in Some Aspects of the Economic History of India (1860-1945)* (New York: Asia Publishing House, 1963), especially chs. 2 & 5; Michelle Burge McAlpin, *Subject to Famine: Food Crises and Economic Change in Western India, 1860-1920* (Princeton: Princeton University Press, 1983). The only recognition of this phenomenon that I have found in the Indian Ocean context is in UNESCO, *Historical relations across the Indian Ocean*, The general history of Africa: Studies and documents 3 (Paris: UNESCO, 1980), p. 173.

4. James de Vere Allen, "A proposal for Indian Ocean studies," in ibid., p. 141.

5. For an invaluable introduction to the problem of sources, see *I.C.I.O.S. Proceedings*, 6 (Perth. 1979). On the related importance of collaborative research in tackling this kind of regional study, see Michel Mollat, "Historical contacts of Africa and Madagascar with South and South-East Asia: the role of the Indian Ocean," in UNESCO, *Historical relations*, pp. 56-58; Paul Ottino, "L'Océan Indien comme domaine de recherché," *L'Homme*, 14/3-4 (1974), pp. 143-151.

6. See B. Lewis, et al, eds.. *The Encyclopaedia of Islam*, New Ed., III (Leiden & London: Brill, 1971), p. 34, for figures.

7. I am grateful to Ann D. Alpers for drawing my attention to this last point.

8. Auguste Toussaint, "The role of trade in the settlement of Mauritius," in UNESCO, *Historical relations*, pp. 119-120.

9. Raymond Decary, *Les voyages du chirurgien Avine à l'Île de France et dans la mer des Indes au debut du XIX siècle* (Paris: G. Durassié, 1961), p. 19.

10. Hubert Gerbeau, "The part played by agriculture in the settlement of Reunion," in UNESCO, *Historical relations*, p. 128. For a provisioning voyage from Réunion in 1830, see Francisco Santana, ed., *Documentação Avulsa Moçambicana no Arquivo Histórico Ultramarino*, II (Lisbon: Centro de Estudos Históricos Ultramarinos, 1967), pp. 438-439 #204/1-3.

11. C.P.T. Laplace, *Voyage autour du monde par les mers de l'Inde et de Chine . . . pendant les années 1830, 1831 et 1832* (Paris: Imprimerie royale, 1833), I, pp. 102-103.

12. Gerald S. Graham, *Great Britain in the Indian Ocean* (Oxford: Clarendon Press, 1967), pp. 88, 93.

13. Joseph B.F. Osgood, *Notes of Travel or Recollections of Majunga, Zanzibar, Muscat, Aden, and Other Eastern Ports* (Salem: G. Creamer, 1854), pp.7-8; J.E. Wilson, "Notes on the West Coast of Madagascar," *Journal of the Royal Geographical Society* (hereafter *JRGS*), 36 (1866), p. 245.

14. Phares M. Mutibwa, *The Malagasy and the Europeans* (London: Longman, 1974), p. 259; Hubert Deschamps, *Histoire de Madagascar* (Paris: Berger-Levrault, 1961), p. 212.
15. William Milburn, *Oriental Commerce* (London: Black, Parry & Co., 1813), I, p. 72.
16. Epidariste Colin. "Notice sur Mozambique," in [Conrad] Malte-Brun. *Annales des Voyage, de la Géographie et de l'histoire*, IX (Paris: F. Buisson, 1809), p. 315.
17. See, e.g., James Prior, *Voyage along the Eastern Coast of Africa, to Mozambique, Johanna, and Quiloa . . . in the Nisus Frigate* (London: Sir R. Philips & Co., 1819), p. 37; W.F.W. Owen, *Narrative of Voyages to explore the shores of Africa, Arabia, and Madagascar, performed in H.M. Ships Leven and Barracouta* (London: R. Bentley, 1833), II, pp. 100-102.
18. Public Record Office, London [now National Archives of the United Kingdom, Kew], Admiralty 1/69, #63, Joseph Nourse to John William Croker, at sea in the Mozambique Channel, 15 December 1823.
19. Arquivo da Casa da Cadaval, Cod. 826 (M VI 32), D. Fr. Bartolomeu dos Mártires, "Memoria Chorographica da Provincia e a Capitania de Moçambique na Costa d'Africa oriental Conforme o estado em que se achava no anno de 1822," fl. 31-32.
20. Santana, ed., *Documentação*, I (Lisbon: Centro de Estudos Históricos Ultramarinos, 1964), p. 878 #119; ibid., II, p. 804 #37, p. 805 #40 & #43, p. 818 #81, p. 819 #85, & p. 902 #91; ibid., III (Lisbon: Centro de Estudos Históricos Ultramarinos, 1974), p. 158 #120/1-2, p. 166 #137, p. 983 #167, & p. 984 #170.
21. Charles Guillain, *Documents sur l'histoire. la géographie et le commerce de la partie occidentale de Madagascar* (Paris: Imprimerie royale, 1845), pp. 196-197, 280.
22. Lyons McLeod, *Madagascar and its People* (London: Longman, Green, Longman, Roberts & Green, 1865), p. 246.
23. dos Mártires, "Memoria Chorographica," fl. 26, 31-32.
24. Santana, ed., *Documentação*, II, p. 820 #89.
25. Prior, *Voyage*, p. 55; Public Record Office, London. Colonial Office 415/7, A. No. 172 (31-33), Captain Pilkinhome's Journal; Santana, ed., *Documentação*, I, p. 703 #82-83; ibid., II, p. 32 #47, p. 703 #82-83, p. 760 #251, p. 804 #38, p. 805 #41-42, p. 806 #45-47, p.808 #52, p. 818 #80, p. 819 #83, p. 823 #101, p. 827 #117; ibid., III, p.15 #15, p. 152 #101, p. 678 #144, p. 752 #41 & #43, p. 978 #149, p. 979 #150 & #152, p. 980 #154, p. 981 #160, p. 982 #162 & #164, p. 985 #173, p. 991 #196, p. 998 #211, p. 999 #215, & p. 1000 #218; Marie Armand Pascal d'Azevec et al, *Iles de l'Afrique* (Paris: Firmin Didot frères, 1848), pp. 117 & 120. For *sambo*, see Chapter 8 below.
26. Academia das Ciências de Lisboa, Azul Ms 847. fl. 12; Santana, ed., *Documentação*, II, p. 703 #81; ibid., III, p. 678 #145, p. 752 #42 & #44, p. 808 #16/1, p. 851 #105, p. 189 #195, p. 977 #144, p. 981 #158, p. 984 #171, p. 986 #178-179, p. 987 #182-183, p. 988 #185 & #187, p. 989 #190, p. 990 #192-193, p. 991 #197, p. 997 #207-208, p. 998 #212-213, p. 999 #214, p. 1000 #219.
27. For the Indian ports, see ibid., III, p. 678 #146, p. 986 #177, p. 1001 #222; for the Mozambican ports, see Prior, *Voyage*, p. 25; Santana, ed., *Documentação*, II,

p. 198 #112/1, p. 199 #113, p. 373 #79, p. 824 #105; ibid., III, p. 288 #165, p. 978 #146, p. 979 #153, p. 981 #157, p. 989 #189. For a representative indication of food imports at Mozambique during the first four months in 1858, see Francisco Maria Bordalo, "Ensaio sobre a Estatistica de Moçambique," in F.M. Bordalo & J.J. Lopes de Lima. *Ensaios sobre a Estatistica das Possessões Portuguezas no Ultramar*, II, 4 (Lisbon: Imprensa Nacional, 1859), p. 74.

28. Santana, ed., *Documentação*, II, pp. 942-943 #9/1-3, pp. 951-952 #15/1. For a modern study of the devastating drought that created this famine, see Malyn Newitt, "Drought in Mozambique, 1823-1831," *Journal of Southern African Studies*, 15 (1988), pp. 15-35.

29. Jeronymo Romero, *Supplemento á Memoria Descriptiva e Estatistica de Districto de Cabo Delgado com uma Noticia Acerca do Estabelecimento da Colonia de Pemba* (Lisbon: Typographia Universal, 1860), pp. 122-123, 127-129, 80, 82-84, 130.

30. Fortuné Albrand, "Extrait d'un Memoire sur Zanzibar et sur Quiloa," *Bulletin de la Société de Géographie*, 2e Série, 10 (1838), p. 75; Milburn, *Oriental Commerce*, II, pp. 65-66.

31. Norman R. Bennett & George E. Brooks, Jr., *New England Merchants in Africa: A History through Documents, 1802 to 1865* (Boston: Boston University Press, 1965), p. 157; C.E.B. Russell, *General Rigby, Zanzibar and the Slave Trade* (London: George Allen & Unwin, 1935), pp. 392-343.

32. Osgood, *Notes*, p. 23; Russell, *General Rigby*, p. 339.

33. Guillain, "Côte de Zanguebar et Mascate, 1841," *Revue Coloniale* (1843), pp. 541-542, & *Documents sur l'histoire, la géographie et le commerce de l'Afrique orientale* (Paris: A. Bertrand,, 1856), II, pp. 533-539; Archives Nationales, Section d'Outre-Mer (hereafter ANSOM), Paris [now Aix-en-Provence], Océan Indien 2/10(2), 8-9. 11-12, & Océan Indien 5/23(3); C.S. Nicholls, *The Swahili Coast* (London: George Allen and Unwin, 1971), pp. 349-350, 352-353, 371, chart at p. 374; Frederick Cooper, *Plantation Slavery on the East Coast of Africa* (New Haven & London: Yale University Press, 1977), p. 64; Russell, *General Rigby*, pp. 338-339, 344; Richard F. Burton, "The Lake Regions of Central Equatorial Africa . . . ," *JRGS*, 29 (1859), pp. 433-434, 446; Helge Kjekshus, *Ecology Control and Economic Development in East African History* (London: Heinemann, 1977), p. 32; Ministère des Affaires Etrangères, Paris, Correspondence Consulaire et Commerciale (hereafter MAE, CCC), Zanzibar 4/39v., Gaillard de Ferry to MAE, Zanzibar, 13 December 1877.

34. Cooper, *Plantation Slavery*, pp. 84-85, 97, 100-101; Marguerite Ylvisaker, *Lamu in the Nineteenth Century: Land, Trade, and Politics* (Boston: African Studies Center, Boston University, 1979), pp. 105, 109-111, 116; see also MAE, CCC, Zanzibar 3/348v., A.C. Guillois to MAE. Zanzibar, 10 December 1873; see Chapter 4 in this volume.

35. John Iliffe, *A Modern History of Tanganyika* (Cambridge: Cambridge University Press, 1979), p. 71.

36. Guillain, "Côte," p. 537; ANS0M, Océan Indien 5/23(2-3); MAE, CCE, Zanzibar 3/7, 47 & 72, Jablonski, Zanzibar, 31 December 1865, 1866 & 1867; ibid., 3/104, Eugène Bure, Zanzibar, 31 December 1868. Bennett & Brooks, *New*

England Merchants, p. 533, provide grain and rice export figures in Maria Theresa dollars for 1861/1862-1864/1865, without indicating their destination.

37. Guillain, "Côte," p. 536; MAE, CCC, Zanzibar 2/356, Jablonski, 28 December 1863, giving a figure of 16,500 francs worth exported to Arabia, or about 2% of the total value of sesame exports from Zanzibar that year. At the extrapolated price per kg of French exportations that same year, this would yield approximately 5,000 kg to Arabia.

38. Archives de la Congregation du Saint-Esprit [Arch.C.S.Sp.], Paris [now Chevilly-Larue], 196-A/XII, Anton Horner to État de l'Oeuvre de la Sainte-Enfance, Zanzibar, 31 December 1877 & 1878; ibid., Horner to Laverrière, Zanzibar, 6 April 1878; Arch.C.S.Sp. 196-B/IV, Horner to Penvenne, Zanzibar, 7 February 1878.

39. Arch.C.S.Sp., 196-A/XII, Etienne Baur to Directeur de l'Oeuvre de la Sainte-Enfance, Zanzibar, 5 December 1880; ibid., Baur to État de l'Oeuvre de la Sainte-Enfance, Zanzibar, 31 December 1880.

40. Milburn, *Oriental Commerce*, I, pp. 83, 86-89, 99; John Lewis Burckhardt, *Travels in Arabia* (London: H. Colburn, 1829), pp. 15, 28, 32-33, 44.

41. Richard Pankhurst, *Economic History of Ethiopia 1800-1935* (Addis Ababa: Haile Sellassie I University Press, 1968), pp. 366, 378; R. Wellsted, "Observations on the Coast of Arabia between Ras Mohamed and Jiddah," *JRGS*, 6 (1836), pp. 90-91.

42. Milburn, *Oriental Commerce*, I, pp. 106, 109; Burckhardt, *Travels*, pp. 29-30, 32, 34-35; Wellsted, "Observations," p. 90.

43. Burckhardt, *Travels*, p. 28; Pankhurst, *Economic History*, pp. 365, 371, 377.

44. Burckhardt, *Travels*, pp. 420-422; Wellsted, "Observations," pp. 56, 61-62, 66, 73, 79; see also Burton, *Personal Narrative of a Pilgrimmage to El Medinah and Meccah*, 2nd ed. (London: Longman, Brown, Green, Longmans, and Roberts, 1857), II, p. 9.

45. Henry Salt, *A Voyage to Abyssinia ... in the Years 1809 and 1810* (London: F.C. & J. Rivington, 1814), pp. 106, 191, Appendix V, p. lxx. Mokha imported rice from India, dates from the Persian Gulf, and even some sugar from Mauritius in the middle of the century. See Osgood, *Notes*, p. 180; Charles J. Cruttenden, "Narrative of a Journey from Mokhá to San'á by the Tarik-esh-Sham, or Northern Route, in July and August, 1836," *JRGS*, 8 (1838), p. 272.

46. Alexander Burnes, "On the Maritime Communications of India, as carried on by the Natives, particularly from Kutch, at the mouth of the Indus," *JRGS*, 6 (1836), p. 27.

47. James Bird, "Observations on the Manners of the Inhabitants who occupy the Southern Coast of Arabia and Shores of the Red Sea; . . . ," *JRGS*, 4 (1834), p. 199; Stafford Bettesworth Haines, "Memoir, to accompany a Chart of the South Coast of Arabia, from the Entrance of the Red Sea to Misenat, in 50°43'25" E.," *JRGS*, 9 (1839), pp. 136-137, 147, 149-150, 154.

48. See R.J. Gavin, *Aden under British Rule 1839-1967* (New York: Barnes & Noble Books, 1975), pp. 52, 56-57, 102, 104-105, 107, 118; Z.H. Kour, *The History of Aden 1839-72* (London: Cass, 1981), p. 76; Osgood, *Notes*, p. 126. Dates also were sent to Aden from other Hadramaut ports, and provisions also came from

its own hinterland, of course. See S.B. Miles & Werner Hunzinger, "Account of an Excursion into the interior of Southern Arabia," *JRGS*, 41 (1871), p. 211.

49. F.M. Hunter, *An Account of the British Settlement of Aden in Arabia* (London: Cass, 1968 [1877]), pp. 63-69, 72, 91-98.

50. Gavin, *Aden*, pp. 186-187; Pankhurst, *Economic History*, p. 426; Walter B. Harris, *A Journey through the Yemen and Some General Remarks upon that Country* (Edinburgh: W. Blackwood and sons, 1893), p. 138.

51. Lieut. Barker, "On Eastern Africa," *JRGS*, 18 (1848), pp. 133-134; Cruttenden, "On Eastern Africa," *JRGS*, 18 (1848), pp. 136-139 and "Memoir on the Western or Edoor Tribes, inhabiting the Somali Coast of N.-E. Africa, with the Southern branches of the family of Darrood, resident on the banks of the Webbe Shebeyli, commonly called the River Webbe," *JRGS*, 19 (1849), pp. 64-67; Burton, *First Footsteps in East Africa* (London: J.M. Dent, 1910 [1856]), p. 33 n. 1.

52. Miles, "On the Neighbourhood of Bunder Marayah," *JRGS*, 42 (1872), pp. 61-63, 70; Georges Revoil, *Voyage au Cap des Aromates (Afrique Orientale)* (Paris: E. Dentu, 1880), pp. 271-287.

53. Pankhurst, *Economic History*, pp. 418, 421, 426.

54. Haines, "Memoir of the South and East Coasts of Arabia," *JRGS*, 15 (1845), pp. 105, 119, 125; J.P. Saunders, "A Short Memoir of the Proceedings of the Honourable Company's Surveying Brig 'Palinurus,' during her late Examination of the Coast between Ras Morhat and Ras Seger, and between Ras Fartak and the Ruins of Mesinah," *JRGS*, 16 (1846), pp. 175, 182-183.

55. J.R. Wellsted, "Memoir on the Island of Socotra," *JRGS*, 5 (1835), pp. 200, 215.

56. Wellsted, "Narrative of a Journey into the Interior of Oman, in 1835," *JRGS*, 7 (1837), p. 103; Osgood, *Notes*, pp. 75-76, 82-83; Lieut. Whitelock, "Descriptive Sketch of the Islands and Coast situated at the Entrance of the Persian Gulf," *JRGS*, 8 (1838), p. 175; William Gifford Palgrave, *Narrative of a Year's Journey Through Central and Eastern Arabia (1862-1863)*, 3rd ed. (London: Macmillan and Co., 1866), II, p. 296.

57. Robert Geran Landen, *Oman since 1856: Disruptive Modernization in a Traditional Arab Society* (Princeton: Princeton University Press, 1967), p. 145.

58. Ibid., p. 142. For a recent detailed analysis of the production and export of dates for the global economy, see Matthew Scott Hopper, "The African Presence in Arabia: Slavery, the world economy, and the African diaspora in eastern Arabia, 1840-1940" (unpublished Ph.D. dissertation, UCLA, 2006), ch. 3.

59. Milburn, *Oriental Commerce*, I, p. 123; Palgrave, "Observations made in Central. Eastern, and Southern Arabia during a Journey through that Country in 1862 and 1863," *JRGS*, 34 (1864), pp. 138-139; J.G. Lorimer, *Gazetteer of the Persian Gulf, 'Oman, and Central Arabia*, I, 2 (Calcutta: Superintendant Government Printing, 1915), Appendix D, pp. 2294-2307.

60. Wellsted, "Narrative," p. 103; Osgood, *Notes*, p. 76.

61. Milburn, *Oriental Commerce*, I, pp. 143-148, 155-160, 202-214, 219, 221, 299, 315, 317-318, 322-323, 329, 332-333, 336; see also G.B. Kempthorne, "Notes made on a Survey along the Eastern Shores of the Persian Gulf in 1828," *JRGS*, 5 (1835), p. 263, on rice imports from Kutch and the Malabar coast at Karachi; N. Benjamin, "Arab Merchants of Bombay and Surat (c. 1800-1840)," *Indian*

Economic and Social History Review, 13/1 (1976), pp. 85-95, for the importance of Arab shipping during this period and at p. 91, for their imports of shark fins and exports of grain.

62. Alan Villiers, *Sons of Sinbad* (New York: Charles Scribner's Sons, 1940), pp. 419-428.

Notes to Chapter 3

1. Ronald Latham, trs., *The Travels of Marco Polo* (London: Penguin Books, 1958), p. 301.

2. H.A.R. Gibb, trs. and ed., *The Travels of Ibn Battuta A.D. 1325-1354*, The Hakluyt Society, 2nd series, no. 117 (Cambridge: Cambridge University Press, 1962), II, p. 379.

3. G.S.P. Freeman-Grenville, *The French at Kilwa Island* (Oxford: Clarendon Press, 1965), p. 91.

4. James Prior, *Voyage along the Eastern Coast of Africa, to Mozambique, Johanna, and Quiloa ... in the Nisus Frigate* (London: Sir Richard Phillips and Co., 1819), p. 46.

5. Captain [Philip Howard] Colomb, *Slave-Catching in the Indian Ocean* (New York: Longmans, Green & Co., 1873), p. 348.

6. Alan Villiers, *Sons of Sinbad* (New York: Charles Scribner's Sons, 1940), p. 227.

7. Fernand Braudel, *The Mediterranean and the Mediterranean World in the Age of Philip II* (New York: Harper Torchbooks, 1975), I, pp. 148-167, quoted at 148 and 160.

8. See, e.g., John K. Thornton, *Africa and Africans in the Making of the Atlantic World, 1400-1800*, 2nd edition (New York: Cambridge University Press, 1998), pp. 1, 28-31, 33-35.

9. Auguste Toussaint, *History of the Indian Ocean* (London: Routledge and Kegan Paul, 1966), pp. 3-5, quoted at 4.

10. K.N. Chaudhuri, *Trade and Civilisation in the Indian Ocean from the Rise of Islam to 1750* (Cambridge: Cambridge University Press, 1985). This tendency is further reinforced in Chaudhuri's companion volume, *Asia before Europe: Economy and civilisation of the Indian Ocean from the rise of Islam to 1750* (Cambridge: Cambridge University Press, 1990).

11. Kenneth McPherson, *The Indian Ocean: A History of People and the Sea* (Delhi: Oxford University Press, 1993), pp. 3, 14, and 122-136.

12. UNESCO, *Historical relations across the Indian Ocean* (Paris: UNESCO, 1980); S. Chandra, ed., *The Indian Ocean: Explorations in History, Commerce and Politics* (New Delhi: Sage Publications, 1987); Giorgio Borsa, ed., *Trade and Politics in the Indian Ocean: Historical and Contemporary Perspectives* (New Delhi: Manohar, 1990); S. Chandra, B. Arunachalam, and V. Suryanarayan, eds., *The Indian Ocean and Its Islands: Strategic, Scientific, and Historical Perspectives*, (Delhi, Sage Publications, 1993); Rudrangshu Mukherjee and Lakshmi Subramanian, eds., *Politics and Trade in the Indian Ocean World: Essays in Honour of Ashin Das Gupta* (Delhi: Oxford University Press, 1998). Nor do islands figure significantly in the most recent history by Michael Pearson, *The*

Indian Ocean (London & New York: Routledge, 2003).

13. See, e.g., D.R. Stoddart, ed., *Coral Islands of the Western Indian Ocean* (Washington, DC, Smithsonian Institution, 1970); G.S. Cubitt, *Islands of the Indian Ocean* (Cape Town: C. Struik, 1975); P.M. Allen and J.M. Ostheimer, *Africa and the Islands of the Western Indian Ocean*, California Institute of Technology, Munger Africana Library Notes no. 35 (Pasadena, 1976); M.D. Richmond, ed., *A Guide to the Seashores of Eastern Africa and the Western Indian Ocean Islands* (Stockholm: SIDA/SAREC, 1997). Cf. the very colonial photographic essay by T.V. Bulpin, *East Africa and the Islands* (Cape Town: Howard B. Timmins, [1956]).

14. Jean-Louis Guébourg, *Petites îles et archipels de l'océan Indien* (Paris: Éditions Karthala, 1999), p. 508.

15. A.M.H. Sheriff, "The East African coast and its role in maritime trade," in G. Mokhtar, ed., *General History of Africa*, II (Paris: UNESCO, 1981), p. 559.

16. Ibid., p. 562. For a modern study of Socotra, see Zoltan Biedermann, *Soqotra: Geschichte einer christlichen Insel im Indischen Ozean vom Altertum bis zur frühen Neuzeit* (Wiesbaden: Harrassowitz Verlag, 2006).

17. Mark Horton, *Shanga: The archaeology of a Muslim trading community on the coast of East Africa* (London: British Institute in Eastern Africa, 1996), p. 407.

18. See Pierre Vérin, *Histoire ancienne du Nord-Ouest de Madagascar* (Antananarivo: Université de Madagascar, *Taloha 5—Revue du Musée d'Art et d'Archéologie*, numero special (1972), pp. 35-64; Claude Allibert, "Cités-États et têtes de pont dans l'archipel des Comores," *Omaly sy Anio*, 33-36 (1991-1992), pp. 115-132.

19. Charles R. Boxer, and Carlos de Azevedo, *Fort Jesus and the Portuguese in Mombasa, 1593-1729* (London: Hollis and Carter, 1960); Alexandre Lobato, *Ilha de Moçambique: panorama histórico* (Lisboa: Agência-Geral do Ultramar, 1967).

20. C.S. Nicholls, *The Swahili Coast: Politics, Diplomacy and Trade on the East African Littoral 1798-1856* (London: George Allen & Unwin Ltd, 1971); Abdul Sheriff, *Slaves, Spices & Ivory in Zanzibar* (London: James Currey, 1987).

21. Horton, *Shanga*.

22. Randall L. Pouwels, "The East African Coast, c. 780 to 1900 C.E.," in Nehemia Levtzion and Randall L. Pouwels, eds., *The History of Islam in Africa* (Athens: Ohio University Press, 2000), pp. 251-271.

23. Horton, *Shanga*, p. 419.

24. Gibb, *Travels of Ibn Battuta*, II, pp. 380-381.

25. Vérin, *Les Comores* (Paris: Éditions Karthala, 1994), pp. 45-76.

26. See chapters by David C. Sperling, "The Coastal Hinterland and Interior of East Africa" and Edward A. Alpers, "East Central Africa," both in Levtzion and Pouwels, eds. *The History of Islam in Africa*, pp. 273- 302 and 303-325.

27. See, e.g., Vérin, "Madagascar," in Mokhtar, ed., *General History of* Africa, II, pp. 693-717. For a valuable summary of the different schools of thought and current thought, see Campbell, "The Debate over Malagasy Origins," *ZIFF Journal*, 2 (2005), pp. 5-14.

28. Gwyn Campbell, "The Genetic Evidence for Caste Endogamy in Madagascar," presented to the workshop on "Slave Systems in Asia and the Indian Ocean:

Their structure and change in the 19th and 20th centuries," Université d'Avignon, 2000.

29. Cited in Henry T. Wright, et al, "The Evolution of Settlement Systems in the Bay of Boeny and the Mahavavy River Valley, north-western Madagascar," *Azania*, 31 (1996), pp. 40-41.

30. Nigel Worden, "The Indian Ocean Origins of Cape Colony Slaves: A Preliminary Report," presented to the workshop on "Slave Systems in Asia and the Indian Ocean: Their structure and change in the 19th and 20th centuries," Université d'Avignon, 2000; J.T. Hardyman, "The Madagascar slave-trade to the Americas (1632-1830)," *Stvdia* (Lisbon), 11 (1963), pp. 501-521. Thomas Vernet, "Les Cités-États Swahili de archipel de Lamu, 1585-1810: Dynamiques endogènes, dynamiques exogènes (unpublished Ph.D. thesis, Université de Paris I, 2005), pp. 170-192, presents new evidence for the slave trade from northwestern Madagascar to the Swahili coast during this period.

31. Alpers, "The French Slave Trade in East Africa (1721-1810)," *Cahiers d'Études Africaines*, 37 (1970), 80-124; J.M. Filliot, *La traite des esclaves vers les Mascareignes au XVIIIe siècle* (Paris: ORSTOM, 1974), Mémoire No. 72.

32. Hubert Gerbeau, "Quelques aspects de la traite illégale des esclaves à l'Île Bourbon au XIXe siècle," *Mouvements de populations dans l'océan indien* (Paris: H. Champion, 1979), pp. 279-308; Richard B. Allen, "The Mascarene Slave-Trade and Labour Migration during the Eighteenth and Nineteenth Centuries," *Slavery & Abolition*, 24, 2 (2003), pp. 33-50 and "Licentious and Unbridled Proceedings: The Illegal Slave Trade to Mauritius and the Seychelles during the Early Nineteenth Century," *Journal of African History*, 42 (2001), pp. 91-116. My thanks to Richard Allen for generously sharing this last paper with me before publication.

33. I describe both systems at greater length in Alpers, "Becoming 'Mozambique': Diaspora and Identity in Mauritius," in Vijayalakshma Teelock and Edward A. Alpers, eds., *History, Memory, and Identity* (Port-Louis: Nelson Mandela Centre for African Culture and University of Mauritius, 2001), pp. 117-155.

34. Campbell, "Madagascar and the Slave Trade, 1810-1895," *Journal of African History*, 22 (1981), pp. 203-227; Campbell, "Madagascar and Mozambique in the Slave Trade of the Western Indian Ocean 1800-1861," in Gervase William Clarence-Smith, ed., *The Economics of the Indian Ocean Slave Trade in the Nineteenth Century* (London: Frank Cass, 1989), pp. 166-193; Campbell, "The East African Slave Trade, 1861-1895: The 'Southern' Complex," *International Journal of African Historical Studies*, 22 (1989), pp. 1-26.

35. Chapter 7 in this volume; Jean Martin, *Comores: quatre îles entre pirates et planteurs*, I (Paris: L'Harmattan, 1983), pp. 81-110.

36. Ibid., I, pp. 124-131.

37. J.S. Mangat, *A History of the Asians in East Africa c. 1886 to 1945* (Oxford: Clarendon Press, 1969); Joana Pereira Leite, "Diáspora Indiana em Moçambique," *Economia Global e Gestão*, 2 (1996), pp. 67-108. An important recent overview is Thomas R. Metcalf, *Imperial Connections: India in the Indian Ocean Arena, 1860-1920* (Berkeley: University of California Press, 2007), pp. 165-203.

38. Sophie Blanchy, *Karana et Banians–Les communautés commerçantes d'origine*

indienne à Madagascar (Paris: L'Harmattan, 1995).

39. There is an extensive literature on Indians in Mauritius, but see especially Saloni Deerpalsingh, and Marina Carter, eds., *Select Documents on Indian Immigration –Mauritius, 1834-1926*, 3 vols. (Moka: Mahatma Gandhi Institute, 1994-1996); Hugh Tinker, *A New System of Slavery: The Export of Indian Labour Overseas 1830-1920* (Oxford: Oxford University Press, 1974); Huguette Ly-Tio-Fane Pineo, *Lured Away: The Life History of Indian Cane Workers in Mauritius* (Moka: Mahatma Gandhi Institute, 1984); Marina Carter, *Servants, Sirdars and Settlers: Indians in Mauritius, 1834-1874* (Delhi and New York: Oxford University Press, 1995).

40. Surendra Bhana, ed., *Essays on Indentured Indians in Natal* (Leeds: Peepal Tree Press, 1990); Bill Freund, *Insiders and Outsiders: The Indian Working Class of Durban 1910-1990* (Portsmouth, NH: Heinemann, 1995), especially chapters 1-2. See also Metcalf, *Imperial Connections*, pp. 136-164.

41. See Armoogum Parsuraman, *From Ancestral Cultures to National Culture— Mauritius* (Moka: Mahatma Gandhi Institute, 1988), pp. 62-64.

42. Maurice Schrive and Noël J. Gueunier, "'Histoire du Peuple': Souvenirs sur l'esclavage des Makoa du nord de Madagascar," *Études Océan Indien*, 15 (1992), p. 195.

43. Alpers, "Islam in the Service of Colonialism? Portuguese Strategy during the Armed Liberation Struggle in Mozambique," *Lusotopie 1999*, pp. 165-184.

44. William Finnegan, *A Complicated War: The Harrowing of Mozambique* (Berkeley: University of California Press, 1992), pp. 33-34; Alex Vines, *Renamo: Terrorism in Mozambique* (Bloomington and Indianapolis: Indiana University Press, 1991), pp. 67-68; Vérin, *Les Comores*, pp. 214-216.

45. See "Comoros: African Union Flies in to Demand Elections," http://allafrica.com/stories/200706250188.html; for the recent AU intervention in the Comoros, see "AU troops arrive in the Comoros," BBC News, 11 March 2008, http://news.bbc.co.uk/1/hi/world/africa/7289318.stm

Notes to Chapter 4

1. Earlier versions of this article were presented at the First Congress of the Somali Studies International Association, Muqdisho, July 1980, the annual meeting of the African Studies Association, Philadelphia, November 1980, and the September 1982 conference of the African Studies Association of the United Kingdom. I have benefited by comments at all three presentations. In transcribing Soomaali names and words I have attempted to follow the official orthography, which was adopted in 1972, though scholarly usage is by no means uniform.

2. Among his many important papers, three which are especially pertinent here are James de Vere Allen, "Swahili culture and the nature of east coast settlement," *International Journal of African Historical Studies*, 14, 2 (1981), pp. 306-34; "The 'Shirazi' problem in east African coastal history," *Paideuma*, 28 (1982), pp. 9-27; and his unpublished "Settlements on the East African coast: origins, development and spread." I am grateful to my colleague Merrick Posnansky for sharing this last paper with me.

3. Randall Lee Pouwels, "Islam and Islamic leadership in the coastal communities of East Africa, 1700 to 1920" (unpublished Ph.D. thesis, UCLA, 1979). Although after I wrote this article Pouwels published his revised dissertation as the seminal *Horn and Crescent: cultural change and traditional Islam on the East African Coast, 800-1900* (Cambridge; Cambridge University Press, 1987), all citations in this chapter are from the dissertation.

4. Frederick Cooper, *Plantation Slavery on the East Coast of Africa* (New Haven and London: Yale University Press, 1977); Marguerite Ylvisaker, *Lamu in the Nineteenth Century: Land, Trade, and Politics* (Boston: African Studies Center, Boston University, 1979); Ramachandran Menon, "Zanzibar in the nineteenth century: aspects of urban development in an East African coast town" (unpublished M.A. thesis, UCLA, 1978).

5. See, for example, Cooper, "Africa and the world economy," *The African Studies Review,* 24, 2/3 (1981), pp. 13-15.

6. For a convenient summary of the evidence, see Andre Nègre, "A propos de Mogadiscio au moyen âge," *Annuaire de l'Université d'Abidjan,* série 1 (Histoire), V (1977), pp. 5-38; also Neville Chittick, "Mediaeval Mogadishu," *Paideuma,* 28 (1982), pp. 45-62.

7. Lee V. Cassanelli, *The Shaping of Somali Society: Reconstructing the History of a Pastoral People, 1600-1900* (Philadelphia: University of Pennsylvania Press, 1982), ch. 3.

8. *Documentos sobre os Portugueses em Moçambique e na África Central/Documents on the Portuguese in Mozambique and Central Africa,* I (Lisbon: Centro de Estudos Históricos Ultramarinos and National Archives of Rhodesia and Nyasaland, 1962), pp. 71, 537-539 and V (Lisbon: Centro de Estudos Históricos Ultramarinos and National Archives of Rhodesia and Nyasaland, 1966), p. 381.

9. John R. Jensen, ed., *Journal and Letter Book of Nicholas Buckeridge 1651-1654* (Minneapolis: University of Minnesota Press, 1973), p. 46.

10. Cassanelli, *Shaping,* pp. 73-74, 93-94.

11. Ugo Ferrandi, *Lugh: Emporio commerciale sul Giuba* (Roma: Società geografica italiana, 1903), p. 215.

12. India Office Records, London: Marine, L/MAR/c/586, report of Lieutenant M. Hardy, September 181 I, fl. 170 and v. The records of the India Office are now housed in the British Library.

13. Ibid., report of Captain Thomas Smee, 6 April 1811, fl. 93. The identity of this Soomaali chief cannot be determined, as a result of both Smee's corrupt rendering of his patronymic and the conflicting genealogies extant in Charles Guillain, *Documents sur l'histoire, la géographie et Ie commerce de l' Afrique Orientale,* II (Paris: A. Bertrand, 1856), p. 525; Luigi Robecchi-Bricchetti, *Somalia e Benadir* (Milano: Aliprandi, 1899), pp. 389-390; and Giuseppe Caniglia, *Genti di Somalia* (München: Rieger'sche Universitäts buchhandlung, 1921), pp. 58-65.

14. Smee's report, fl. 95.

15. W. F. W. Owen, *Narrative of Voyages to Explore the Shores of Africa, Arabia, and Madagascar* (London: R. Bentley, 1833), I, pp. 355, 359.

16. C. S. Nicholls, *The Swahili Coast* (London: George Allen & Unwin, 1971), p. 297.

17. Owen, *Narrative*, I, pp. 357-358.
18. See Chapter 5 in this volume.
19. See Cassanelli, *Shaping*, pp.156-159.
20. Guillain, *Documents*, II, pp. 590-591.
21. Ibid. II, p. 526, and III, p. 142. According to Islao Mahadala there was a major drought in the nineteenth century that necessitated the importation of food from Zanzibar: interviewed in Shingaani, 15 November 1980. My research in Muqdisho was carried out in collaboration with the Soomaali Academy of Arts and Science, whose officers provided invaluable support and who assigned me an energetic team of local counterparts without whose assistance all field work would have been impossible. To Maxamed Cabdi Allamagan, Axmed Yuusuf Faarax, and Ciismaan Yuusuf Maxamed I am thus indebted for carrying out and transcribing all of these interviews, as well as for translating some of them. At UCLA I was no less indebted to Saeed Muktag Samatar for translating the bulk of this material. My research began while teaching at the Somali National University, College of Education, Lafoole, with assistance from a Fulbright Senior Scholar Fellowship and received further support from the Research Committee (now the Committee on Research) of the Academic Senate of UCLA.
22. Cassanelli, *Shaping*, pp. 135-146, 187. For a recent history of Geledi, see Virginia Luling, *Somali Sultanate: the Geledi city-state over 150 years* (Piscataway, NJ: Transaction Publishers, 2002).
23. Caniglia, *Genti*, p. 62.
24. Giovanni Cerrina-Feroni, *Benadir* (Roma: Tip. del Ministero degli affari esteri, 1911), pp. 27-28.
25. Guillain, *Documents*, II, p. 527; W. Christopher, "Extract from a Journal by Lieut. W. Christopher . . . on the E. Coast of Africa. Dated 8th May, 1843," *Journal of the Royal Geographical Society*, 14 (1844), pp. 93, 99, who also calls the rival to Imam Axmed a nephew.
26. Guillain, *Documents*, II, p. 527; Christopher, "Extract," pp. 90, 93, 99. Cf. interview with Islao Mahadala for general confirmation of this split.
27. See Ferrandi, *Lugh*, pp. 138-139.
28. Guillain, *Documents*, II, pp. 527, 528 n. 1, 547 n. 1.
29. Christopher, "Extract," p. 98; Guillain, *Documents*, II, p. 511.
30. Ibid. II, pp. 525-526.
31. Ibid. II, p. 504.
32. Ibid. II, pp. 529-530.
33. Christopher, "Extract," pp. 87-88.
34. Guillain, *Documents*, II, pp. 507, 514, 516, 520, 526.
35. Esmond B. Martin and T. C. I. Ryan, "The slave trade of the Bajun and Benadir Coasts," *Transafrican Journal of History*, 9, 1/2 (1980), pp. 103-132.
36. Guillain, *Documents*, II, pp. 532-533; Archives Nationales, Section d'Outre-Mer [hereafter ANSOM], Paris [now Aix-en-Provence]: Océan Indien, 2/10 (2), Guillain, "Exploration de la cote orientale d'Afrique . . . pendant les années 1846-47-48 & 49: Rapport commercial–Ière partie," pp. 7-9; *British Parliamentary Papers (Slave Trade)*, 91 (cited hereafter as BPP 91, etc.), p. 268; "Produce

of the Zanzibar Dominions on the Coast and adjacent islands imported in Zanzibar in 1867-68," *Zanzibar Blue Books 1875-1880,* India Office Library, pp. 96-97, cited in Walter Brown, "A pre-colonial history of Bagamoyo" (unpublished Ph.D. thesis, Boston University, 1971), pp. 250, 253; Giorgio Sorrentino, *Ricordi del Benadir* (Napoli: Tip. A. Trani, 1912), p. 381.

37. Cassanelli, *Shaping*, pp. 137, 140.
38. ANSOM, Océan Indien 2/10 (2), Guillain, "Exploration," p. 57.
39. Christopher, "Extract," pp. 85, 87.
40. Guillain, *Documents*, II, pp. 530-531; ANSOM, Océan Indien 2/10 (2), Guillain, "Exploration," pp. 68, 13.
41. BPP 91, p. 268.
42. John Kirk, "Visit to the coast of Somali-land," *Proceedings of the Royal Geographical Society*, 27 (1873), p. 341.
43. BPP 53, p. 337, Kirk, "Memorandum on the Somali slave trade," in Kirk to Granville, Zanzibar, 31 May 1873.
44. Brown, "Bagamoyo," pp. 250, 253.
45. Sorrentino, *Ricordi*, p. 381.
46. Cooper, *Plantation Slavery*, esp. pp. 84-86, 100-101.
47. Christopher, "Extract," pp. 85, 79, 80.
48. J. L. Krapf, *Travels, Researches, and Missionary Labors During an Eighteen Years' Residence in Eastern Africa* (London: Frank Cass, 1968 [1860]), p. 112; C.E.B. Russell, *General Rigby, Zanzibar and the Slave Trade* (London: George Allen & Unwin, 1935), p. 190; BPP 92, 315, Minutes of Evidence taken before the Royal Commission on Fugitive Slaves, Captain George L. Sullivan, 11 March 1876, Q. 297-298; BPP 7, p. 28, "The slave trade on the east coast of Africa," Select Committee Report, 1871, H. A. Sullivan, para. 357.
49. Kirk, "Visit," p. 342.
50. BPP 53, pp. 337-8, Kirk, "Memorandum;" BPP 91, pp. 381, 440, H. B. Frere, "Report on a visit to Bagamoyo and the Somali Coast," 5 April 1873; BPP 92, 315, Minutes of Evidence, Rear-Admiral Arthur Cumming, 11 March 1876, Q. 202-206.
51. Martin and Ryan, "Slave trade," p. 122.
52. BPP 53, p. 338, Kirk, "Memorandum;" BPP 91, p. 440, Frere, "Report."
53. Cassanelli, *Shaping*, pp. 169-170. For the cholera epidemic, see also interview with Islao Mahadala and stories associated with the Xaji Cali Arbow Xuseenka mosque on the edge of Xamarweyn.
54. Georges Revoil, "Voyage chez les Benadirs, les Çomalis, et les Bayouns en 1882-1883," *Le Tour du Monde*, 49 (1885), p. 39.
55. Ibid., p. 36; cf. the illustration in Guillain's *Atlas,* which depicts a camel operating such a press.
56. Sorrentino, *Ricordi*, p. 22; interviews with Ciisman Nuur Adde, Xamarweyn, 23 May 1980, and with Maolin Maow Xamuud, Xamarweyn, 25 March 1980.
57. Interview with Islao Mahadala; Chapter 5 below.
58. I. M. Lewis, *Peoples of the Horn of Africa: Somali, Afar and Saho* (London: International African Institute, 1955), pp. 31-33, 51-55; Allen, "Settlements," p. 72.
59. Sorrentino, *Ricordi*, pp. 203-204, 52.

60. Robecchi-Bricchetti, *Dal Benadir - Lettre illustrate alla Società Antischiavista d'Italia* (Milano: Società Editrice "La Poligrafica", 1904), p. 58.
61. Ibid., pp. 68-69.
62. Ibid., pp. 108, 63.
63. Quoted in Cassanelli, *Shaping*, p. 225.
64. Guillain, *Documents*, II, p. 530; Nicholls, *Swahili Coast*, p. 292.
65. Cooper, *Plantation Slavery*, p. 140.
66. Guillain, *Documents*, II, p. 529.
67. Ministère des Affaires Étrangères, Paris: Correspondence Politique, Zanzibar 3/109 and v, Jablonski to M.A.E., Zanzibar, 11 January 1863; Russell, *Rigby*, pp. 96-97.
68. Guillain, *Documents*, II, p. 527.
69. Cassanelli, *Shaping*, p. 175; see also, BPP 51, 60, Captain S. M. Savine Pasley to Commodore Chas. T. Hillyar, 29 November 1866, which suggests from information gathered at Baraawe that the sultan of Geledi's attitude towards the sultan of Zanzibar may have reflected a diminution in his own political authority; Caniglia, *Genti*, p. 64.
70. BPP 91, p. 381, Frere, "Report;" Nicholls, *Swahili Coast*, p. 292.
71. Revoil, "Voyage," pp. 36, 38; cf. Allen, "Settlements," pp. 6, 63-64.
72. Robecchi-Bricchetti, *Somalia*, p. 593 n. 1.
73. Cooper, *Plantation Slavery*, 140 and n. 1.
74. Sorrentino, *Ricordi*, 425; see Robecchi-Bricchetti, *Somalia*, 195, for a photograph of Tharia Topan's commercial establishment at Baraawe.
75. Sorrentino, *Ricordi*, 13-14, 64-5, 84, 170-171, 388; for parallel practice at Luuq, see Ferrandi, *Lugh*, 341-5. The Chief *Qadi* of Muqdisho was at this time drawn from the *reer* Faaqi of Xamarweyn: Cerrina-Ferroni, *Benadir*, 28.
76. Sorrentino, *Ricordi*, 429, 134.
77. Robecchi-Bricchetti does not provide any specific figures for the *vania* population of Muqdisho, lumping them together with Arabs in both Shingaani (200) and Xamarweyn (270). He also includes an unknown category of people called Indavuena, which was a nickname for the Zanzibar governor of Muqdisho, Suliman bin Ahmed, and may have been applied to all of the Zanzibaris there, 50 of whom resided in Shingaani and 40 in Xamarweyn: Robecchi-Bricchetti, *Dal Benadir*, p. 71; Bahasan, "Mogadishu—down the corridors of history," *Heegan*, 21 March 1981, p. 3. In 1907 the Italian Governor claimed that Indian traders lived exclusively in Xamarweyn: Cerrina-Ferroni, *Benadir*, p. 22.
78. Revoil, "Voyage," pp. 38, 49-50, 52.
79. Robecchi-Bricchetti, *Somalia*, p. 107. See also, Vico Mantegazza, *Il Benadir* (Milano: Fratelli Treves, 1908), p. 135.
80. Allen, "Settlements," p. 59.
81. Pouwels, "Islam and Islamic leadership," ch. 5, quoted at p. 212. See also, T. O. Ranger, *Dance and Society in Eastern Africa* (Berkeley & Los Angeles: University of California Press, 1975); Pamela Weaver Landberg, "Kinship and community in a Tanzanian coastal village (East Africa)" (unpublished Ph.D. thesis, University of California, Davis, 1977), chs. 11 and 12.
82. Guillain, *Documents*, II, pp. 511-514, 546-547.

83. Revoil, "Voyage," p. 38.
84. Robecchi-Bricchetti, *Somalia*, pp. 114-17; Sorrentino, *Ricordi*, pp. 401, 33-34; Cerrina-Ferroni, *Benadir*, pp. 28-31, 23-28.
85. Cassanelli, *Shaping*, ch. 6, especially pp. 207-53.
86. Pouwels, "Islam and Islamic leadership," pp. 223-234.
87. Revoil, "Voyage," p. 55, and engraving on p. 41.
88. Interview with Islao Mahadala; Lewis, *Peoples*, pp. 62, 64-65; Gherardo Pàntano, *Nel Benadir—La Città di Merca e la Regione Bimal* (Livorno: S. Belforte, 1910), p. 60; J. M. Gray, "Nairuzi or Siku ya Mwaka," *Tanganyika Notes and Records*, 37 (1955), pp. 1-21; Margaret Strobel, *Muslim Women in Mombasa 1890-1975* (New Haven & London: Yale University Press, 1979), pp. 81-84.
89. Sorrentino, *Ricordi*, pp. 340-341, 102-105, and photographs on pp. 61 and 101; see Mantegazza, *Benadir*, p. 141, for reference to the violence that sometimes marked *Lab.*
90. See, for example, A. H. J. Prins, *The Swahili-Speaking Peoples of Zanzibar and the East African Coast* (London: International African Institute, 1967), p.115; J.W.T. Allen, ed., *The Customs of the Swahili People* (Berkeley & Los Angeles: University of California Press, 1981), pp. 192-193.
91. Interview with Islao Mahadala; cf. Strobel, *Muslim Women*, ch. 8. I have developed this theme more fully in Edward A. Alpers, "Dance and society in nineteenth-century Muqdisho," in Thomas Labahn, ed., *Proceedings of the Second International Congress of Somali Studies: University of Hamburg, August 1-6, 1983*, II: Archaeology and History (Hamburg, 1984), pp. 127-144.
92. See Revoil, "Voyage," p. 62.
93. Interview with Islao Mahadala; Prins, *Swahili-Speaking Peoples,* p. 115; Abdul Hamid el-Zein, *The Sacred Meadows* (Evanston: Northwestern University Press, 1974); G.E.T. Wijeyewardene, "Some aspects of village solidarity in Ki-Swahili speaking communities of Kenya and Tanganyika" (unpublished Ph.D. thesis, Cambridge University, 1961); Pouwels, "Islam and Islamic leadership," pp. 593-598.
94. See, for example, August H. Nimtz, Jr., *Islam and Politics in East Africa* (Minneapolis: University of Minnesota Press, 1980), p. 98.

Notes to Chapter 5

1. These include Renée Boser-Saravaxénis, *Les tissues de l'Afrique occidentale* (Bâle: Pharos-Verlag H. Schwabe, 1972) and *Recherche sur l'histoire des textiles traditionnels tissés et teints de l'Afrique occidentale* (Basel: Naturforschende Gesellschaft, 1975); Brigitte Menzel, *Textilien aus Westafrika*, 3 vols. (Berlin: Museum für Völkerkunde, 1972-1973); John Picton and John Mack, *African Textiles: Looms, Weaving and Design* (London: Brisith Museum Publications, 1979).
2. Interview with Shaykh Suufi Aamac Nuur, Muqdisho, 4 June 1980. For the inscription, see Enrico Cerulli, *Somalia: Scritti Editi ed Inediti*, I (Roma: Istituo Poligrafico dello Stato, 1957), pp. 7-8.

3. H.A.R. Gibb, trs. and ed., *The Travels of Ibn Battuta*, The Hakluyt Society, 2nd series, no. 117 (Cambridge: Cambridge University Press, 1962), II, p. 374.

4. Charles Guillain, *Documents sur l'histoire, la géographie et le commerce de l'Afrique orientale* (Paris: A. Bertrand, 1856), II, p. 531. For the Abgal invasion, see Lee Cassanelli, *The Shaping of Somali Society: Reconstructing the History of a Pastoral People, 1600-1900* (Philadelphia: University of Pennsylvania Press, 1982), pp. 73-74, 106-107. *Toob* is derived from Arabic and is widely used; *futa* appears to be a Benaadir dialect term.

5. Georges Revoil, "Voyage chez es Benadirs, les Çomalis, et les Bayouns en 1882-1883," *Le Tour du Monde*, 49 (1885), p. 35.

6. See Chapter 4 in this volume.

7. Guillain, *Documents*, II, pp. 520, 531-532. Cf. A.G. Hopkins, *An Economic History of West Africa* (London: Lomgman, 1973), pp. 121, 250.

8. W. Christopher, "Exract from a Journal by Lieut. W. Christopher ... 8th May 1843," *Journal of the Royal Geographical Society*, 14 (1844), p. 101.

9. Guillain, *Documents*, II, p. 532.

10. Ministère des Affaires Étrangères (Paris), Correspondence consulaire et commerciale (hereafter MAE, CCC), Zanzibar 2/251, Jablonski to Minister, Zanzibar, 2 February 1862.

11. Revoil, "Voyage," pp. 35-36. Cf. Philip Curtin, *Economic Change in Precolonial Africa* (Madison: University of Wisconsin Press, 1975), pp. 213-214.

12. Luigi Robecchi-Bricchetti, *Somalia e Benadir* (Milano: Aliprandi, 1899), p. 604 n.2.

13. See Picton and Mack, *African Textiles*, pp. 50, 99-102, 133; Marion Johnson, "Technology, Competition, and African Crafts," in Clive Dewey and A.G. Hopkins, eds., *The Imperial Impact* (London: Athlone Press, 1978), p. 259; cf. H. Ling Roth, "Studies in Primitive Looms," *Journal of the Royal Anthropological Institute*, 47 (1917), p. 49. Interview with Shaykh Suufi. Also see Vinigi Grottanelli, "Asiatic Influences on Somali Culture," *Ethnos*, 12, 4 (1947), pp. 156-157.

14. See Eberhard Fischer and Haku Shah, *Simple Weft-Ikat from South Gujarat, India* (Calico Museum of Textiles, [1973]); Chapter 1 in this volume.

15. As opposed to the situation for most of West Africa and for rural southern Somalia: Johnson, "Technology," p. 267.

16. Guillain, *Documents*, II, p. 532; Archives Nationales, Section Outre-Mer (Paris): Océan Indien 2/10 (2), Guillain, "Exploration de la côte orientale d'Afrique ... Rapport commercial, 1ère partie," p. 31; Christopher, "Extract," pp. 59, 91, 82; J.L. Krapf, *Travels, Researches and Missionary Labours during an Eighteen Years' Residence in Eastern Africa* (London: Trübner, 1860), p. 113. For Geledi, see the recent book by Virginia Luling, *Somali Sultanate: the Geledi city-state over 150 years* (Piscataway, NJ: Transaction Publishers, 2002).

17. Revoil, "Voyage," p. 35.

18. Robecchi-Bricchetti, *Somalia*, p. 604, n.2.

19. Interview with Shaykh Suufi; Ferdinando Bigi, "Recenti sviluppi e prospettive della cotonicoltura in Somalia," *Rivista di Agricoltura Subtropicale e Tropicale*, 47, 7-9 (1953), p. 296.

20. Robecchi-Bricchetti, *Somalia*, pp. 83, 84, 606, quoting Giorgio Mylius.

21. On the high cost of Gujarati cotton before the cotton famine, see Alexander Mackay, *Western India: Reports addressed to the Chambers of Commerce of Manchester, Liverpool, Blackburn, and Glasgow*, ed. James Robertson (London: N. Cooke, 1853), pp. 155-172. For the period after 1860, see Anthony S. Chullikal, *Economic Progress and Price Behaviour, India-United Kingdom 1860-1966* (Louvain: Université Catholique de Louvain, 1968), pp. 60-66.
22. Chapter 4 above.
23. See Frederick Cooper, *Plantation Slavery on the East Coast of Africa* (New Haven and London: Yale University Press, 1977); Jonathan Glassman, *Feasts and Riot: Revelry, Rebellion, and Popular Consciousness on the Swahili Coast, 1856-1888* (Portsmouth, NH: Heinemann, 1995).
24. Guillain, *Documents*, II, p. 532 (1,000); MAE, CCC, Zanzibar 2/251v., Jablonski to Minister, Zanzibar, 2 February 1862 (800); Robecchi-Bricchetti, *Somalia*, p. 604 n.2 (1,000); Giorgio Sorrentino, *Ricordi di Benadir* (Napoli: Tip. A. Trani, 1912), p. 403 (1,000); interview with Shaykh Suufi.
25. Guillain, *Documents*, II, p. 532; Robecchi-Bricchetti, *Somalia*, p. 604 n.2, 605; Sorrentino, *Ricordi*, pp. 17, 403.
26. As testified to in Guillain (1847-1848) and Jablonski (1862), as well as by Grotta-nelli, *Pescatori dell'Oceano Indiano* (Roma: Cremonese, 1955), pp. 186-187, citing Von der Decken (1865) and Mauch (1867).
27. Vittorio Bòttego, *L'esplorazione del Giuba* (Roma: Società ed. Nazionale, 1900), pp. 332-334; Ugo Ferrandi, *Lugh: Emporio commerciale sul Giuba* (Roma: Società Geografica Italiana, 1903), pp. 215, 368; Gustavo Chiesi, *La colonizzazione Europea nell'Est Africa* (Torino: Unione tip.-editrice Torinese, 1909), p. 350.
28. Ferrandi, *Lugh*, pp. 215, 368.
29. Revoil, "Voyage," p. 60; Sorrentino, *Ricordi*, pp. 227, 388.
30. Robecchi-Bricchetti, *Somalia*, pp. 84, 86.
31. Chiesi, *Colonizzazione*, pp. 347-348.
32. For the dramatically declining cost of American raw cotton by the 1890s, see M.B. Hammond, *The Cotton Industry: An Essay in American Economic History*, Publications of the American Economic Association, New Series, No. 1 (1897), p. 332; for the threefold expansion of American cotton cloth exports, see U.S. Department of Treasury, Bureau of Statistics, *Foreign Commerce and Navigation of the United States* (Washington, D.C., 1893), p. 134 and (Washington, D.C., 1902), p. 152. For a recent study of the price of raw cotton, see Gavin Wright, *Old South, New South: Revolutions in the Southern Economy since the Civil War* (New York: Basic Books, 1986). My thanks to Naomi Lamoreaux for this reference.
33. Revoil, "Voyage," p. 36. Carthamus also yields a rose dye.
34. Interview with Shaykh Suufi.
35. Robecchi-Bricchetti, *Somalia*, pp. 604-605; Sorrentino, *Ricordi*, p. 16.
36. Ibid., p. 84; Chiesi, *Colonizzazione*, p. 348. Cf. Johnson, "Technology," p. 265, for yarn imports to West Africa.
37. Chiesi, *Colonizzazione*, p. 351.
38. Ibid., p. 352. Cf. T. Carletti, *I Problemi del Benadir* (Viterbo: n.p., 1912), p. 124;

Angelo Cortinois, *La Somalia Italiana* (Milano: Francesco Vallardi, 1913), pp. 74-75; and Giuseppe Piazza, *Il Benadir* (Roma: Bontempelli & Invernizzi, 1913), p. 38.

39. See Sorrentino, *Ricordi*, pp. 421, 432; Gherardo Pàntano, *Nel Benadir: La Città di Merca e la Regione Bimal* (Livorno: S. Belforte, 1910), pp. 22, 111; Carletti, *Attraverso il Benadir* (Viterbo: Tip. Agnesotti, 1910), p. 29.

40. Corrado Zoli, *Oltre Giuba: Notizie Raccolte a cura del Commissariato Generale nel Primo Anno do occupazione Italiana (1925-1926)* (Roma: Sindacato Italiano Arti Grafiche, 1927), pp. 356-357. Earlier descriptions of these cloths with their trademarks are in Bòttego, *L'esplorazione*, p. 333, and Ferrandi, *Lugh*, pp. 361-363.

41. Giuseppe Stefanini, *In Somalia: note e impressioni di viaggio* (Firenze: Le Monnier, 1922), p. 39.

42. Pàntano, *Nel Benadir*, p. 120; interview with Shaykh Suufi. *Bengala* was a type of colored Indian cloth of which this was presumably a copy.

43. Zoli, *Oltre Giuba*, p. 358; cf. William Travis, *The Voice of the Turtle* (London: George Allen & Unwin, 1967), p. 162.

44. F.M. Hunter, *An Account of the British Settlement of Aden in Arabia* (London: Cass, 1968 [1877]), p. 105; cf. Johnson, "Technology," p. 263, for West Africa.

45. Pàntano, *Nel Benadir*, p. 120; Stefanini, *In Somalia*, p. 39.

46. Pàntano, *Nel Benadir*, pp. 27-29, 34-36.

47. See Nello Puccioni, *La Popolazioni Indigene della Somalia Italiana* (Bologna: I. Cappelli, 1937), p. 87.

48. Robecchi-Bricchetti, *Somalia*, pp. 84, 87; Chiesi, *Colonizzazione*, p. 350; Carletti, *Problemi*, p. 124; Pàntano, *Nel Benadir*, pp. 22, 111.

49. Luigi Cufino, *Nell'Oceano Indiano: Rendiconto di una missione inviata della Società Africana d'Italia, Febraio-Giugno 1914* (Napoli: Società Africana d'Italia, 1916), p. 112; Carlo Riveri, *Relazione presentata dall'avv. Carlo Riveri il Ottobre 1921 sulla situazione generale della Somalia Italiana* (Roma, n.d.), p. 97. There is no indication of the number of pieces in each bale.

50. Pàntano, *Nel Benadir*, p. 29, quoting Carletti, *Attraverso*, p. 24; Pietro Barile, *Colonizzazione Fascista nella Somalia Meriodionale* (Roma: Società Italiana Arte Grafiche, 1935), p. 144.

51. Puccioni, *Popolazioni*, p. 87; Guido Corni, *Somalia Italiana*, I (Milano: Editoriale Arte e Storia, 1937), pp. 326, 330; interview with Shaykh Suufi.

52. I.M. Lewis, *The Modern History of Somaliland* (London: Weidenfield & Nicholson, 1965), p. 110 [same pagination in later editions]. Cf. Johnson, "Technology," pp. 265-266.

53. Lewis, *Modern History*, pp. 117-118; International Bank for Reconstruction and Development, *The Economy of the Trust Territory of Somaliland* (Washington, D.C., 1957), pp. 40, 36, 62.

54. Unless otherwise noted, the following three paragraphs, including quotations, are from the International Labour Office [ILO], Expanded Programme of Technical Assistance, *Report to the Government of the Republic of Somalia on the Development of Handicrafts and Small-Scale Industries*, ILO/TAP/Somalia/R.2 (Geneva, 1963), pp. 20-21, §68-73.

55. Ibid., pp. 84-85, §345.
56. Interview with Shaykh Suufi.
57. See also Travis, *Voice*, pp. 162-163.
58. Somali Democratic Republic, UDHIS, *The Cooperative Movement in the Somali Socialist Revolution* (Mogadishu, 1978), pp. 12-13.
59. ILO, Jobs and Skills Programme for Africa, *Economic Transformation in a Socialist Framework: An Employment and Basic Needs Oriented Development Strategy for SOMALIA* (Addis Ababa, 1977), pp. 151-152, 197, 201, 337.
60. Ibid., p. 155.
61. Cf. the similarly narrow margin of survival among handloom weavers in the Yemen and India: Shlomo Dov Goitein, "Portrait of a Yemeni Weavers' Village," *Jewish Social Studies*, 17, 1 (1955), p. 12; K.S. Venkataraman, *The Hand-loom Industry in South India* (Madras: Diocesan Press, 1940), pp. 29, 183-186; and R.G. Kakade, *A Socio-Economic Survey of Weaving Communities in Sholapur* (Poona: D.R. Gadgil for the Gokhale Institute of Politics and Economics, 1947), pp. 147-166.
62. Personal communication from Cali Maxamed Sugaal.

Notes to Chapter 6

1. That we know anything at all about the *kitimiri* spirit possession cult is due to the intellectual curiosity of Père Anton Horner, who served as the first vice-prefect apostolic of Zanzibar and directed the mission of the Holy Ghost Fathers [Spiritans] in East Africa from 1863 to his death in 1880. Horner was a careful ethnographer, despite his Eurocentric prejudices, and his description of *kitimiri* accords well with later descriptions of similar spirit possession cults. It is contained in a long letter to his metropolitan superior, Monsignor Jean-Joseph Gaume, who was Apostolic Pronotary to Paris, as part of a larger analysis of Zanzibar society. See Archive de la Congrégation du St. Esprit [Arch.C.S.Sp.], Paris [now outside of Paris at Chevilly-Larue], Box 196-A/XII, Horner to Gaume, Zanzibar, 1 July 1869, pp. 24-30. I am indebted to the late Père Bernard Nöel, *archiviste* of this important private collection, for permission to consult its records during June 1978. My research during this period was generously supported by a fellowship from the National Endowment for the Humanities. Two discussions of Swahili spirit possession that refer to and take some issue with my interpretation in this article as originally published are Linda Giles, "Possession Cults on the Swahili Coast: A Re-examination of Theories of Marginiality," *Africa*, 57, 2 (1987), pp. 234-258 and Tapio Nisula, *Everyday Spirits and Medical Interventions: Ethnographic and historical notes on therapeutic conventions in Zanzibar Town*, Transactions of the Finnish Anthropological Association No. 43 (Saarijärvi: Gummerus Kirjapaino Oy, 1999), pp. 87-96.
2. Margaret Strobel, *Muslim Women in Mombasa 1890-2975* (New Haven: Yale University Press, 1979), esp. ch. 2.
3. John Gray, *History of Zanzibar from the Middle Ages to 1856* (London: Oxford University Press, 1962), pp. 156-169; C.S. Nicholls, *The Swahili Coast* (London: George Allen & Unwin, 1971), pp. 30-31, 281-282; see John Middleton and Jane

Campbell, *Zanzibar: Its Society and Its Politics* (London: Oxford University Press, 1965), pp. 26-28, for a description of soils.

4. Mtoro bin Mwinyi Bakari, *The Customs of the Swahili People,* ed. and trans. J.W.T. Allen (Berkeley: University of California Press, 1981), chs. 15-17, for a representative Swahili man's delineation of the sexual division of labor, in this case of Bagamoyo.

5. For a statement of this theoretical position, see Karen Sacks, "Engels Revisited: Women, the Organization of Production, and Private Property," in Reyna Reiter, ed., *Toward an Anthropology of Women* (New York: Monthly Review Press, 1975), pp. 211-234, and Janet Bujra, "Introductory: Female Solidarity and the Sexual Division of Labour," in Patricia Caplan and Janet Bujra, eds., *Women United, Women Divided* (London: Tavistock, 1978), pp. 13-45.

6. I have tried to work out some of these ideas in "State, Merchant Capital and Gender Relations in Southern Mozambique to the End of the Nineteenth Century: Some Tentative Hypotheses," *African Economic History*, 13 (1985), pp. 23-55. For a comparative example, see Kate Young, "Modes of Appropriation and the Sexual Division of Labour: A Case Study from Oaxaca, Mexico," in Annette Kuhn and AnnMarie Wolpe, eds., *Feminism and Materialism* (London: Routledge and Kegan Paul, 1978), pp. 124-154.

7. Ramachandran Menon, "Zanzibar in the Nineteenth Century: Aspects of Urban Development in an East African Coastal Town" (unpublished M.A. thesis, U.C.L.A., 1978), pp. 41-44, 62-63, 73. For a more recent detailed examination of the history of Zanzibar Town, see Abdul Sheriff, ed., *The History & Conservation of Zanzibar Stone Town* (Zanzibar: Department of Archives, Museums & Antiquities/London: James Currey/Athens: Ohio University Press, 1995).

8. Menon, "Zanzibar," p. 36.

9. Ibid., pp. 44-46.

10. Ibid., p. 71.

11. Karen Sacks, *Sisters and Wives* (Urbana: University of Illinois Press, 1982); Eleanor Leacock, "Interpreting the Origins of Gender Inequality: Conceptual and Historical Problems," *Dialectical Anthropology*, 7 (1983), pp. 263-284.

12. Randall Lee Pouwels, "Islam and Islamic Leadership in the Coastal Communities of Eastern Africa, 1700 to 1914" (unpublished Ph.D. thesis, U.C.L.A., 1979), especially Part III. See also the seminal book that emerged from the revised dissertation, Randall L. Pouwels, *Horn and Crescent: Cultural change and traditional Islam on the East African Coast, 800-1900* (Cambridge: Cambridge University Press, 1987).

13. Pouwels, "Islam and Islamic Leadership," pp. 187-188.

14. B.G. Martin, "Notes on Some Members of the Learned Classes of Zanzibar and East Africa in the Nineteenth Century," *African Historical Studies,* 4, 3 (1971), p. 540.

15. For a devastating critique of the concept of the "status of women," see Barbara Rogers, *The Domestication of Women* (London: Kegan Paul, 1981), pp. 29-32; also Michelle Zimbalist Rosaldo, "The Use and Abuse of Anthropology: Reflections on Feminism and Cross-Cultural Understanding," *Signs*, 5, 3 (1980), p. 401.

16. J. Spencer Trimingham, *Islam in East Africa* (Oxford: Clarendon Press, 1964), p. 85.
17. A.H.J. Prins, *The Swahili-Speaking Peoples of Zanzibar and the East African Coast* (London: International African Institute, 1967), p. 62.
18. W.H. Ingrams, *Zanzibar: Its History and Its People* (London: Witherby, 1931), pp.148-150, 160, who notes in conclusion that "such a thing would be unlikely to happen nowadays." For the seventeenth- and eighteenth-century queens of Zanzibar, see also John Gray, *History of Zanzibar*, pp. 51-54, 83.
19. For a thesis subscribing to the theory of sexual parallelism, see Karla O. Poewe, *Matrilineal Ideology* (London: Academic Press, 1981).
20. Martin, "Notes," pp. 531-534.
21. Cf. Patricia Caplan, "Gender, Ideology and Modes of Production on the Coast of East Africa," *Paideuma*, 28 (1982), pp. 29-43.
22. Hans Koritschaner, "Ngoma ya Sheitani: An East African Native Treatment for Psychical Disorder," *Journal of the Royal Anthropological Institute*, 50 (1936), p. 209; Isaria N. Kimambo, *A Political History of the Pare of Tanzania, c. 1500-1900* (Nairobi: East African Publishing House, 1969), pp. 189-190; Steven Feierman, *The Shambaa Kingdom; A History* (Madison: University of Wisconsin Press, 1974), pp. 200-202; cf. Gerhard Lindblom, *The Akamba in British East Africa; an ethnological monograph*, 2nd ed. (Uppsala: Appelbergs boktryckeri aktiebolag, 1920), pp. 230-240, and Grace Harris, "Possession 'Hysterics' in a Kenya Tribe," *American Anthropologist*, 59 (1957), pp. 1046-1066. Neither Lindblom nor Harris addresses the question of *mbepho* and *pepo* possession, respectively, among the Kamba and Taita, but it seems quite possible that the latter adopted the concept from the coast, too.
23. Mary Douglas, *Implicit Meanings* (London: Routledge & Kegan Paul, 1975), pp. 64-61.
24. Joseph B.F. Osgood, *Notes of Travel or Recollections of Majunga, Zanzibar, Muscat, Aden, and Other Eastern Ports* (Salem: G. Creamer, 1854), pp. 28-29. Both Pouwels and Strobel have suggested to me that the launching of toy boats might have occurred at the conclusion of the Swahili New Year, but so far as I have been able to determine, Osgood was not at Zanzibar at that time of year, which in the mid-nineteenth century was the month of August. See John Gray, "*Nairuz* or *Siku ya Mwaka*," *Tanganyika Notes and Records*, 38 (1955), pp. 1-22, and "Nairuzi—Some Additional Notes," *Tanganyika Notes and Records*, 41 (1955), pp. 69-72.
25. Ingrams, *Zanzibar*, pp. 484-485; Caplan, *Choice and Constraint in a Swahili Communityy* (London: Oxford University Press, 1975), p. 140; Michael Joshua Lambek, "Human Spirits: Possesion and Trance Among the Malagasy Speakers of Mayotte (Comoro Islands)" (unpublished Ph.D. dissertation, University of Michigan, 1978), I, p. 74. Lambek's revised dissertation has been published as *Human Spirits: A Cultural Account of Trance in Mayotte* (Cambridge: Cambridge University Press, 1981), but all of my references are to the original dissertation.
26. Carl Velten, *Desturi za Wasuaheli na khabari na desturi za shari'a za Wasuaheli* (Göttingen: Vandenhoeck & Ruprecht, 1903), p. 162; translated in Mtoro bin

Bakari, *Customs*, p. 109.
27. J.L. Krapf, *A Dictionary of the Suaheli Language* (London: Trübner & Co,, 1882), p. 312.
28. J.E.E. Craster, *Pemba, The Spice Island of Zanzibar* (London: T.F. Unwin, 1913), p. 305; Robert P. Gray, "The Shetani Cult Among the Segeju of Tanzania," in John Beattie and John Middleton, eds., *Spirit Mediumship and Society in Africa* (London: Routledge & Kegan Paul, 1969), p.174; see also Caplan, *Choice and Constraint*, p. 100. My research for this paper has made me realize the enormous complexity of the historical dissemination and local adaptation of various possessing spirits. Pemba is the most important East African source of these spirits and consequently certain spirits, such as the category of *kibwengu*, which are land spirits on Pemba, become sea (*bahari*) or seashore (*pwani*) spirits elsewhere: for example, Koritschoner, "Ngoma ya Sheitani," p. 211; Charles Sacleux, *Dictionnaire Swahili-Français* (Paris: Institut d'Ethnographie, 1939), pp. 350, 765; Caplan, *Choice and Constraint*, p. 112.
29. Sacleux, *Dictionnaire*, p. 872: "*Mgonjwa akisema kiArabu, hatta neno modya, huambiwa ana pepo ya t.*"
30. Arch.C.S.Sp. 196-A/XII, Horner to Gaume, Zanzibar, 1 July 1869, 24; Velten, *Desturi*, p. 162; Mtoro bin Bakari, *Customs*, p. 109.
31. Velten, *Desturi*, pp. 13-15; Mtoro bin Bakari, *Customs*, p. 11; Sacleux, *Dictionnaire*, p. 872. Slightly different varieties of *tari* are apparently used for the *tari* dance and *maulidi* celebrations: see Ingrams, *Zanzibar*, pp. 400, 405. Among the Swahili of Mombasa, part of the wedding celebrations involved a dance called *tari la ndia* ("street *tari*"): Sir Mbarak Ali Hinawy, "Notes on Customs in Mombasa," *Swahili*, 34, 1 (1964), p. 18; See also Hans Zache, "Sitten and Gebräuche der Suaheli," *Zeitschrift für Ethnologie*, 31 (1899), pp. 80, 85.
  The earliest reference to the Prophet's *maulidi* is made by Horner in the 1860s, but Kirkman has recently published a fine description of a private circumcision *maulidi* with tom-toms (probably a variety of *tari*) dating to 1838, though its author does not give it any name. See Gaume, *Voyage*, 215; James S. Kirkman, ed., "The Zanzibar Diary of John Studdy Leigh, Part 1," *International Journal of African Historical Studies*, 13, 2 (1980), pp. 291-292. On *maulidi* celebrations of the Prophet's birthday, see Jan Knappert, *Swahili Islamic Poetry* (Leiden: Brill, 1971), I, ch. 2, esp. pp. 41-48.
32. L.W.C. van den Berg, *Le Hadramout et les Colonies Arabes dans l'Archipel Indien* (Batavia: imprimerie du gouvernement, 1886), p. 91.
33. Ibid., p. 85; Becker, "Materials," 34, 43, 46; Martin, "Notes," 530; Pouwels, "Islam and Islamic Leadership," pp. 451-457, 510 n. 2.
34. Monica Wilson, "The Wedding Cakes: A Study of Ritual Change," in J.S. La Fontaine, ed., *The Interpretation of Ritual* (London: Tavistock Publications, 1972), pp. 192-200, quoted at p. 200.
35. On sexual relations and jealousy in Swahili society, see Strobel, *Muslim Women*, pp. 48-51, 86-89.
36. Lyndon Harries, *Swahili Poetry* (Oxford: Clarendon Press, 1962), pp. 227-233, translating the text in Sacleux, *Dictionnaire*, pp. 1108-1112; cf. Pouwels, "Islam and Islamic Leadership," pp. 505-506, translating the shorter version collected by

Sh. Abdallah Salih Farsy, "Baadhi ya Wanavyuoni wa Kishafii wa Mashariki ya Afrika," unpublished MS, 4.

37. Emily Reute, *Memoirs* of *an Arabian Princess* (New York: Appleton, 1886), p. 6; Norman R. Bennett, ed., *The Zanzibar Letters of Edward D. Ropes, Jr. 1862-1892* (Boston: African Studies Center, Boston University, 1973), p. 96 n. 267. For a recent, definitive edition of Reute's memoir, see Sayyida Salme/Emily Reute, *An Arabian Princess between Two Worlds*, ed. with an introduction by E. Von Donzel (London/New York/Köln: E.J. Brill, 1993).

38. See Strobel, *Muslim Women,* pp. 73-76.

39. Velten, *Desturi,* 147-148; Mtoro bin Bakari, *Customs,* 100.

40. Reute, *Memoirs*, pp. 215-216.

41. There is an extensive modern literature on *zaar* possession in Islamic Northeast Africa, including I.M. Lewis, "Spirit Possession in Northern Somaliland," in Beattie and Middleton, eds., *Spirit Mediumship,* pp. 189-219; Lucie Wood Saunders, "Varieties in Zar Experience in an Egyptian Village," in Vincent Crapanzano and Vivian Garrison, eds., *Case Studies in Spirit Possession* (New York: Wiley, 1977), pp. 177-191; Soheir A. Morsy, "Sex Differences and Folk Illness in an Egyptian Village," in Lois Beck and Nikki Keddie, eds., *Women in the Muslim World* (Cambridge, MA: Harvard University Press, 1978), pp. 599-616; Pamela Constantinides, "Women's Spirit Posssession and Urban Adaptation in the Muslim Northern Sudan," in Caplan and Bujra, eds., *Women United*, pp. 185-205.

42. Christiann Snouck Hurgronje, *Mekka in the Latter Part of the Nineteenth Century*, trs. J.H. Monahan (Leiden and London: Brill, 1930), p. 100; Paul Kahle, "Zâr-Beschwörungen in Egypten," *Der Islam,* 3 (1912), pp. 4-7; Constantinides, "Women's Spirit Possession," p. 186; Enrico Cerulli, "Zar," *Encyclopaedia of Islam* (Leiden: Brill, 1936), IV, p. 1217. See also William T. Amatruda, "The Ethiopian Slave Trade c. 1800-1914: An Overview," paper for the Seminar in African History, UCLA, December 1971; Ralph A. Austen, "The Islamic Red Sea Slave Trade: An Effort at Quantification," paper for the Fifth International Conference on Ethiopian Studies, University of Chicago, April 1978. For a more recent calculation by Austen see his "The 19th Century Islamic Slave Trade from East Africa (Swahili and Red Sea Coasts): A Tentative Census," in William Gervase Clarence-Smith, ed., *The Economics of the Indian Ocean Slave Trade in the Nineteenth Century* (London & Totowa, NJ: Frank Cass, 1989), pp. 21-44.

43. Snouck Hurgronje, *Mekka*, p. 101; Kahle, "Zâr-Beschwörungen," pp. 2, 7-8; and Constantinides, "Women's Spirit Possession," pp. 195-196, who notes that the exception to female leadership in *zaar* is homosexual males. Among Somali women these female leaders are called *alaaqad*: Lewis, "Spirit Possession," p. 204.

44. For Abyssinian slaves at the Omani court, see Frederick Cooper, *Plantation Slavery on the East Coast of Africa* (New Haven & London: Yale University Press, 1977), p. 198. The *habashi* or Abyssinian spirit that was noted in the twentieth century on the coast is generically distinct from *zaar* possession, being no more than one among many exotic spirits in Swahili possession. See R. Skene,

"Arab and Swahili Dances and Ceremonies," *Journal of the Royal Anthropological Institute,* 47 (1917), p. 429, noting that while little was known of the *habashi* spirit at Malindi, it was "believed to have possessed people in Zanzibar and Kismayu;" Sacleux, *Dictionnaire,* p. 765, where he includes the enigmatic sentence: "*pèpo ya Habucia hupungiwa tandiko, kwani hawèsi kukaa cini.* The *habashi* spirit is always exorcised spread out [on a mat], because it/the patient cannot sit on the ground." Skene, "Arab and Swahili Dances," p. 421, notes the possibility of elderly women serving as *mafundi* or *waganga,* as does Koritschoner, "Ngoma ya Sheitani," p. 214. Skene even names at least one such woman (out of twelve *mafundi* known to him) on p. 423. F.M.T. Topan, "Oral Literature in a Ritual Setting: The Role of Spirit Songs in a Spirit-Mediumship Cult of Mombasa, Kenya" (unpublished Ph.D. dissertation, University of London, 1972), p. 114, found that women outnumbered men as *waganga* in the cult that he studied, but remarked that "it is significant that it is men who have much more 'spiritual' power than women" and who, therefore, had overwhelmingly the largest number of female adherents (seven men had twenty-nine followers, while seventeen women had only four followers).

45. Edward Steere, *A Handbook of the Swahili Language as Spoken at Zanzibar,* 4th ed., revised by A.B. Hellier (London: The Sheldon Press, 1955 [1870]), p. 170; Krapf, *Dictionary,* p. 260.

46. Ingrams, *Zanzibar,* p. 454. There were two fundi who apparently specialized in *kitimiri* spirit possession at Mombasa in 1912: see Public Record Office, London [now National Archives of the United Kingdom, Kew], Foreign Office 367/304, Clarke to Grey, 20 August 1912, enclosing list compiled by H.R. Cartwright, Commandant of Police. I am grateful to Margaret Strobel for sending me this reference, which was passed along to her by Frederick Cooper.

47. Topan, "Oral Literature," pp. 117-120; Sacleux, *Dictionnaire,* pp. 640, 412.

48. Strobel, *Muslim Women,* pp. 196-206.

49. Velten, *Desturi,* p. 162; Mtoro bin Bakari, *Customs,* pp. 109-110, 286 n. 17; Pouwels, "Islam and Islamic Leadership," pp. 349 n. 134, and 400-404, for a discussion of Omani-derived astrology (*falak*), Krapf, *Dictionary,* p. 368; cf. Caplan. *Choice and Constraint,* p. 107, for a distinction between *kupiga ramli* and *kutazamia* as Quranic and non-Quranic forma of divination.

50. Caplan, *Choice and Constraint,* p. 107.

51. Harries, *Swahili Poetry,* p. 231, v. 16.

52. R.F. Gray, "Shetani Cult," p. 177.

53. The available statistics are woefully inadequate, but see Menon, "Zanzibar," 45-52, 91 and n. 76; Cooper, *Plantation Slavery,* pp. 184-186.

54. Cf. Skene, "Arab and Swahili Dances," p. 422; R.F. Gray, "Shetani Cult," pp. 177, 179; Caplan, *Choice and Constraint,* p. 120; Topan, "Oral Literature," p. 98; Strobel, *Muslim Women,* p. 169.

55. On the link between the turban and putting on Arab airs, see Ingrams, *Zanzibar,* p. 309, and 310 for *msuruaki,* also Prins, *Swahili-Speaking Peoples,* p. 112. For facial decoration, cf. Velten, *Desturi,* p. 146; Mtoro bin Bakari, *Customs,* p. 99. For a helpful analysis of color symbolism among a closely related people, see Marja-Liisa Swantz, *Ritual and Symbol in Transitional Zaramo Society with*

Special Reference to Women (Lund: Gleerup, 1970), pp. 241-255.

56. Horner translates these words as though they related to the word *tayari*, "ready," but they are part of a vocabulary peculiar to spirit exorcism and seem to indicate being in a state of deep personal need. See Frederick Johnson, *A Standard Swahili-English Dictionary* (Oxford: Oxford University Press, 1939), pp. 389, 445; cf. Velten, *Desturi*, p. 156, who translates *taileni* as "*loben*," "to praise," as does J.W.T. Allen in Mtoro bin Bakari, *Customs*, p. 105. Existing clients of a cult are usually called *wateja*, but Horner does not record this term. See Johnson, *Standard Dictionary*, p. 308.

57. This passage is a difficult one in Horner's MS (p. 28): "*Mwana mavoua, anakuita, pande mrima, nikouene.*" First, he inserts a "v" in *maua*, suggesting possible confusion with a Pemba sea spirit called *mvua*, "rain": Craster, *Pemba*, p. 305. Second, the use of *mrima*, that is *mlima*, "mountain," is peculiar. In Swahili spirit possession the spirit is said to rise up to the head (*kupanda kichwani*) and, on the other hand, certain land spirits, for example *Kilimandja* – which is named by Horner – are said to live on the tops of mountains and to possess women. In the overall context of Horner's description, I have decided provisionally to allow a symbolic equation of *mrima/mlima* with *kichwa*, while admitting that this is done primarily for convenience. See, for example, Velten, *Desturi*, p. 146; Mtoro bin Bakari, *Customs*, p. 99; Skene, "Arab and Swahili Dances," p. 421. It is also worth noting that neither Mtoro bin Bakari, *Customs*, p. 110, nor Ingrams, *Zanzibar*, p. 407, includes a small iron bell among the instruments played at the *ngoma ya kitimiri*.

58. Velten, *Desturi*, p. 161; also Caplan, *Choice and Constraint*, p. 119.

59. Topan, "Oral Literature," pp. 284-286, who names two spirits of the *kipemba* "tribe."

60. Lambek, "Human Spirits," I, p. 54 and n.7. Cf. Skene, "Arab and Swahili Dances," p. 431, for names of spirits of the *kiarabu* "tribe," among others; and R.F. Gray, "Shetani Cult," pp. 171 and 181, who notes that spirits have individual names and personalities, as well as genealogies, but does not provide any in his article.

61. Skene, "Arab and Swahili Dancers," pp. 431, 430; Topan, "Oral Literature," p. 118. Cf. Mtoro bin Bakari, *Customs*, p. 79. We must recognize, however, that notions about possession by female spirits may well have changed between 1869 and 1913, when Skene made his observations, especially if gender roles had continued to rigidify during this period. It may also be significant that it was the *kiarabu* spirits which are gender identified in view of my contention that *ustaarabu*, and the enforcement of *shari'a* hardened gender differences.

62. Ingrams, *Zanzibar*, pp. 149-150, 160. There is also an islet called Mwana Mwana immediately to the north of Tumbatu Island, off the northwest coast of Zanzibar Island (Unguja).

63. Lambek, "Human Spirits," I, pp. 54 and 84 n. 8.

64. The definitive analysis is by J.F. Baré, *Pouvoir des Vivants, Langage des Morts: Idéo-Logiques Sakalava* (Paris: François Maspero, 1977).

65. Craster, *Pemba,*, p. 313; R.F. Gray, "Shetani Cult," p. 176.

66. J. Tkacsch, "Mahra," *Encyclopaedia of Islam* (Leiden and London: Brill, 1934),

III, pp. 138-144; also Tkatsch, "Sokotra," ibid., IV, 476-481. Mahri is the adjectival form of Mahra; Socotra Island was formally subordinate to the Mahri Sultanate of Qishn and was politically and economically dependent upon Oman from the late 1830s, which may also explain the link with Zanzibar.

67. Paret, "*Ashab at-Kahf*," *Encyclopaedia of Islam*, new edition (Leiden and London, 1960), I, p. 691.

68. Abdullah Yusuf Ali, *The Meaning of the Glorious Qur'an*, 3rd ed. (Cairo: Dar al-Kitab al-Masri, 1938), pp. 733, 735.

69. See, for example, Alla'Din Ali Ibn Ahmed Ibn Ibrahim al-Bagdadi, *The Kasin Commentary* (Cairo, 1317/1899-1900), III, 194, which was originally written in 725/1324-1325. My thanks go to Mahmoud El Sheikh for locating and translating this and other commentaries in Arabic on the *Surat al-kahf* for me.

70. Muhammad Muhammad al-Madani, *The Useful Stories (As We See Them in the Quran)* (Cairo, 1383-1384/1964), p. 62; see also Ibn Katir, *The Commentary of Ibn Katir* (Beirut, 1385-1386/1966), IV, p. 374, and Louis Massignon, "Les 'Sept Dormants' Apocalypse de l'Islam," (1950) in Massignon, *Opera Minora, III* (Beirut: Dar al-Maaref, 1963), pp. 105-106, 108. Many years after writing this article I purchased an interesting popular booklet in Port-Louis, Mauritius, on the Seven Sleepers by Mohamed Yasin Owadally, *As'hab-ul-kahf, The Shocking Story of the Sleepers* (Vacoas: Éditions Le Printemps, 1998) that bears witness to the continuing significance of this miraculous story of their resurrection and the faithful dog who guarded them.

71. Trimingham, *Islam in East Africa*, p. 80; Krapf, *Dictionary*, p. 121.

72. Abdullah Yusuf Ali, *Glorious Qur'an*, p. 730 n. 2334; Massignon, "Les 'Sept Dormants'," p. 114, and "Le Culte Liturgique e Populaire des VII Dormants Martyrs d'Ephèse (Ahl al-Kahf): Trait d'Union Orient-Occident Entre l'Islam et le Chrétienté," (1961), réuni par Y. Moubarac, in Massignon, *Opera Minora, III*, p. 143.

73. Massignon, "Les 'Sept Dormants'," p. 104.

74. Knappert, *Swahili Islamic Poetry*, p. 87.

75. Massignon, "Le Culte Liturgique," pp. 167-170, 171-173. Massignon (p. 145) documents the public recitation of the eighteenth sura in Egypt and Saudi Arabia only. Mr. El Sheikh has provided me with verification from the Sudan.

76. C.H. Becker, "Materials for the Understanding of Islam in German East Africa," ed. and trs. B.G. Martin, *Tanzania Notes and Records*, 68 (1958), pp. 52-57.

77. Edmond Doutté, *Magie et Religion dans l'Afrique du Nord* (Alger: Typ. A. Jourdan, 1908), pp. 198, 270-271.

78. Paret, "*Ashab at-kahf*," p. 691; Johnson, *Standard Dictionary*, p. 210.

79. Massignon, "Les 'Sept Dormants,'" 108.

80. Wilson, *Religion and the Transformation of Society* (Cambridge: Cambridge University Press, 1971), p. 75.

81. Rosaldo, "Women, Culture, and Society: A Theoretical Overview," in Michelle Zimbalist Rosaldo and Louise Lamphere, eds., *Women, Culture and Society* (Stanford: Stanford University Press, 1974), pp. 17-42 at 17-18; see also Peggy R. Sanday, "Female Status in the Public Domain," in ibid., pp. 189-206. Cf. the re-

evaluations of each in Rosaldo, "Use and Abuse," pp. 389-417, and Sanday, *Female Power* and *Male Dominance* (Cambridge: Cambridge University Press, 1981).

82. Sacks, "Engels Revisited," p. 231. This is echoed by Bujra, "Introductory," p. 32, as well as by Sacks, *Sisters and Wives*, and Leacock, "Interpreting."

83. Beck and Keddie, "Introduction," in Beck and Keddie, *Women*, p. 25; cf. Caplan, *Choice and Constraint*, pp. 121-122, and "Gender," pp. 32-36.

84. See, for example, Olivia Harris and Kate Young, "Engendered Structures: Some Problems in the Analysis of Reproduction," in Joel S. Kahn and Josep R. Llobera, eds., *The Anthropology of Pre-Capitalist Societies* (London: Macmillan, 1981), pp. 109-147, especially p. 131; Jane I. Guyer, "The Raw, the Cooked, and the Half-baked: A Note on the Division of Labor by Sex," Boston University, African Studies Center Working Papers No. 48 (1981).

85. Lewis, *Ecstatic Religion* (Harmondsworth: Penguin Books, 1971).

86. Lewis, "Patterns of Protest Among Non-Western Women," in Raymond Price and Dorothy Barrier, eds., *Configurations* (Lexington, MA: Lexington Books, 1974), p. 100.

87. Bujra, "Introductory," pp. 14-15; see also Caplan, *Choice and Constraint*, pp. 122-123, on the influence of male shamans over their female clients; Beattie and Middleton, "Introduction" to their *Spirit Mediums*, p. xxvii.

88. Sacks, *Sisters and Wives*, p. 195. Indeed, as Topan, "Oral Literature," p. 98, makes clear, women are possessed as wives, not sisters, and thus "most commonly, it is husbands who have to meet such expenses" as are involved in spirit exorcism. On cult fees as "a major redistributive economic institution," cf. Wim H.J. van Binsbergen, "Regional and Non-regional Cults of Affliction in Western Zambia," in R.P. Werbner, ed., *Regional Cults* (London: Academic Press, 1977), p. 151.

89. Roger Gomm, "Bargaining from Weakness; Spirit Possession on the South Kenya Coast," *Man*, New Series, 10, 4 (1975), pp. 540-541.

90. Topan, "Oral Literature," pp. 451-452.

91. See, for example, Raymond Prince, "Forward," in Crapanzano and Garrison, eds., *Case Studies*, pp. xi-iii; Crapanzano, "Introduction," in ibid., pp. 20-21.

92. Lewis, "Spirit Possession," p. 204, and other sources cited in n. 41 above.

93. Charles W. Rechenbach, *Swahili-English Dictionary* (Washington, DC: The Catholic Universities of America Press, 1967), p. 227, second entry under *kitimiri*, the first being "name of an evil spirit."

94. Cf. Skene's attribution in "Arab and Swahili Dances," p. 420, with those of Koritschoner, "Ngoma ya Sheitani," p. 210, and especially Caplan. *Choice and Constraint*, pp. 121-122.

95. Lambek, "Spirits and Spouses; Possession as a System of Communication Among the Malagasy Speakers of Mayotte," *American Ethnologist*, 7 (1980), pp. 318-331.

96. Lambek, "Human Spirits," II, ch. 12, p. 409. This whole chapter is extremely nuanced and suggestive for further historical research.

97. Godfrey Dale, *The Peoples of Zanzibar* (Westminster: Universities' Mission to Central Africa, 1920), p. 34; cf. Koritschoner, "Ngoma ya Sheitani," p. 209.

98. R.F. Gray, "Shetani Cult," p. 185.
99. Saunders, "Variants," esp. p. 189.
100. R.F. Gray, "Shetani Cult," p. 185.
101. Feierman, *Shambaa Kingdom,* p. 200.
102. Beattie and Middleton, "Introduction," pp. xxviii-xxix; Constantinides, "Women's Spirit Possession."
103. Lambek, "Human Spirits," I, p. 80. For Lambek's most recent exploration of the relationship between spirit possession and history, see Lambek, *The Weight of the Past: Living with History in Mahajanga, Madagascar* (New York & Houndsmill: Palgrave Macmillan, 2002).
104. In writing this paper I was made unusually aware of my considerable intellectual debt to three former students, Ramachandran Menon, Randall Pouwels, and Margaret Strobel, as well as to Kathleen Sheldon, who was then working with me. For assistance with particular aspects of this paper I am also grateful to my colleagues, Nikki Keddie and Michael Morony, and to my former student, Mahmoud Abdul Rahman El Sheikh. The original version was presented at the conference on African Women in History at the University of Santa Clara, 15-16 May 1981, and subsequently benefited by comments from the audience and from close critical readings by both Pouwels and Strobel. The present version was discussed at the November 1983 meeting of the UCLA Women's Studies Program's Faculty Seminar on Women, Culture and Theory, on which occasion particularly helpful suggestions were mode by Ann Bergren, the late Hilda Kuper, and Kathryn Kish Sklar. I am also indebted to Luise White for numerous invaluable suggestions and for generally sharing her ideas with me.

Notes to Chapter 7

1. Hubert Deschamps, *Histoire de Madagascar*, 2e ed. (Paris: Berger-Levrault, 1961), p. 107. For purposes of economy I have not included information on the general organization of the expeditions, for which see Pierre Vérin, "Histoire ancienne du Nord-Quest de Madagascar," *Taloha 5*, Numéro spécial (1972), pp. 155-156.
2. Eugène de Froberville, "Historique des invasions madecasses aux îles Comores et la côte orientale d'Afrique," *Annuaire des Voyages et de la Géographie*, 11 (Paris, 1845), pp. 194-208; Charles Guillain, *Documents sur l'histoire, la geographie et le commerce de la partie occidentale de Madagascar* (Paris: Imprimerie royale 1845). pp. 199-201. The definitive study of the Malagasy raids on the Comoros is Jean Martin, *Comores: quatre îles entre pirates et planteurs*, I (Paris: L'Harmattan, 1983), pp. 81-110.
3. For this Muslim trading network, see Edward A. Alpers, *Ivory and Slaves in East Central Africa* (Berkeley: University of California Press and London: Heinemann, 1975), pp. 75, 132-133, 183-184; Nancy Jane Hafkin, "Trade, Society, and Politics in Northern Mozambique, c. 1753-1913" (unpublished Ph. D. dissertation, Boston University, 1973), passim. For the slave trade across the Mozambique Channel, see subsequent publications by Gwyn Campbell, "Madagascar and Mozambique in the Slave Trade of the Western Indian Ocean 1800-1861," in

William Gervase Clarence-Smith, ed., *The Economics of the Indian Ocean Slave Trade in the Nineteenth Century* (London: Frank Cass, 1989), pp. 166-193, "Madagascar and the Slave Trade, 1810-1895," *Journal of African History*, 22 (1981), pp. 203-227, and "The East African Slave Trade, 1861-1895: The 'Southern' Complex," *International Journal of African Historical Studies*, 22 (1989), pp. 1-26.

4. Alfredo Brandão Cro de Castro & Joaquim José Lapa, *Elementos para um Diccionario Chorographico da Provincia de Moçambique* (Lisbon: Adolpho, Modesto & Ca., 1889), p. 2; José Justino Teixeira Botelho, *História Militar e Política dos Portugueses em Moçambique*, I (Lisbon: Centro Tipografico Colonial, 1934), pp. 595-596; Alpers, *Ivory and Slaves*, p. 383.

5. Arquivo Histórico Ultramarino, Lisbon, Moçambique, Caixa 38 (hereafter AHU, Moç., Cx.), Antonio da Silva Pinto to Francisco Guedes de Carvalho e Meneses da Costa, Ibo, 24 February 1801.

6. AHU, Moç., Cx. 37, same to same, Ibo, 10 July 1800. If the leader of this expedition was indeed the Sultan of Mayotte, then he would have been Saleh bin Mohamed, a Zanzibar Arab who had married into the ruling family. See "Histoire de Mayotte et des Sakkalava depuis l'invasion de Radama dans le royaume de Boueni, par le cheikh Ioussouf ben el-Moallem-Moussa, de la grande Comore," collected by V. Noel in 1840 and translated from the Arabic in Noel, "Recherches sur les Sakkalava," *Bulletin de la Société de Géographie*, 2ème Série, 20 (1843), pp. 41-55. Francisco Santana, ed., *Documentação Avulsa Moçambicana do Arquivo Histórico Ultramarino*, III (Lisbon: Centro de Estudos Históricos Ultramarinos, 1974), p. 241 #56, unaccountably attributes this raid to the Sultan of Anjouan and also misdates it to 1801. For a much earlier incident involving a boat from Mohilla [Mwale] Island with 72 men, nearly half of whom were armed, which was part of a "squadron which was going to make war in Anjouan, but which was blown off course in a storm and arrived at Ibo," see AHU, Moç., Cx. 12, Caetano Alberto Judice to Governor-General, Ibo, 20 April 1766.

7. AHU, Cod. 1372, fl. 7v, Isidro Almeida Sousa e Sà to Visconde de Anadia, Moç., 9 July 1805, basing his report on an unlocated communication from the Sultan of Anjouan. Cf. the treatment by Guillain, *Madagascar*, p. 200 who misdates this event to 1807 and states that the *Bonne-Mère* (*Boa Mãe*) flew French colors and was captained by a man named Legars. The Portuguese Governor-General's letter explains that the vessel had been purchased by Vicente Guedes da Silva e Sousa from a Frenchman called Tessero (Tisserot?) and specifically expressed his shock at the insult that these barbarians made against the Portuguese flag. It would not be at all surprising, however, if the captain was still French, as this was common practice in the Mozambique slave trade of this period.

8. AHU, Cod. 1372, fl. 7v, Sousa e Sà to Anadia, Moç., 9 July 1805; fl. 11v-12, Francisco de Paula a Albuquerque Amaral Cardoso to same, Moç., 6 January 1806; & fl. 28v, Interim Governing Triumvirate to same, Moç., 10 October 1807; Guillain, *Madagascar*, p. 200. Since the Portuguese only learned of the *Emboscada*'s fate from a Portuguese ship's captain who got his information from

a Sakalava whom he encountered at Mauritius and who claimed to have been present at the attack, it is understandable that French sources might be more detailed on this point, though Guillain misdates the incident to 1805.

9. AHU, Moç., Cx. 48, Interim Governing Triumvirate to Antonio Alberto Pereira, Moç., 20 September 1808, and same to Anadia, Moç., 10 November 1808 (also in AHU, Cod. 1372, fl. 32v-33); AHU, Moç., Cx. 54, Jeronimo Fernandes Viana to Interim Governing Triumvirate, Ibo, 16 February 1810. For a recent analysis of these raids in the Kerimba Islands, see Carlos Lopes Bento, *As Ilhas de Querimba ou de Cabo Delgado* (Lisbon: Universidade Técnica de Lisboa, Instituto Suerior de Ciências Sociais e Políticas, 1993), II, ch. 10.3, "As incursões malgaxes," http://geocities.yahoo.com.br/quirimbashistoria/index.htm accessed on 11/1/2005.

10. AHU, Moç., Cx. 54, petition of the inhabitants of the Cape Delgado Islands, 5 July 1810, enclosed in Francisco Antonio de Sousa Cesar to Antonio de Melo Castro a Mendonça, Ibo, 28 December 1810; AHU, Moç., Cx. 55, same to same, Ibo, 18 [April] 1811, See also, AHU, Moç., Cx. 56, José da Silva Delgado to same, Ibo, 15 July 1812, seeking a military post and citing previous service against the Sakalava at Pangani, on the mainland north of Ibo.

11. AHU, Moç., Cx. 53, Sousa Cesar to same, Ibo, 28 December 1810; for what little we know about João de Morais, see Alpers, *Ivory and Slaves*, pp. 146, 182, 190. Traditions regarding the ransoming of relatives who had been enslaved during these raids and taken away to Madagascar were current in some families on Ngazija four decades ago; see [Antoine Maurice] Fontoynont & [Emmanuel] Raomandahy, "La Grande Comore," *Mémoires de l'Académie Malgache*, 23 (Tananarive: Impr. moderne de l'Emyrne, Pitot de la Beaujardière, 1937), p. 17.

12. AHU, Moç,, Cx. 52, Pereira to Interim Governing Triumvirate, Ibo, 1 April 1809; Henry Salt, *A Voyage to Abyssinia . . .* (London: F. C. and J. Rivington, 1814), p. 79. Guillain's account of the 1807 Sakalava expedition that encountered a French slaving vessel at sea, sacked it, and then was decimated by smallpox contracted from the African slaves on board appears to be a telescoped version of what contemporary Portuguese sources describe more accurately as separate incidents in 1805 and 1808-1809. See Guillain, *Madagascar*, pp. 200-201.

13. Biblioteca Nacional de Lisboa, Fundo Geral, Cod. 8470, no 6, Sultão Alaui Bono Mussene Bono Omaro Sultan Muenhe Fane to Mendonça, [1811]. Hafkin, "Trade, Society, and Polities," pp. 211-213, identifies the writer of this letter with the first m'bilinzi Sultan of Angoche, Alawi Musheni. But in view of both Gevrey's reconstruction that Alawi ruled as Sultan of Anjouan from c. 1804-1820 and two subsequent letters from 1820 sent to Mozambique by Sultan Alawi of Anjouan, I am inclined to reject Hafkin's identification. See A. Gevrey, *Essai sur les Comores* (Pondichery: B.A. Saligny, 1870), pp. 187, 189; AHU, Moç., Cx. 66, Sultão Alave Oxeny, Rey de Anjouane, to Governor-General of Mozambique, n.d.., but responded to on 28 March 1820 according to a note overleaf, Sultane Alavy Bunu Ussene to same, [Anjouan], 5 October 1820. Resolution of this problem awaits scholarly translation of the original letter written in Arabic script, as both Dr. Hafkin and I have necessarily worked from the contemporary Portuguese translation accompanying it. The haphazard rendering of names in

these translations is manifest from the variations in the two later letters to which I have referred.

14. AHU, Moç., Cx. 56, Mendonça to Caetano José Resende, Moç., 1 March 1812; AHU, Moç., Cx. 54 & Cod. 1478, fl. 238v, Manuel Onofre Pantoja to Marcos Caetano de Abreu e Meneses, [Ibo], 16 March 1814; AHU, Moç., Cx. 58, Abreu e Meneses to Antonio de Araujo de Azevedo, Moç., 29 October 1814. Bwana Kombo, who was an Arab living at Anjouan, a regular port of call for British East Indiamen making the inner passage, had gained a reputation as a friend of the English, who dubbed him "Bombay Jack." See James Prior, *Voyage along the East Coast of Africa . . . in the Nisus Frigate* (London: Sir R. Philips & Co., 1819), pp. 22, 29-30, 45-65 passim. Despite some derogatory remarks about the Portuguese which are recorded by Prior, Bwana Kombo was known equally as a friend of them in 1812. See AHU, Moç., Cx. 56, unsigned letter of introduction for Bombajaque, Moç., 12 [April] 1812. What this suggests, of course, is that Bwana Kombo was a very effective ambassador for Anjouan. His embassy to Mauritius in 1814 was an important step in effecting the Anglo-Malagasy Treaty of 1817 which was designed to end the export slave trade from Madagascar and with it the raids on the Comoro Islands. See below, n. 31. For a superb recent discussion of the impact of the English connection with Nzwani, see Jeremy Prestholdt, *Domesticating the World: African Consumerism and the Genealogies of Globalization* (Berkeley: University of California Press, 2008), pp. 13-33.

15. AHU, Moç., Cx, 59 & Cod. 1380, fl. 157-160, Abreu e Meneses to Azevedo, Moç., 17 December 1815; Santana, *Documentação*, II (Lisbon: Centro de Estudos Históricos Ultramarinos, 1967), p. 894. For the favorable reaction of the Portuguese Crown to the defense of Ibo, see AHU, Moç., Cx. 59, Marques de Aguiar to Abreu e Meneses, Rio de Janeiro, 16 October 1816. The implied large size of the canoes used in this expedition points to Betsimisaraka participation, since in all the major sources large canoe construction is only explicitly reported for eastern Madagascar. See Vérin, "Histoire ancienne," p. 157; Gevrey, *Essai*, pp. 210-211.

16. AHU, Moç., Cx. 59 & Cod. 1478, fl, 242v, Antonio da Costa Portugal to Abreu e Meneses, Ibo, 6 March 1816.

17. AHU, Moç., Cx. 59, Abreu e Meneses to José Antonio Caldas, Moç., n.d., but clearly 1816.

18. Ibid. and Cod. 1478, fl 243 & v, Costa Portugal to Abreu e Meneses, Ibo, 14 March 1816.

19. AHU, Cod. 1374, fl. 96-97, Caldas to same, Ibo, 3 December 1816; AHU, Cod. 1380, fl. 169, Abreu e Meneses to Conde da Barca, Moç., 16 December 1816; Vérin, "Histoire ancienne," p. 155. For Sancul during this period, see Hafkin, "Trade, Society, and Politics," ch. 5.

20. AHU, Cod. 1374, fl. 96-97, Caldas to Abreu e Meneses, Ibo, 3 December 1816. According to Froberville, "Historique," p. 198, "When the number of men assembled at the place of rendezvous is very great, two divisions are formed which direct themselves towards different points." This would seem to explain the two fleets of Sicandar and Nassiri in 1816-1817.

21. AHU, Cod. 1377, fl. 210, Cavalcanti de Albuquerque to Sultão Assane, Moç.,

29 March 1817, replying to an earlier letter which has not been located; Fortuné Albrand, "Extrait d'un Memoire sur Zanzibar et sur Quiloa," *Bulletin de la Société de Géographie,* 2ème Série, 10 (1838), p. 82; G.S.P. Freeman-Grenville, *The East African Coast–Select Documents from the first to the earlier nineteenth century* (Oxford: Clarendon Press 1962). p. 224.

22. AHU, Moç., Cx. 60, Caldas to Abreu a Meneses, Ibo, 29 January 1817; ibid., same to Cavalcanti de Albuquerque, Ibo, 6 July 1817, enclosing Falume Asani Falume to Caldas, Tungui, 24 May 1817; ibid., Caldas to Abreu e Meneses, Ibo, 29 January 1817, naming João Leite Pereira of Vamizi, the mother of Dona Francisca Onofre Correa of Arimba, and people who returned to the mainland settlement of Pangani after weathering the October battle at Ibo in the security of the fort. As for King Hasan, his success against the Sakalava in 1815 may have encouraged him to sever his largely nugatory ties with the Portuguese, but the ravages of 1817 caused him to seek military assistance from them. His appeal was couched both in terms of fealty and a threat to attach himself to the Sultan of Kilwa, who had been an Omani vassal since 1815. The Governor-General dismissed him as being completely untrustworthy. See AHU, Moç., Cx. 60, Cavalcanti de Albuquerque to Caldas, Moç., 26 July 1817. Tungui remained a semi-independent frontier zone between Busaidi Zanzibar and Portuguese Mozambique until 1887. See John Gray, *History of Zanzibar from the Middle Ages to.1856* (London: Oxford University Press, 1962), pp. 175-179.

23. AHU, Moç., Cx. 60, petition of Jose Pereira Machado, n.d., but granted at Moç., 10 January 1817; ibid. & Cod. 1478, fl. 252 & v, Caldas to Cavalcanti de Albuquerque, Ibo, 26 March 1817; AHU, Moç., Cx. 60, same to same, Ibo, 6 May 1817, enclosing Caldas, "Relação das Ilhas que estão no districto deste Governo," Ibo, 6 May 1817, in which only three of twenty-six are listed as populated (Matemo, Ibo, and Querimba) and seven show signs of having formerly been populated; ibid., reply, Moç., 14 June 1817.

24. Ibid., Caldas to Cavalcanti de Albuquerque, Ibo, 13 November 1817; ibid. & Coda 1478, fl. 263 & v, same to same, Ibo, 1 December 1817.

25. Biblioteca Nacional de Lisboa, Fundo Geral, Cod. 8470, fl. 71, Salimo Bono Sahi Bono Saiude Usaiude Seleman to Governor of Mozambique, Zanzibar (?), n.d. The details of this letter greatly clarify later accounts of this battle, both written and oral, but must necessarily remain provisional until the Arabic script original text receives proper scholarly translation. See Albrand, "Extrait," p. 82; W.F.W. Owen, *Narrative of Voyages to explore the shores of Africa, Arabia, and Madagascar ...* (London: R. Bentley, 1833), I, pp. 372-373, and the use of these by Froberville, "Historique," pp. 199-200; for oral traditions about this defeat, see Freeman-Grenville, *Select Documents,* pp. 224 (Kilwa) & 298 (Kua, Juani); Kadhi Amur Omar Sandi (translated by D.W.I. Piggott), "Mafia - History and Traditions," *Tanganyika Notes and Records,* 12 (1941), pp. 26-27 (Kua, Juani). The Kua traditions are extremely confused and at base represent part of a deeper attempt to account for this disaster and others by relating them to the bitter communal rivalry between Kua and Kisimani, Mafia.

26. AHU, Cod. 1380, fl. 229-230, Amaro Guedes da Silva da Sousa & Fr. José Nicolau de Jésus Maria Pegado to Conde dos Arcos, Moç., 18 January 1819.

27. AHU, Moç., Cx. 64, Caldas to Interim Governors, Ibo, 20 February 1819; ibid., José Alves Barbosa to Caetano José Cordeiro, Moç., 8 July 1819; ibid., Cordeiro to Interim Governors, Ibo, 23 September 1819; Arquivo da Casa da Cadaval, Portugal, Cod. 826 (M VI 32), D. Fr. Bartolomeu dos Màrtires, "Memoria Chorographica da Provincia e a Capitania de Moçambique na Costa d'Africa Oriental Conforme o estado em que se achava no anno de 1822," fl. 39-42. It is possible that the Moma rumor was the result of Malagasy traders there, as Màrtires mentions that they sometimes traded directly to Mozambique. See ibid., fl. 31-32. The mid-channel disaster which Màrtires reports would seem to have been that related to Thomas Boteler, who visited Mozambique in 1823, but who in his subsequent account possibly confused it with the 1816 expedition of Sicandar's fleet of 71 *lakas* of a reported 150 that were being readied earlier in the year, since he reports that of 260 boats which left Madagascar, only 68 reached the Kerimba Islands. Boteler was later cited by Froberville, who has since provided the basis for this bit of incorrect detail on the raids: Thomas Boteler, *Narrative of a Voyage of Discovery to Africa and Arabia* ... (London: R. Bentley, 1836), II, p. 69; Froberville, "Historique," p. 199.

28. Deschamps, *Histoire*, p. 108; Vérin, "Histoire ancienne," p. 162. A Merina garrison was established at Mahajanga in 1824, for which see Gwyn Campbell's recent *An Economic History of Imperial Madagascar, 1750-1895* (Cambridge: Cambridge University Press, 2005), pp. 162, 164.

29. Santana, *Documentação*, III, pp. 349-350. Bwana Kombo and his brother, Omar Abubakr, visited Mozambique at the beginning of 1820; by the end of the year both had died, Bwana Kombo's brother having first succeeded him as consul at Anjouan after his death. See AHU, Moç., Cx. 66, Sultão Alave Oxeny, Rey de Anjoane, to Governor-General of Mozambique, n.d., but responded to on 28 Mars 1820 in a letter carried by Prince Mwenye Mweri Sidi Ali; AHU, Moç., Cx. 67, João da Costa de Brito Sanches to Arcos, Moç., 22 December 1820, including a reference to a royal order of 29 June 1819 which seems to have established the appointment of these Comorian consuls. For the identification of the Balambos as Merina, see Vérin, "Histoire ancienne," p. 166 n. 1.

30. AHU, Moç., Cx. 67, Brito Sanches to Arcos, Moç., 23 November 1820, enclosing "Copia da Tradução de huma Carta enviada pelo vizir de São Lourenço, Bona ussene Bone Abdulà, 18 October 1820. This is the same Antalaotse governor of Mahajanga who was executed on 22 July 1824 after the town fell to the army of Radama I. His letter would seem to throw a different light on received accounts of Radama's 1820 campaign against the Sakalava. See Vérin, "Histoire ancienne," pp. 166-167.

31. dos Mártires, "Memoria," fl. 39-42. For the significance the Anglo-Malagasy alliance in repressing the maritime expeditions, see Deschamps, *Histoire*, pp. 153-159.

32. R.K. Kent, *Early Kingdoms in Madagascar, 1500-1700* (New York: Holt, Rinehart and Winston,1970), p. 203; Vérin, "Histoire ancienne," pp. 153, 162-163.

33. Salt, *Voyage*, p. 76. Fischer was Captain of the HMS *Racehorse*, which took Salt to Mozambique from the Cape.

34. Verin, "Histoire ancienne," pp. 155-160; Also A. Monteiro, "Pesquisas arque-

ológicas nos estabelecimentos de Kiuya, M'buezi a Quisiva," *Monumenta*, 2 (1966), pp. 51-56, who describes several Sakalava tombs at the mouth of the Ruvuma River; but cf. C.S. Nicholls, *The Swahili Coast* (London: George Allen & Unwin, 1971), p. 130, though the two published of her three sources do not mention the Betsimisaraka. Colin is cited by Gevrey, *Essai*, pp. 210-211, from [Conrad] Malte-Brun, *Annales des Voyages, de la Géographie et de l'histoire*, XIII; Froberville, "Historique," p. 197, uses the same passage, but without citation, though the mistake may be Gevrey's.

35. Verin, "Histoire ancienne," pp. 153, 160, 163. For an important new perspective on the Swahili slaving network linking northwestern Madagascar to the Comoros and the coast involving slaves, see Thomas Vernet, "Les Cités-Etats Swahili de l'archiel de Lamu, 1585-1810: Dynamiques endogènes, dynamiques exogènes" (unpublished Ph.D. thesis, Université de Paris I, 2005), pp. 170-192.

36. Guillain, *Madagascar*, p. 33; for the dates of Queen Ravahiny, see H. Rusillon, "Notes d'histoire Sakalava," *Bulletin de l'Académie Malgache*, Série 2, 6 (1922-1923), chart between pp.178-179.

37. Fressanges is quoted most accessibly by Vérin, "Histoire ancienne," pp, 161-152; for *chelingues*, see Albrand, "Extrait," p. 75. For a contemporary commercial guide to trade at Bombetoka Bay, see William Milburn, *Oriental Commerce* (London: Black, Parry & Co., 1813), I, p. 72, citing a source dated to 1802.

38. AHU, Cod. 1372, fl. 7v, Sousa e Sà to Anadia, Moç., 9 July 1805. In general, boat size is not mentioned in the East African sources on the raids, though the two oral versions of the history of Kua, Juani, specify that the Sakalava *lakas* were small, a point of detail which conflicts sharply with the letter from Zanzibar that describes the battle in Msimbati Bay; see Freeman-Grenville, *Select Documents*, p. 298; Kadhi Amur, "Mafia," p. 25.

39. George McCall Theal, ed., *Records of South-Eastern Africa*, IX (London: Government of the Cape Colony, 1903), pp. 5, 12-13; AHU, Moç., Cx. 56, Robert Stafford to Melo Castro e Mendonça, Cape of Good Hope, 10 July 1812; Prior, *Voyage*, pp. 22-23.

40. W.H. Smythe, *The Life and Service of Captain Philip Beaver, late of Her Majesty Ship Nisus* (London: J. Murray, 1829), p. 256 ; Prior, *Voyage*, pp. 63-64; Boteler, *Narrative*, II, p. 59.

41. Epidariste Colin, "Notice sur Mozambique," in Malte-Brun, *Annales*, IX (Paris: F. Buisson, 1809), p. 315; AHU, Moç., Cx. 46, Rodrigo Berri to Sousa e Sà, [1805]; AHU, Moç., Cx. 50, Caetano José Resende to Melo Castro a Mendonça, Ibo, 27 October 1807. Macaloe is north of Ibo, just offshore from Pangani.

42. AHU, Cod. 1379, fl. 66, *registo de despacho*, 8 January 1811. It could well be that traders from Bombetoka continued to identify themselves to Europeans as being under the protection of Ravahiny for years after her death because of her great prestige, but if this brief and casual notation is correct, then we are faced with a reassessment of her date of death, a point of detail which can only be resolved by those whose knowledge of Sakalava history is more profound than mine. The continued eminence of the "Queen of Bombetoka" may also account for a reference to her success in war in 1820, by which date she was certainly dead and her grandson, Andriamanesiarivo, reigned. Cf. the explanation given by Vérin,

"Histoire ancienne," p. 166, for this anomaly.

43. For the Muslim slave trade to Madagascar from Mozambique see Hafkin, "Trade, Society, and Politics," *passim*; for the Antankara and Tsimihety, see Deschamps, *Histoire*, pp. 101-102. In the middle of the eighteenth century a marriage alliance was made between the Zana-Malata founder of the Betsimisaraka kingdom, Ratsimilaho or Ramaromanompo, and the kingdom of Boeny. What the ramifications of this alliance between the Zana-Malata and the Volamena dynasty might have been during the era of the maritime raids is a question that remains to be examined. See ibid., p. 106.

44. Cited in Raymond Decary, *Coutumes Guerrieres et Organisation Militaire chez les Anciens Malgaches* (Paris: Éditions maritimes et d'outremer, 1966), I, pp. 134-131.

45. In this context it is worth noting "the important services made to this State [of Mozambique] on the occasions of the Sakalava when they twice sought to invade the Island of Ibo ... with his person and people, offering his powder, shot, and foodstuffs," claimed by a trader from Anjouan. See AHU, Moç.., Cx. 66, petition of Saide Homar Bonu Cheane, n.d., but received at Moç., 16 December 1820. The petitioner identifies himself as being of the "Casta Mujojo," which at this time could mean any coastal Muslim or Comorian, but his letter was handled at Mozambique by the "Consul de Nação Arabe" and the Anjouan consul.

46. Fontoynont & Raomandahy, "La Grande Comore," p. 17.

47. See A.H.J. Prins, *Didemic Lamu: Social Stratification and Spacial Structure in a Muslim Maritime Town* (Groningen: Instituut voor Culturele Antropologie der Rijks-universiteit, 1971); Peter Lienhardt, "Introduction" to Hasani bin Ismail, *The Medicine Man: Swifa ya Nguvumali* (Oxford: Clarendon Press, 1968).

48. For early Anjouan appeals, see Gevrey, *Essai,* p. 187, & Vérin, "Histoire ancienne," pp. 158-159; for Alawi's history, see Gevrey, *Essai*, pp. 187, 189. The earliest general Comorian appeal to the Portuguese for assistance "against the continual invasions of the Sakalava pirates," an interesting choice of words considering the origins of the Zana-Malata, came from Mohilla: AHU, Moç., Cx. 26, O Principe dos Mulates (with untranslated Arabic signature) to Senhores, n.d. [in a folder marked 1785].

49. For details, see Noel, "Recherches," pp. 41-55. No less riddled with internecine struggles during the nineteenth century is the history of Ngazija, for which see Fontoynont & Raomandahy, "La Grande Comore," pp. 25-29. For Andriantsoly's history, see Deschamps, *Histoire*, pp. 159-160, 170-171 ; Vérin, "Histoire ancienne," pp. 167-168. He also appears in the Portuguese documentation, before his final defeat by Ranavalona I, when he was still based at Anorontsangana: Santana, *Documentação*, III, pp. 166-167 #138. For a more detailed analysis of Andriantsoli's career, see Martin, *Comores*, I, pp. 132-162; see also the recent contribution by Jean-Claude Hebert, "Mayotte au XVIIIe siècle. Des pirates européens aux pirates malgaches, en passant par les sultans batailleurs et les traitants d'esclaves français," in *Esclavage, razzias et deportations: aspects d'une histoire de Mayotte. Actes de la conference sur l'abolition de l'esclavage*, Archives Orales, Cahiers, no 4 et 5 (Mayotte: Éditions du Baobab, June 1998), pp. 11-95, at pp. 57-68.

Notes to Chapter 8

1. This paper, now slightly revised, was originally presented at the Colloque marquant le XXème anniversaire de la création du CNDRS [Centre National de Documentation et de Recherche Scientifique], Moroni, République Fédérale Islamique des Comores, 27-28 January 1999. I am most grateful for the support and hospitality of the CNDRS during my visit, especially to its Director General at the time, Djaffar Mmadi, and to Hachimo Soendi, who guided me around the island of Ngazija. Thanks also to Jean-Claude Penrad for his comments on the paper and for bringing it to the attention of the editors of *Cahiers d'Études Africaines*, where it was originally published.

2. For the earlier history of these exchanges, see Malyn Newitt, "The Comoro Islands in the Indian Ocean Trade before the 19th Century," *Cahiers d'Études Africaines*, 89-90, 1-2 (1983), pp. 139-165.

3. See, e.g., original letters in Arabic with Portuguese translations in Biblioteca Nacional de Lisboa, Reservados, Fundo Geral [BNL, FG], Cod. 8470, fls. 1, 3, 6 (a, b, e, f), 70, 95-96.

4. For the era of the Malagasy raids, see Jean Martin, *Comores: quatre îles entre pirates et planteurs* (Paris: L'Harmattan, 1983), I, ch. 2; Chapter 7 in this volume.

5. With the notable exception of correspondence from the Sakalava interloper, Andriantsoli, to the Governor of Mozambique in 1829, for which see Barbara Dubins, "A Political History of the Comoro Islands, 1795-1886" (unpublished Ph.D. dissertation, Boston University, 1972), p. 138.

6. BNL, FG, Cod. 8470, fl. 27, Sultane Chei Mondar Bon Sultan Chei Abo Bacar to Governor-General, 20 June 1828; fl. 37, Sultan of Anjouan, 11 December 1829. The odd wording of the Portuguese translation, "alguns escravos velhos ou moleques pequenos para a minha agricultura," which I suspect is a mistake for something like "mature slaves or boys" in the Arabic original, makes a strong argument for modern translations of the documents in this important codex. For Shaykh Mukhtar bin Abubakr, see Martin, *Comores*, citations in Index; the Sultan of Nzwani at this time was Abdallah II bin Alawi (1823-1836): see ibid., I, p. 141 and citations in Index.

7. My thanks to Iain Walker for explaining this to me in an email dated 17 Aug 1999. See also Charles Sacleux, *Dictionnaire Swahili-Français* (Paris: Institut d'Ethnologie, 1939), p. 690.

8. James Prior, *Voyage along the Eastern Coast of Africa, to Mozambique, Johanna, and Quiloa . . . in the Nisus Frigate* (London: Sir R. Philips & Co., 1819), p. 55; Public Record Office, London [now National Archives of the United Kingdom, Kew] Colonial Office 415/7, A. No. 172 (31-33), Captain Pilkinhome's Journal; Francisco Santana, ed., *Documentação Avulsa Moçambicana no Arquivo Histórico Ultramarino* I (Lisbon: Centro de Estudos Históricos Ultramarinos, 1964), pp. 703 #82-83; ibid., II (Lisbon: Centro de Estudos Históricos Ultramarinos, 1967), pp. 32 #47, 760 #251, 804 #38, 805 #41-42, 806 #45-47, 808 #52, 818 #80, 819 #83, 823 #101, 827 #117: ; ibid., III (Lisbon: Centro de Estudos Históricos Ultramarinos, 1974), pp. 152 #101, 678 #144, 752 #41 & #43, 978 #149, 979 #150 & #152, 980 #154, 982 #162 & #164, 985 #173, 991

#196, 998 #211, 999 #215, and 1000 #218; Marie Armand Pascal d'Azevec et al, *Iles de l'Afrique* (Paris: Firmin Didot frères, 1848), pp. 117 and 120. For a broad discussion of the trade in foodstuffs, including information on western Madagascar and Comorian links to Zanzibar, see Chapter 2 above.

9. B.F. Leguevel de Lacombe, *Voyage à Madagascar et aux îles Comores 1823 à 1830* (Paris: L. Desessart, 1840), II, p. 331.

10. Santana, *Documentação*, III, pp. 981 #160 and 15 #15.

11. Ibid., II, pp. 337-339 #5/2.

12. Leguevel de Lacombe, *Voyage*, II, pp. 316-317; for Husayn see Martin, *Comores*, citations in Index.

13. Santana, *Documentação*, III, pp. 163-164 #132, parentheses in original. For further details, see Dubins, "Political History," pp. 102-103, 105, 108-109.

14. Ibid., III, p. 159 #121. Jean Martin argues that this incident was part of Mwinyi Mkuu's attempt to gain recognition from the Portuguese of his authority over the entire island, which as his letter clearly indicates, he did not exercise. See Martin, *Comores*, I, pp. 356-360, 587-588 n. 19-20. Dubins, "Political History," pp. 207-208, confirms the identification of Quitanda.

15. Santana ed., *Documentação*, II, pp. 942-943 #9/1-3, and pp. 951-952 #15/1. For the history of this period of famine, see Newitt, "Drought in Mozambique 1823-1831," *Journal of Southern African Studies*, 15, 1 (1988), pp. 15-35.

16. Leguevel de Lacombe, *Voyage*, II, pp. 322-323; Martin, *Comores*, I, pp. 126, 432-433 n. 49.

17. Ibid., I, pp. 124-131; see also BNL, FG, Cod. 8470, fl. 48.

18. Martin, *Comores*, I, pp. 163, 462 n. 118; also Oumar Aboubakari Housséni (1865), *Histoire des Îles: Ha'Ngazidja, Hindzou'ani, Maïota et Mwali*, ed. Kana-Hazi (St.Denis, La Réunion: Djahazi Édition, 1997), pp. 75, 80.

19. I have seen only a transcription of the letter in Portuguese from João Távares de Almeida to Said Omar, Moçambique, 24 July 1861. I am indebted to Emeritus Professor Martin Ottenheimer, Kansas State University, for sharing his copy of this document, which he located in the Comoros. For Said Omar, see Martin, *Comores*, I, pp. 209-211 and subsequent citations.

20. There is a single reference to a *pangaio* embarking in January 1828 from Ibo, in the Kerimba Islands, for Nzwani in Jeronymo Romero, *Supplemento á Memoria Descriptiva e Estatistica do Districto de Cabo Delgado com uma Noticia ácerca do Estabelecimento da Colonia de Pemba* (Lisbon: Typographia Universal. 1860), p. 123.

21. For specific references to the Comoros, see Alpers, *Ivory and Slaves in East Central Africa* (London: Heinemann & Berkeley: University of California Press, 1975), p. 214; Gill Shepherd, "The Comorians and the East African Slave Trade," in James L. Watson, ed., *Asian and African Systems of Slavery* (Berkeley & Los Angeles: University of California Press, 1980), pp. 75-80; Martin, *Comores*, I, pp. 259-260; José Capela and Eduardo Medeiros, "La traite au départ du Mozambique vers les îles françaises de l'Océan Indien, 1720-1904," in U. Bissoondoyal and S.B.C. Servansing, eds., *Slavery in South West Indian Ocean* (Moka, Mauritius: Mahatma Gandhi Institute, 1989), pp. 268-270.. For the wider context, with scattered references to the Comoros, see Gwyn Campbell,

"Madagascar and Mozambique in the Slave Trade of the Western Indian Ocean 1800-1861," in William Gervase Clarence-Smith, ed., *The Economics of the Indian Ocean Slave Trade in the Nineteenth Century* (London: Frank Cass, 1989), pp. 166-193, "Madagascar and the Slave Trade, 1810-1895," *Journal of African History*, 22 (1981), pp. 203-227, and "The East African Slave Trade, 1861-1895: The 'Southern' Complex," *International Journal of African Historical Studies*, 22 (1989), pp. 1-26. For a recent study on indentured labor at the nearby island of Nossi-Bé, see Jehane-Emmanuelle Monnier, *Esclaves de la canne à sucre: Engagés et planteurs a Nossi-Bé, Madagascar 1850-1880* (Paris: L'Harmattan, 2006).

22. Nancy Jane Hafkin, "Trade, Society, and Politics in Northern Mozambique, c. 1753-1913" (unpublished Ph.D. Dissertation, Boston University, 1973), pp. 56-57, square brackets in Hafkin's original citation of Sultan Said Bakr's letter. For more on this individual, the son of Sultan Mwinyi Mkuu of Bambao, see Martin, *Comores*, citations in Index.

23. Ibid., II, p. 223; for the identification of Sito (Sitou in Martin), see Ministério das Colónias, Comissão de Cartografia, *Dicionário Corografico da Província de Moçambique*, 1.° Fascículo, "Territórios de Cabo Delgado (Companhia do Nyassa)" (Lisboa: Tip. Cristóvão Augusto Rodrigues, 1919), pp. 115 and 163.

24. This pattern of residential segregation would seem to have persisted into the 20th century on Nzwani, according to Vasile Tara and J.-C. Woillet, *Connaissance des Îles: Madagascar, Mascareignes et Comores* (Paris: Société continentale d'éditions modernes illustrées, 1969), p. 355.

25. Shepherd, "The Comorians," pp. 80-99, quoted at 92 and 81, probably drawing upon A. Gevrey, *Essai sur les Comores* (Pondichery: B.A. Saligny, 1870; republished Antananarivo, 1980), p. 84, for filed teeth and tatooing. For an example of how easily recognizable were such slaves, see Eugène de Froberville, "Notes sur les Moeurs, coutumes et traditions des Amakoua, sur le commerce et la traite des esclaves dans l'Afrique orientale," *Bulletin de la Société de Géographie*, 3ème Série, 8 (1847), pp. 311-329.

26. Martin, *Comores*, I, p. 44; see also Claude Robineau, *Société et Économie d'Anjouan (Océan Indien)* (Paris: Office de la recherché scientifique et technique outré-mer, 1966), pp. 56-57, also in his "L'Islam aux Comores: Une étude d'histoire culturelle de l'île d'Anjouan," *Revue de Madagascar*, 35 (1966), pp. 24-25.

27. Martin, *Comores*, I, pp. 53, 55.

28. Ibid., I, pp. 227 and 493 n. 184, quoted at pp. 230, 494 n. 197, which also mentions an African leader named Paria. For a recent essay on this uprising see Isabelle Denis, "Forced labour and the 1856 revolt on Mayotta," in Edward A. Alpers, Gwyn Campbell and Michael Salman, eds., *Resisting Bondage in Indian Ocean Africa and Asia* (London & New York: Routledge, 2007), pp. 40-48.

29. Martin, *Comores*, II, pp. 226-227, 361 n. 270.

30. Ibid., II, p. 176.

31. Ibid., 1, p. 468, n. 150.

32. Guillain's figures are cited in Claude Allibert, *Mayotte: Plaque Tournante et Microcosme de l'Océan Indien Occidental, Son Histoire avant 1841* (Paris: Anthropos, 1984), p. 116; the original source is Charles Guillain, "Mayotte,"

Revue de l'Orient, 9 (1851), p. 225.

33. Martin, *Comores*, I, p. 206.
34. Gevrey, *Essai*, pp. 253, 277-278.
35. Ibid., p. 82. For my ideas about the M'Chambara, see Elias C. Mandala, *Work and Control in a Peasant Economy: A History of the Lower Tchiri Valley in Malawi 1859-1960* (Madison: University of Wisconsin Press, 1990), pp. 67-80. For comparison, see the detailed reconstruction of East African slaves sources for nineteenth-century Madagascar by Campbell, "The Origins and Demography of Slaves in Nineteenth Century Madagascar: A Chapter in the History of the African Ancestry of the Malagasy," in Ignace Rakoto, ed., *L'Esclavage à Madagscar: Aspects historiques et résurgences contemporaines* (Antananarivo: Institut de Civilisations, Musée d'Art et d'Archaeologie, 1997), pp. 5-37.
36. Heudebert cited in Allibert, *Mayotte*, p. 116.
37. See Tara and Woillet, *Connaissance des Îles*, p. 355.
38. Gevrey, *Essai*, p. 82.
39. Sacleux cited in Allibert, *Mayotte*, pp. 116, 152, 228.
40. See Noël J. Gueunier, "Documents sur la langue makhuwa à Madagascar et aux Comores (fin XIXe-début XXe siècles)," in *Fanadevozana ou esclavage: Colloque international sur l'esclavage à Madagascar* (Antananarivo: Institut de Civilisations, Musée d'Art et d'Archaeologie, 1996), pp. 309-321, at 313; for a Makhuwa text from western Madagascar, see Gueunier, with J.M. Katupha, *Contes de la côte ouest de Madagascar* (Antananarivo: Ambozantany and Paris: Karthala, 1991), pp. 78-96.
41. Mohamed Ahmed Chamanga and Noël-Jacques Gueunier, *Le dictionnaire Comorien-Français et Français-Comorien du R.P. Sacleux* (Paris: SELAF, 1979), pp. 23-24.
42. Leguevel de Lacombe, *Voyage*, I, p. 111; J. Capmartin and E. Colin, "Essai sur les îles Comores," in [Conrad] Malte-Brun, *Annales des Voyages de la géographie et de l'histoire*, III (Paris: F. Buisson, 1810), p. 149.
43. Gevrey, *Essai*, p. 84.
44. François Bensignor and Zainab Elyas, "Musique des Comores," <http://www.chez.com/rita/fram.htm>. See also, Hervé Chagnoux and Ali Haribou, *Les Comores* (Paris: Presses Universitaires de France, 1980), pp. 45-46. For *maloya*, see Robert Chaudenson, ed., *Encyclopédie de la Réunion*, 5 (Saint-Denis: Livres-Réunion, 1981), pp. 101-103.
45. See Margaret Strobel, *Muslim Women in Mombasa, 1890-1975* (New Haven: Yale University Press, 1979), pp. 13-14. Pierre Vérin, *Les Comores* (Paris: Karthala, 1994), p. 253, specifically mentions the important unpublished thesis of Damir ben Ali, "Musique et Société aux Comores" (École des Hautes Études en Sciences Sociales, 1977), which I have not yet seen.
46. L. Aujas, "Notes historiques et ethnographiques sur les Comores," *Bulletin de l'Académie Malgache*, 9 (1911), p. 141. For *trumba* spirits in Mayotte the indispensable source is Michael Lambek, especially his *Human Spirits: A cultural account of trance in Mayotte* (Cambridge: Cambridge University Press, 1981), pp. 152-159, and *Knowledge and Practice in Mayotte: Local Discourses of Islam,*

Sorcery, and Spirit Possession (Toronto: University of Toronto Press, 1993), esp. pp. 31-68. Although Lambek addresses cultural diversity in Mayotte and includes an appendix on "Additional classes of possession spirits in Mayotte" in *Human Spirits*, pp. 186-190, he does not record any mainland African possession spirits. For references to *mzuka* and *dungumaro* in their wider Swahili context, see Sacleux, *Dictionnaire Swahili-Français*, pp. 658, 176.

47. Sophie Blanchy, Mwanaesha Cheikh, Moussa Said, Masséande Allaoui, and Moussa Issihaka, "Thérapies traditionnelles aux Comores," *Cahiers des Sciences Humaines*, 29/4 (1993), pp. 763-790, and "Rituels de Protection dans l'Archipel des Comores," *Islam et Sociétés au Sud du Sahara*, 10 (1996), pp. 121-142, quoted at p. 124. According to Vérin, however, African spirits in the Comoros are known as *sera*; see Vérin, *Les Comores*, p. 131. For *rohani* as a specifically Arab possessing spirit associated with the sea elsewhere in East Africa, see J.E.E. Craster, *Pemba, the Spice Island of Zanzibar* (London: T.F. Unwin, 1913), p. 305; Robert F. Gray, "The Shetani Cult among the Segeju of Tanzania," in John Beattie and John Middleton (eds.), *Spirit Mediumship and Society in Africa* (London: Routledge & Kegan Paul, 1969), p. 174.

48. For a regional overview of this history, see Alpers, "East Central Africa," in Nehemia Levtzion and Randall Pouwels (eds.), *The History of Islam in Africa* (Athens: Ohio University Press, 2000), pp. 302-325. For a recent revisionist perspective that parallels much of what follows below, see Liazzat J.K. Bonate, "Traditions and Transitions: Islam and Chiefship in Northern Mozambique, ca. 1850-1974 (unpublished Ph.D. dissertation, University of Cape Town, 2007), chs. 1-2.

49. See Randall Pouwels, *Horn and Crescent: Cultural Change and Traditional Islam on the East African Coast, 800-1900* (Cambridge: Cambridge University Press, 1987), Chs. 6-8.

50. Hafkin, "Trade, Society, and Politics," p. 48 n. 41.

51. Carlos Roma Machado, "Mussa-Quanto o Namuali (O Napoleão de Angoche)," *Boletim da Sociedade de Geografia de Lisboa*, 38, 1-2 (1920), p. 63; Eduardo do Couto Lupi, *Angoche* (Lisboa: Typographia do Annuario Commercial, 1907), p. 183; João de Azevedo Coutinho, *Do Nyassa a Pemba* (Lisboa: Typographia da Companhia Nacional Editora, 1893), pp. 10-11.

52. Arquivo Histórico de Moçambique, Maputo, Secção Especial N.o 20, Cota S.E.. 2 III p 6, Portugal, Província de Moçambique, SCCI, *Prospecção das Forças Tradicionais–Distrito de Moçambique*, Secret, submitted by Director of the Services Fernando da Costa Freire, Lourenço Marques, 30 December 1969, enclosing José Alberto Gomes de Melo Branquinho, Nampula, 22 April 1969, "Relatório da Prospecção ao Distrito de Moçambique (Um estudo das estruturas das hierarquias tradicionais e religiosas, e da situação político-social), hereafter Melo Branquinho, "Relatório," pp. 18, 343-346.

53. Hafkin, "Trade, Society, and Politics," p. 56.

54. Melo Branquinho, "Relatório," pp. 83-84.

55. Álvaro Pinto de Carvalho, "Notas para a História das Confrarias Islâmicas na Ilha de Moçambique," *Arquivo* (Maputo), 4 (1988), pp. 61-63, where additional details of these fissions are included. There is no mention of Shaykh Ma'ruf's

visit to Mozambique Island in the abridged translation of Sayid Ahmad b. 'Abd al-Rahman's *Manaqib al-Sayyid Muhammad b. Ahmad b. Abi Bakr al-Shadhili al-Yashruti* (Cairo, 1934) by Paul Guy and Abdourahamane bin Cheik Amir, *La Vie et l'Oeuvre du Grand Marabout des Comores, Said Mohamed ben Ahmad al Ma'arouf* (Tananarive, 1949); indeed, its author claims (p. 11) that after Shaykh Ma'ruf's return from exile in Zanzibar, he made no further voyages; for references to his brother, see pp. 9-10. An alternative or perhaps simply mistaken version of these events, which cites a different oral source of information and dates the introduction of the Yashrutiyya at Mozambique Island to 1905, is included in Melo Branquinho, "Relatório," pp, 358-360. See also B.G. Martin, *Muslim Brotherhoods in Nineteenth-Century Africa* (Cambridge: Cambridge University Press, 1976), pp. 152-158. For the dating of Sultan 'Ali's exile, see Martin, *Comores*, II, p. 152. For a recent short overview of this aspect of Ngazija's history, see Anne K. Bang, *Sufis and Scholars of the Sea: Family Networks in East Africa, 1860-1925* (London: RoutledgeCurzon, 2003), pp. 52-56.

56. Melo Branquinho, "Relatório," p. 370.
57. Ibid., pp. 353-354, 409; Shaykh Issa's Comorian roots are not mentioned in Carvalho, "Notas," p. 63.
58. Melo Branquinho, "Relatório," pp. 360-363, 366. This is still the only reference I have seen to the Gazila [al-Ghazali?] center and welcome any suggestions regarding information on its history and activities.
59. Ibid., p. 408.
60. *Ilha de Moçambique: Danze e canti della costa settentrionale*, Folklore 7, Musiche dal Nuovo Mondo: Mozambico, compiled by Erasmo Treglia (Instituto de Comunicação Social, Maputo; ARPAC, Arquivos do Patrimónío Cultural, Maputo; Centro Internazionale Cicrocevia & Sudnord Records, 1995), p. 8 of accompanying notes in Portuguese; Tracks 1, 5, and 11 on this CD are examples of *tufo*. For a fascinating analysis of *tufo*, see Signe Arnfred, "Tufo Dancing: Muslim Women's Culture in Northern Mozambque," *Lusotopie 2004*, pp. 39-65. My thanks to the author for sharing this paper with me in its unpublished 1999 version.
61. Arquivo Histórico de Moçambique, PP 1145, Associação Maometana Comoreana (Association Mahometane Comoréene), *Estatutos* (Lourenço Marques, 5 May 1931), p. 5, Cap. I, Art. 1(a), and Cap. III, Art. 4.
62. For the full story, see Alpers, "Islam in the Service of Colonialism? Portuguese Strategy during the Armed Liberation Struggle in Mozambique," *Lusotopie 1999*, pp. 165-184. The following paragraph is based upon sources cited in this paper. For more recent discussions, see Lorenzo Macagno, "Les noveaux oulémas: La recomposition des autorités musulmanes au nord du Mozambique," *Lusotopie*, 14 (2007): pp. 151-177; Bonate, "Tradition and Transition," chs. 4-6.
63. See, e.g., the fascinating preliminary study by José Kagobo, "Réseaux d'*ulama* <<swahili>> et liens de parenté: Une piste de recherche," in Françoise Le Guennec-Coppens and Pat Caplan, eds., *Les Swahili entre Afrique et Arabie* (Paris: Karthala, 1991), pp. 59-72. Anne Bang's *Sufis and Scholars of the Sea* is a major addition to this literature.
64. William Finnegan, *A Complicated War: The Harrowing of Mozambique*

(Berkeley: University of California Press, 1992), pp. 33-34; Alex Vines, *Renamo: Terrorism in Mozambique* (London, Bloomington and Indianapolis: Indiana University Press, 1991), pp. 67-68; Verin, *Les Comores*, pp. 214-216.

Notes to Chapter 9

1. Auguste Toussaint, *History of the Indian Ocean* (London: Routledge and Kegan Paul, 1966), p. 8.
2. Michael N. Pearson, "Littoral Society: The Case for the Coast," *The Great Circle*, 7, 1 (1985), pp. 1-8.
3. Pearson, *The Indian Ocean* (London and New York: Routledge, 2003), p. 5.
4. Kenneth McPherson, "Cultural Exchange in the Indian Ocean Region," *Westerly*, 29, 4 (1985), p. 6; McPherson, *The Indian Ocean: A History of People and the Sea* (Delhi: Oxford University Press, 1993), p. 122.
5. K.N. Chaudhuri, *Trade and Civilisation in the Indian Ocean: An Economic History from the Rise of Islam to 1750* (Cambridge: Cambridge University Press, 1985), p. 20.
6. Sugata Bose, "Space and Time on the Indian Ocean Rim: Theory and History," in Leila Tarazi Fawaz and C.A. Bayly, eds., *Modernity and Culture: From the Mediterranean to the Indian Ocean* (New York: Columbia University Press, 2002), pp. 368, 370.
7. A.J. da Silva Costa, *Guia do Canal de Moçambique* (Lisboa: Imprensa Nacional, 1878), p. 9.
8. Frederick Barnard describes the wreck of a slaver that left Quelimane, the main Portuguese town on the north bank of the Zambezi River, on the rocks of Bassas da Índia, which at high tide are almost completely submerged. "The current had drifted them close to the breakers before they knew their danger, and they had barely time to get out of her before she opened and went down," losing 700 slaves on board and most of her crew: [Frederick Lamport] Barnard, *A Three Years Cruise in the Mozambique Channel* (London: Dawsons of Pall Mall, 1969 [1848]), pp. 153-154.
9. *U.S. Navy Regional Climatic Study of the Mozambique Channel and Adjacent Waters*. prepared by Naval Oceanography Command Detachment, Asheville, N.C. under the authority of Commander Naval Oceanography Command, Stennis Space Center, MS 39529-5000, July 1989, p. v; Silva Costa, *Guia*, p. 9, gives the distance as 213 miles.
10. Ibid.; C. Diniz, *Informações sobre a Costa N. de Moçambique* (Lisboa: Imprensa Nacional, 1890).
11. *U.S. Navy*, pp. iv-v.
12. Ibid., p. vi; Silva Costa, p. 14.
13. Ibid., p. 15.
14. Ibid., p. 16.
15. *U.S. Navy*, p. viii; Silva Costa, pp. 10-11.
16. *U.S. Navy*, p. x.
17. Silva Costa, pp. 11-12.
18. Barnard, *A Three Years Cruise*, pp. 120-132.; also Pascoe Grenfell Hill, *Fifty*

Days on Board a Slave-Vessel in the Mozambique Channel, in April and May, 1843 (London: John Murray, 1844).

19. Pierre Vérin, *The History of Civilisation in North Madagascar* (Rotterdam and Boston: A.A. Balkema, 1986), pp. 32-52; Chantal Radimilahy, "Ancient iron-working in Madagascar," in Thurstan Shaw et al, eds., *The Archaeology of Africa: Food, metals and towns* (London and New York: Routledge, 1993), pp. 478-483; R.E. Dewar, "The Archaeology of the Early Settlement of Madagascar," in J. Reade, ed., *The Indian Ocean in Antiquity* (London and New York: Kegan Paul International; London: The British Museum, 1996), pp. 471-486; Pearson, *The Indian Ocean*, pp. 60-61; cf. S. Crook, *Distant Shores: By traditional canoe from Asia to Madagascar* (London: Impact Books, 1990), p. 7; Milo Kearney, *The Indian Ocean in World History* (New York and London: Routledge, 2004), p. 22.

20. Pierre Simon, *Ny Fiteny Fahizany: Reconstitution et périodisation du malgache ancien jusuqu'au XIVè siècle* (Paris: Institut des Langues et Civilisations Orientales, 1988); also Trefor Jenkins, et al, "The Genetic Evidence for Caste Endogamy in Madagascar," paper presented to the workshop on "Slave Systems in Asia and the Indian Ocean: Their structure and change in the 19th and 20th centuries," Université d'Avignon, 18-20 May 2000.

21. Christopher Ehret, *An African Classical Age: Eastern & Southern Africa in World History, 1000 B.C. to A.D. 400* (Charlottesville: University of Virginia Press, 1998), pp. 277-280.

22. Ibid., p. 280; A.M. Jones, *Africa and Indonesia: The evidence of the xylophone and other musical and cultural factors* (Leiden: J. Brill, 1971), has suggested that Indonesians also introduced the xylophone to eastern Africa, an assertion that has usually been cited as further evidence of Indonesian influence in eastern Africa, but his argument and methodology have been vigorously challenged by Roger Blench, "Evidence for the Indonesian origin of certain elements of African culture: a review, with special reference to the arguments of A.M. Jones," *African Music*, 6, 2 (1982), pp. 81-93 and "The Ethnographic Evidence for Long-Distance Contacts Between Oceania and East Africa," in Reade, ed., *The Indian Ocean in Antiquity*, pp. 417-438.

23. Geneviève Boulnier-Giraud, *Étude morphologique de la pirouge à balancier aux Comores et dans l'ouest de l'Océan Indien* (Paris: Institut d'Ethnologie, Musée de l'Homme, Archives et Documents, Micro-edition 730091, 1973); Georges Boulnier and Geneviève Boulnier-Giraud, "Chronologie de la pirouge à balancier: le témoignage de l'océan Indien occidentale," *Journal de la Société des Océanistes*, 32, 50 (1976), pp. 89-98; Armando Reis Moura, "Barcos do litoral de Moçambique," *Monumenta*, 8 (1972), pp. 20-24 and Figs. 28-36.

24. Vérin, *History of Civilisation*, pp. 67-79, ch. 8.

25. Henry T. Wright, "Early Seafarers of the Comoro Islands: the Dembeni Phase of the IX-Xth Centuries A.D.," *Azania*, 19 (1984), pp. 13-60.

26. Ricardo Teixeira Duarte, *Northern Mozambique in the Swahili World*, Studies in African Archaeology 4 (Stockholm: Central Board of National Antiquities; Maputo: Eduardo Mondlane University; Uppsala: Uppsala University, 1993).

27. Vérin, *History of Civilisation*, pp. 78-79.

28. G.G. Tibbetts, *Arab Navigation in the Indian Ocean Before the Coming of the Portuguese* (London: Royal Asiatic Society of Great Britain and Ireland, 1971), pp. 218-219, 234-235, 267, 429-435; J. S. Trimingham, "The Arab Geographers and the East African Coast," in H. Neville Chittick and Robert I. Rotberg, eds., *East Africa and the Orient* (New York and London: Holmes & Meier Publishers, Inc., 1975), pp. 115-146.

29. Vérin, "Malgache et Swahili – Culture de Frange et Interférences," in M.-F. Rombi, ed., *Le Swahili et Ses Limites: Ambiguïté des notions reçues* (Paris: Editions Recherche sur les Civilisations, 1989), pp. 175-178; N.J. Gueunier, "Le Swahili à Madagascar," in ibid., pp. 179-182; also Derek Nurse and Thomas Spear *The Swahili: Reconstructing the History and Language of an African Society, 800-1500* (Philadelphia: University of Pennsylvania Press, 1985).

30. Vérin, *History of Civilisation*, pp. 183-186; Raymond K. Kent, "The Kingdom of Samamo in the diary of Paulo Rodrigues da Costa," *Omaly sy Anio*, 16 (1982), pp, 7-12.

31. Vincent Belrose-Huyghues, "La Baie de Boina entre 1580 et 1640 – Une critique des sources anciennes et récentes," *Omaly sy Anio*, 17-20 (1983-1984), p. 175; also John R. Jenson, ed., *Journal and Letter Book of Nicholas Buckeridge 1651-1654* (Minneapolis: University of Minnesota Press, 1973).

32. Chapter 2 in this volume.

33. Kent, "The Kingdom of Samamo," p. 10.

34. Benigna Zimba, *Mulheres Invisíveis: O Género e as Políticas Comerciais no Sul de Moçambique, 1720-1830* (Maputo: Promédia, 2003), ch. 3.

35. Pearson, "Littoral Society," p. 6; also Pearson, *The Indian Ocean*, pp. 37-41.

36. Thomas Vernet, "Le commerce des esclaves sur la côte Swahili, 1500-1750," *Azania*, 38 (2003), pp. 69-97.

37. Jean Martin, *Comores: quatre îles entre pirates et planteurs* (Paris: L'Harmattan, 1983), I, ch. 2; Chapter 7 in this volume; Carlos Lopes Bento, *As Ilhas de Querimba ou de Cabo Delgado* (Lisbon: Universidade Técnica de Lisboa, Instituto Superior de Ciências Sociais e Políticas, 1993), II, ch. 10.3, "As incursões malgaxes," http://geocities.yahoo.com.br/quirimbashistoria/index.htm accessed on 11/1/2005.

38. Gwyn Campbell, "Madagascar and the Slave Trade, 1810-1895," *Journal of African History*, 22 (1981), pp. 203-227; Campbell, "Madagascar and Mozambique in the Slave Trade of the Western Indian Ocean 1800-1861," in William Gervase Clarence-Smith, ed., *The Economics of the Indian Ocean Slave Trade in the Nineteenth Century* (London: Frank Cass, 1989), pp. 166-193; Campbell, "The East African Slave Trade, 1861-1895: The 'Southern' Complex," *International Journal of African Historical Studies*, 22 (1989), pp. 1-26.

39. Maurice Schrive and Nöel J. Gueunier, "Histoire du Peuple'": Souvenirs sur l'esclavage des Makoa du nord de Madagascar, *Études Océan Indien*, 15 (1992), p. 195; Sophie Goedefroit, *A l'ouest de Madagascar: Les Sakalava du Menabe* (Paris: Éditions Karthala/Éditions de l'ORSTOM, 1998), pp. 152-153.

40. Chapter 8 in this volume.

41. Alpers, "Becoming Mozambique: Diaspora and Identity in Mauritius," in Vijayalakshmi Teelock and Edward A. Alpers, eds., *History, Memory and*

Identity (Port-Louis: Nelson Mandela Centre for African Culture and University of Mauritius, 2001), pp. 135-138.

42. Alpers, *Ivory and Slaves in East Central Africa* (London: Heinemann & Berkeley: University of California Press, 1975), pp. 85-94, 113-118, 143-149, 233-234; L.F.D. Antunes, "The Trade Activities of the Banyans in Mozambique: Private Indian Dynamics in the Panel of the Portuguese State Economy (1686-1777)," in K.S. Mathew, ed., *Mariners, Merchants and Oceans: Studies in Maritime History* (New Delhi: Manohar, 1995), pp. 301-331; Pedro Machado, "Without Scales and Balances": Gujarati merchants in Mozambique, 1680s-1800," *Portuguese Studies Review*, 9, 1-2 (2001), pp. 254-288; Sophie Blanchy, *Karana et Banians: Les communautés commerçantes d'origine indienne à Madagascar* (Paris: Editions L'Harmattan, 1995), pp. 33-82, 121-126.

43. António Alberto de Andrade, *Relações de Moçambique Setecentista* (Lisboa: Agência Geral do Ultramar, 1955), p. 97.

44. See Chapter 8 above.

45. Micheline Rasoamiaramanana, *Aspects économiques et sociaux de la vie à Majunga entre 1862 et 1881* (Antananarivo: Université de Madagascar, Études Historiques VI, 1983), p. 87 .

46. Nancy J. Hafkin, "Trade, Society, and Politics in Northern Mozambique, c. 1753-1913" (unpublished Ph.D. Dissertation, Boston University, 1973), pp. 56-57.

47. Ibid.

48. Arquivo Histórico de Moçambique (hereafter AHM), Maputo, Fundo do Século XIX, Distrito de Moçambique, 8-14, M.1(3) #1, Movimento Marítimo, Barra de Moçambique, 26 April-2 May 1874; M.1(3) #2, Movimento Marítimo, 1-30 September 1885, #3, Nota das Embarcações entradas n'este porto hoje 27 de Agosto de 1890, #5, Nota . . . 29 August 1890; M.2(5) #4, José Faustino Francisco Gomez, Alfândega de Moçambique, disembarking vessels for 4 July 1891. AHM, Fundo do Século XIX, Cabo Delgado–Códice 11-1655, Bd2, Registo dos pangaios, bateis, lanchas e individuos a saírem deste porto à capital, 1841-1847.

49. AHM, Fundo do Século XIX, Governo Geral, 8.27, M.1(5), Abdallah, King of Johanna to Governor of Mozambique, 18 March 1884.

50. AHM, Fundo do Século XIX, Governo Geral, 8.27, M.1(6), doc. 2, Governor Papinaud of Mayotte to Governor General of Mozambique, Dzaoudzi, 1 December 1889. For a recent study of *engagés* at Nossi-Bé, see Jehanne-Emmanuelle Monnier, *Esclaves de la canne à sucre: Engagés et planteurs à Nossi-Bé, Madagascar 1850-1880* (Paris: L'Harmattan, 2006).

51. Françoise Le Guennec-Coppens, "Changing Patterns of Hadhdrami Migration and Social Integration in East Africa," in Ulrike Freitag and William Gervase Clarence-Smith, eds., *Hadhrami Traders, Scholars and Statesmen in the Indian Ocean, 1750s-1960s* (Leiden/New York/Köln: Brill, 1997), pp. 157-174; Anne K. Bang, *Sufis and Scholars of the Sea: Family Networks in East Africa, 1869-1925* (London and New York: RoutledgeCurzon, 2003).

52. See Chapter 8 above. For a recent study, see Liazzar J.K. Bonate, "Traditions and Transitions: Islam and Chiefship in Northern Mozambique ca. 1850-1974"

(unpublished Ph.D. dissertation, University of Cape Town, 2007).

53. Pearson, "Littoral Society," p. 7.

54. Ibid.; Matteo Angius and Mario Zamponi, eds., *Ilha de Moçambique: Convergencia de Povos e Culturas–Incontro di Populi e Culture* (Repubblica di San Marino: AIEP editore, 1999).

55. Wright, "Early Seafarers of the Comoro Islands;" Rui Manuel Falcão, "Notas Gerais Sobre a Actividade da Pesca na Ilha de Moçambique," *Arquivo: Boletim Semestral do Arquivo Histórico se Moçambique*, 4 (1988), pp. 23-30; Vérin, *Les Comores* (Paris: Éditions Karthala, 1994), pp. 40-42; Goedefroit, *A l'ouest de Madagascar*, pp. 370-374.

56. This comment mirrors Anthony Reid's observation on the South East Asian distinction between upriver and downriver that he made at the conference "Narratives of the Sea: Encapsulating the Indian Ocean World," Nehru Memorial Museum and Library, New Delhi, December 2003. See also Anthony Reid, *Southeast Asia in the Age of Commerce 1450-1680*, I: "The Lands below the Winds" (New Haven and London: Yale University Press.1988), p. 7.

57. Pearson, "Littoral Society," p. 7.

INDEX

235

ABOUT THE AUTHOR

Edward A. Alpers is Professor and Chair of the Department of History at the University of California, Los Angeles, having served as Dean of Honors and Undergraduate Programs at UCLA from 1985 to 1996. He has also taught at the Universities of Dar es Salaam, Tanzania (1966-1968), and the Somali National University, Lafoole (1980), the latter as a Fulbright Senior Scholar. In 1994 he served as President of the African Studies Association and as National Program Chair for its 2001 Annual Meeting in Houston, Texas.

Professor Alpers has published widely on the history of East Africa and the Indian Ocean. His major publications include *Ivory and Slaves in East Central Africa* (1975); *Walter Rodney: Revolutionary and Scholar*, co-edited with Pierre-Michel Fontaine (1982); *Africa and the West: A Documentary History from the Slave Trade to Independence*, with William H. Worger and Nancy Clark (2001); *History, Memory and Identity*, co-edited with Vijayalakshmi Teelock (2001); *Sidis and Scholars: Essays on African Indians*, co-edited with Amy Catlin-Jairazbhoy (2004); *Slavery and Resistance in Africa and Asia*, co-edited with Gwyn Campbell and Michael Salman (2005); *Slave Routes and Oral Tradition in Southeastern Africa*, co-edited with Benigna Zimba and Allen F. Isaacman (2005); *Resisting Bondage in Indian Ocean Africa and Asia*, co-edited with Gwyn Campbell and Michael Salman (2007); and *Cross-Currents and Community Networks: The History of the Indian Ocean World*, co-edited with Himanshu Prabha Ray (2007). His current research focuses on Africans in the Indian Ocean world.

Breinigsville, PA USA
22 October 2009
226268BV00005BA/3/P